VOICE FIRST

T0324254

VOICE FIRST

A Writer's Manifesto

SONYA HUBER

University of Nebraska Press
LINCOLN

The University of Nebraska Press is part of a land-
grant institution with campuses and programs on the
past, present, and future homelands of the Pawnee,
Ponca, Otoe-Missouria, Omaha, Dakota, Lakota, Kaw,
Cheyenne, and Arapaho Peoples, as well as those of the
relocated Ho-Chunk, Sac and Fox, and Iowa Peoples.

Library of Congress Cataloging-in-Publication Data
Names: Huber, Sonya, 1971– author.
Title: Voice first: a writer's manifesto / Sonya Huber.
Description: Lincoln: University of Nebraska Press,
[2022] | Includes bibliographical references and index.
Identifiers: LCCN 2021057715
ISBN 9781496231314 (paperback)
ISBN 9781496232830 (epub)
ISBN 9781496232847 (pdf)
Subjects: LCSH: English language—Rhetoric—
Study and teaching (Higher) | Authorship. | Creation
(Literary, artistic, etc.) | BISAC: LANGUAGE
ARTS & DISCIPLINES / Writing / General
Classification: LCC PE1404 .H835 2022 | DDC
808/.0420711—dc23/eng/20220114
LC record available at https://lccn.loc.gov/2021057715

Set in Garamond Premier by Mikala R. Kolander.
Designed by N. Putens.

CONTENTS

NOTE TO THE READER

Voice is a term that vexes writers and teachers. We use it quite a lot, and we know it when we see it, but most of us have struggled to define where it comes from or how to encourage it. I believe that we often hold this sense of voice as "self" or "essence" a little too tightly. The idea of one "authentic" voice is a holdover from a time when we saw each self as singular, isolated, and separate. These days we're moving beyond ideas of simple subjectivity and objectivity, and we're more likely to see the self as constituted in relation to others, in community.

The idea of an authentic voice also doesn't make sense to me in terms of a writer's process and life. If a writer happens upon that so-called authentic voice, does that mean the previous voices were false or impostors? Would that authentic voice then, once discovered, stay constant and reliable, even as the writer's life spurs change and perspectives evolve?

Even in looking at scholarship—such as *The Writer's Voice* by A. Alvarez, for one example—you can see the way the concept of authentic voice doesn't actually work in practice. Alvarez talks about poet Sylvia Plath having finally come into her authentic voice but then, getting into the details of the poem "The Moon and the Yew Tree," describes it as "a poem in two voices" that "speak out and clash continually through the poem." This comes up a lot: the idea of a voice made of voices.

For that, and many other reasons, I've decided to reclaim the term *voice*, give it a plural, and use it as a tool in the service of writing. As Felicia Rose Chavez describes in her book, *The Anti-Racist Writing*

Workshop, a question about the definition of *voice* or another literary term can be turned into an investigation of process, with the test of "How does your definition influence the way you read and write?"[1] That's the question I've been asking myself. This book is the result of me trying to watch what I'm doing as I write and read, so the inferences here were first based on a sample size of one and then tested through writing and talking with other writers and readers. I've tried to pay attention to and intuit the feeling of writing, of coming into voices, in a way that I hope is generative and that sparks inspiration for other writers and readers.

Voices, to me, are the engines inside us that summon and refract meaning. Paisley Rekdal defines *voice* as "a ceaseless stream of impressions formed through memory, sense, and emotion, all of which trigger more memories and emotions as we internally narrate the story of our lives."[2] I love this sense of a voice river that is the font of story and speech, and to extend the metaphor, that river could have many currents and inlets and eddies that can float leaves or turn into shallow rapids. Voices provide the link between our thoughts and the way those thoughts come out into the world.

Along the way I've had to tackle a few other terms, such as *tone*, that you'll encounter through a new lens in these pages. If you're baffled by the definition of literary terms like *voice* and *style* and *tone* and *diction*, don't worry. Different people have their favorite definitions, and those are helpful because they are approximations of the ideas to use and react against. But language and expression themselves are such shifting, movable creatures that it's fine if the instruments we use to track them are always staggering and racing to catch up.

Often *style* is used to denote a series of party tricks with language, the surface thumbprint of sentences and words that an author tends toward. I won't talk much about style in this book, but I'm assuming that this toolbox—all of a writer's go-to words and phrases and comfortable sentence constructions—is what many writers have meant when they talk about authentic voice. To me style is your toolbox. Voices are the things in your ears that whisper what to build, that react to a cut of lovely cherrywood and say, *Oh, make this a hearth*. To simplify, remember that there's sometimes a separation between what it feels like to write and the terms of analysis used to discuss literary effects. To me voices impel the telling, and the braiding and melody of their resonance and dissonance are what create an urgency in the tale.

Poet Adrienne Rich expressed this same impulse in the poem "Phantasia for Elvira Shatayev," which is about a women's climbing team:

> If in this sleep I speak
> it's with a voice no longer personal
> (I want to say *with voices*)

Her use of the parentheses hedges and shifts her meaning, and then within them she offers a sense of the speaker's own voices in a plural chorus, adding layers, authority, and depth.

No matter what genres you're writing in, the notion of voices in your work may help you explore a full range of options for what you want to write about and how. I think our storehouse of voices crosses genre lines, and the more we train and explore them, the more our writing options will grow.

When I first heard, as a young person who liked to write, that writing was about "finding your voice," I got nervous. That seemed very risky. What if I picked the wrong one? And I had a hard time listening to some of those voices inside myself and appreciating them. I always thought I should sound *different*: smarter, more complex, more restrained. You might have had this feeling too. Many writers I've known in the course of my teaching career have also struggled with this sense that their writing is not *theirs* or that they can't hear or can't bear to hear themselves. It bothers me that many people feel alienated from this essential element of expression, from writing as a way to think and have conversations with our past and present selves. Much of this book is motivated by a desire to invite people who feel they aren't "good" at writing back into engagement with the fire of their own expression. I think having voices might take down the stakes a little, make the binary between "true" and "false" voices kind of irrelevant, and invite writers to *play*.

So, even the subtitle of this book—a manifesto—is a voice correction. I've seen my own tendency to hide, my own desire to be agreeable or not offend, which has often ended up with me not saying anything. I've also often been so stymied by what I thought I should sound like that I decided at certain points not to say anything. To counteract that tendency, I embrace the notion of a manifesto, which urges me to say what I think, to listen to the bold voice inside me, and then to *follow* that voice, to let it grow, to see it and understand it, and to feed it, knowing I can always switch to another one.

Hanging around in three-dimensional life, interviewing and talking to people from all over, I have always been impressed with the music of expression, with the everyday brilliance of language. As a teacher, I'm amazed that one of the best ways to help a fellow writer when they're stuck is to let them talk, to transcribe what they tell me. Spoken language, often combined with the movement of the face, hands, and body, animates and enlivens. We become thought; we feel voice; we act out ideas on the small stage of our being.

I want as many people as possible to get the option of feeling that same kind of fluidity in writing, to feel that writing is theirs, that they can do whatever they want with the alphabet, that they are not at all deficient in the raw material that makes for good, engaging, lively, soulful sentences.

I'm aware that my main assertion—that we have *voices* instead of a voice—flies in the face of much craft-based and scholarly work by authors I respect. I do this while borrowing from many theorists I admire, setting the concept of voice to one side in order to loosen it up a little. Much of the credit for this idea goes to Peter Elbow, whose writing has been so important to me throughout my career as a writer and teacher. You'll find him quoted in many chapters of this book. The teaching of composition has swung away from his theories, often incorporating elements of his work but not fully crediting the expressivist school of thought for its impact on the way we teach today. So, I hope this book might bring Elbow to a new generation of writers and teachers. Elbow has continued to pursue the question of voice in writing, always allowing his investigations to evolve. Please consider this volume as a useful patio or backyard pool to the welcoming home of that theory, except in cases where I've gotten it wrong or misinterpreted him.

As I asked my fellow writers about voice, many of them highlighted the ways in which voice comes into writing: through immersion in subject matter, through deep research, through deep feeling with a subject. I have also sensed this general connection between voice and investment in a piece of writing, and this guide explores and uses the connection between author and subject to discover and exercise a range of voices that can be activated for whatever writing task is at hand.

As poet Jillian Weise pointed out to me, the conception of voice might be taken as ableist, as would any metaphor in which one sense—vision or speech—is relied upon to carry the freight of an entire web of expression. This point has deep implications not only for this book but also for the fields of writing and rhetoric. I urge us all to consider the ways in which our metaphors privilege certain bodies and modes of expression. The challenge, then, is to engage with the long conversation about voice and vision. I work throughout this book to broaden those limiting terms and to note that voice includes expression in all modes of communication. There's voice in signing, in use of communicative technologies, and even in the way we move our eyes and bodies. I apologize in advance for any implication here that privileges certain bodies over others or that appears exclusionary. Throughout this book *speech* represents a particular idiolect or pattern of expression. *Voice* means the mysterious cloud of invisible triggers that both kindle and enliven that expression.

VOICE FIRST

1 *Listening to Voices*

When you're inside a piece of writing that hums and crackles and sparks, when a real person is talking to you from the page, you've encountered a voice. "Voice" is what writing *feels* like. It sets off sympathetic vibrations in readers. It gives us a sense of connection to another live human presence, creating a real and complex moment of communication.

We all naturally speak with voice, which in verbal speech animates the larynx and the lungs; the ribcage and the lips, tongue, and teeth; gestures and expressions. In sign language voice comes from the fingers and posture, and gestures and expressions, or when using an assistive device, voice comes from expression and gesture, from the bodily movement of eyes or fingers using a keyboard, and in each case from the unique string of expression that is produced. The poet Adrienne Rich writes that words written with voice "have the heft of our living behind them."[1]

We have voices already, which makes the guidance to "find" one's voice confusing. Somewhere between the body and mind and the page, this singular voice vanishes like a wisp of fog. Somehow the heft of our living gets stripped from written communication.

My assumption in this guide is that you already have a full range of voices and they are already fantastic. Through these chapters we will name them, exercise them, watch as their stems and roots grow and branch and strengthen. When you can identify the huge range of voices you have, you can make choices about how and when to use them, how to draw on them, which voice to channel, how to create text that sounds like you, with the heft of your living and imagination, with syntax and style and snap and verve.

As Janet Burroway writes, "Begin by knowing, and exploring, the fact that you already have a number of different voices."[2] You can borrow voices, learn to listen to your own, exercise them so they grow stronger, trade them, try others on for size. And you get as many as you want.

When you use one, two more appear. And yet they are all connected and shifting. Once you appreciate all the voices you have to work with, you can mine them, and discover others, for writing in all genres. Your web of voices is you—but it's also other people's impact on you, what you've read, and what you've experienced. As Walt Whitman wrote, you "contain multitudes." And as Felicia Rose Chavez writes, "How we speak is as abundant as we are."[3]

Throughout my years of teaching writing, I have tended to skip the question of voice with my students because it didn't seem to help writers. Instead, I gave writing prompts and asked writers to inhabit perspectives, real and imagined, past, present, and future. As these writers exercised and stretched, they began to feel something flow that had been frozen. They began to inhabit their writing, and that comfort on the page— with all the different selves that sounded like them—often transferred far outside the world of memoir or the personal essay and enlivened their academic writing. But I didn't yet have a theory about why this worked.

If you've read about voice, you might have encountered the idea that it is a singular essence that animates writing, made up of craft and style choices and tone, and that it is somehow connected to our "real self." As a young writer, this advice sounded to me like I had one "authentic" voice, the "real me," with the rest of my expression some-how impure or fake.

I knew that I had a certain style, a set of phrases and an underlying grammar that united much of my writing, but when I thought about my voice, I felt self-conscious. That "one voice" concept made me feel like I couldn't stray far from my roots, like I had one crayon to color with. Following that idea, it seemed like I'd somehow have to incorporate all of my being and influences into one mode of expression so that, no matter what, I'd always sound a little like a midwesterner stuck in the 1980s and my true style was a kind of anchor or tether, one I'd always circle around, with a limited range.

I couldn't tell you much about my "singular voice" beyond a list of words I choose regularly, a few bad habits of sentence construction, and some influences of region and era. But when I think about my range of voices, I see very clearly how I use these strands in different situations. I knew as I grew as a writer that I had a voice that comes from my experience as a small-town midwesterner, a voice that comes from my background as a political organizer, a voice that is shaped by my time in academia, and many more. On a deep level those voices have been shaped by everyone I have listened to and read.

We each have a range of functional voices that help us get through the day in our present life. We have a voice we use to tell the dog how cute she is, which is different than the voice we use at work, and mixing them up is often fun. (*Is bossy-wossy the cutest ever?*)

Every voice we develop is an interface or cognitive tool to help us interact with a specific slice of the world in a specific time and place. All of these voices are definitely connected, and they're united by a whole host of style and tonal habits. We move along throughout our lives, and we discard some of our old voices, or they are used to make new ones.

MY VOICE STORY

I stumbled upon my own experiments with voice when I began literally to stumble with an autoimmune disease. Chronic pain affected my joints, but it also affected my energy, my thinking, and my writing voice.

I began writing a book, but I didn't know it. Instead, I scrawled panicked and sad journal entries between naps, doctors' visits, and angry attempts to wash dishes and do chores with hands that didn't seem to work. Then I had to switch gears constantly to become the assistant professor doing all of her jobs well and calmly. Without that assistant professor role, there would have been no health insurance for me or my five-year-old son and no food.

I watched a gap widen between myself as a professional going to work each day, using almost all the energy I had, and myself as a writer. Before I got sick, the writer voice only needed one or several cups of coffee to get started. I'd sit down at the screen, and words would appear. But after I got sick, I felt like I couldn't think, couldn't zip along and fling handfuls of words at the keyboard. Instead, I pecked one letter at a time, my thoughts unspooling very slowly.

Imagine a river that has dried to a trickle. Everything around that rivulet of water changes in response to the water level. The riverbed accumulates silt, and the water stands in shallow pools. Plants from the banks begin to grow in the mud and algae. Before long, everything about the river looks different.

I fought against this change. I forced myself to write the way I'd always written, escalating a terrible battle between my mind and my body. I got depressed because my writing had always been the one thing about my life that I could control. While I didn't know what would appear on the page or how good it would be or where it would go, I always knew, before, that words would appear.

At the root of this conflict was a lot of anger toward myself and the world and a lot of fear about what my future might bring. I did not want to be where I was, and I didn't want to have to give up writing.

Eventually, as I adapted, I began to look back at my accumulating journal entries about pain. Was there anything there, in the actual experience? Luckily, I was also beginning to understand the nature of disability. I found support from other disabled writers, and the work they'd done to reframe disability as an insight-giving window into reality, rather than a deficit, helped me to begin to rebuild my life and my writing.

I turned back to my writing, looking for the ways in which I was coming to terms with disability. What I was beginning to write, I realized, was unlike what I had thought of as my style. Well, there were definitely elements of my style—not things I necessarily loved about my writing but things that were as deep as my scars and my life story. Yep, I loved *Star Wars*, and the space and sci-fi metaphors abounded. Yep, part of me sounded like the Illinois girl I'll always be, though she was always fencing and jabbing at my professor voice. Looking at those chunks of raw writing was like looking at a mountain laid open, all the geological layers. And yes, my deep abiding love for mixed metaphors was laid on thick in the writing about pain. But combining those pieces had created something new that adapted to my new existence in the world.

When I looked at the pain writing, I saw that the combination of a new experience and some desperation prompted me to play on the page. If everything was ruined, why not let the language rip? I was leaning on some old vices and tricks, amped up tenfold, and trying them in different combinations. And then in other places the writing was so thin and stark, a slow kind of writing I had never needed to do before, and that voice was so direct and clear. I benefited as I wrote, over and over again, from the support of other writers who claimed their bodily experience and described it. And the community helped me appreciate and hear new voices within myself. One voice, which I named Pain Woman, was the beginning of my conscious thinking about voices.

The book that resulted, *Pain Woman Takes Your Keys and Other Essays from a Nervous System*, looks so composed sitting on the shelf with its vibrant multicolored cover. The author in the smiley headshot on the back cover smirks like she knew what she was doing from the beginning. I wish the reader could open the book and see a series of clippings and crumpled fragments fall out and then watch as the words slowly cohere along with my growing understanding of disability and my understanding of my own ableism.

Once I started naming her and other voices, I felt set free. There was no need to hunt for some core voice. I could go wherever I wanted. I could delve deeply into the voice of the junior high mathlete. I could name voices that no one had ever seen. I experienced a massive sense of relaxation in my own work, the end of rigidly trying to control my own style and voice. I began to see that I could weave a few voices together for a writing task, and I began to try on different voices to see which would turn a dripping creek back into a torrent.

In letting myself loose a bit, in looking for the weird voices in my own life and head and letting them out, I found new ways to say things and new perspectives on my life. These weird little pieces were written first for only myself, as roadmaps or stretches. And then something happened that isn't supposed to happen: it ended up that those pieces written in my own private voices *also* connected with other readers. I hadn't been considering readers at all—and certainly not readers who didn't have chronic pain.

I had *not* made a rhetorical choice about audience or purpose. I was consciously trying to talk only to myself, privately, about the new world I inhabited, to understand where I was. I was trying to summon voices from the edges of my own life that would help me interpret the challenges I faced.

I'm not saying that considering audience is always a bad idea. What I am saying, however, is that sometimes we have to listen to ourselves first and use voice *first* as a generative engine rather than a kind of surface question of style or rhetoric.

When we get to choose which voice to use, when we name the voices and exercise them, we can then see more options, make more conscious choices, and find more joy and agency in writing. And the more we write into them, the more they proliferate.

MANY VOICES

One of the cores of Buddhist philosophy is the idea of "no self." That doesn't mean there's a big void between your ears. Instead, that idea says that the "self" is not a core nugget of identity but a constantly shifting experience, like a river. While the self has a name, like a river, and while both the self and the river have a predictable set of behaviors, the actual river is never the same river twice. The self, like voice, is more of a mysterious hovering, shifting collection of experience, a flow.

The memoirist Thomas Larson writes that the core self "can never be found. It can only be activated now and in the succession of nows" that we encounter in the different moments we live and occasionally set down on paper.[4] This "succession of nows" creates a palette of voices that can give you options in your writing, and different voices can deliver very different insights.

The writer Eva Hoffman describes her writing process as sorting through these voices, describing a process that I find very resonant and familiar: "I am writing a story in my journal . . . I make my way through layers of acquired voices, silly voice, sententious voices, voices that are too cool and too overheated. Then they all quiet down, and I reach what I'm searching for: silence. I hold still to steady myself in it. . . . A voice begins to emerge: it's an even voice, and it's capable of saying things straight, without exaggeration or triviality. As the story progresses, the voice grows and diverges into different tonalities and timbres. . . . But the voice always returns to its point of departure, to ground zero."[5] Hoffman has a voice she sees as her baseline. I have three or four. How you relate to your voices, and whether you choose a "core" voice, is up to you.

Barbara Johnson describes the resonance or richness of voice as coming from "splitness or doubleness," which I think implies the necessity of multiple voices.[6] To imagine this, think about plucking one string on a guitar to produce a note. When we strum multiple strings at the same time, then change the pattern and the way we hold those strings in a rhythm, we get music. In writing, that complex strum sound with depth and body is called resonance.

To listen to the resonance among different voices, think about whether there are words you pronounce that other people remark on or notice. As a midwesterner on the East Coast of the United States, I still get remarks on the way I pronounce vowels, saying *roof* and *root* with the *u* sound in *put* rather than the long double *o* sound in *zoo* That's the Midwest with me always, even when I'm standing at a podium giving a talk using formal academic language. We use multiple voices without even knowing it, and the friction and shifting among them is what makes the music of expression.

SILENCED VOICES

Voice is a performance of identity that can generate material and excavate insight, yet we rarely talk explicitly about the struggle to find our voices or the damage done when a voice is derailed. Sometimes we lose the thread of voice. This can happen through overly aggressive criticism of a voice itself rather than a helpful critique of a text and its goals. Losing a voice can be triggered by trauma related to, or external to, writing instruction, including forms of social and systemic oppression. Sometimes our wandering search for the most vital and true voice for our material may not have been encouraged, or we did not encounter models that might have sparked our confidence.

Voice is a flame that has to be protected. There were times in my own life when I let other people tell me what a voice was supposed to sound like. Real-life troubles affected my voice, to the point where I couldn't be honest on the page or feel some of my emotions.

Voice is shaped by experience and by the way we interact with other people. As Matthew Salesses writes in *Craft in the Real World*: "Some authors have been taught to speak quickly if they want to get a word in; others have been taught to hold forth. Breath, too, is about power: it is gendered, raced, etc. To modulate breath means to think about the frequencies we've been taught to speak on, and to tune in to how we transmit information and what kind and to whom."[7]

And our interactions with people are often messed up, infused with power imbalances and judgment, racism and sexism and homophobia and ableism. Words, as we know, can wound individuals and divide nations and communities or can bring people together.

Some people are taught that they have lots of important things to say, so their voices grow strong and wide. Other people are taught that their voices annoy, are grating, are too much and too angry, or too soft, too wrong. So their voices grow thick shields and thistles and grow in circles or even grow deep roots underground and pop up somewhere faraway and safe.

Many voices are judged as technically "incorrect," and power and privilege have shaped those judgments over centuries of injustice and violence. African American Vernacular English, or Black Standard English, as one example, is a complex language. Toni Morrison writes: "It's terrible to think that a child with five different present tenses comes to school to be faced with those books that are less than his own language. And then to be told things about his language, which is him, that are sometimes permanently damaging. . . . This is a really cruel fallout of racism."[8]

Writing in the classroom has often made people self-conscious about their powers of expression, so that they then think they're not good writers or good thinkers. When people feel like they can't express themselves or that they're not qualified to do so, an avoidable tragedy has occurred. I see this every time I tell someone I teach writing and the person I'm talking to—a nurse, a bank teller, an accountant, a plumber—instinctively winces like I'm going to correct the sentences that come out of their mouths with a red pen. It always makes me so sad.

After years of being told "you're doing it wrong," it should be no surprise that writers are a little self-conscious and disconnected from their voices.

Voices are grown by those who have nurtured and supported us, by the way our bodies absorb the sounds and expressions that we've been bathed in. And listening to the voices of our communities—absorbing them as valuable and life-giving elements, as brilliant threads that carry messages for surviving and thriving in their sounds and cadences—can also heal.

BEGINNING TO LISTEN TO OUR VOICES

Even if a person believes they're not a "good writer," they have picked up habits of rhythm, beauty, and economy that ground and animate their communication.

A good tweet, for example, seems like a simple act, but crafting a good post on Twitter, with its tight space limits, requires the writer to borrow the brilliance of spoken expression. The poet Robert Frost wrote that people harvest sounds and idea from a flow of speech, "where they grow spontaneously."[9] Peter Elbow, who has dedicated his writing career to an outside-the-box understanding of voice, writes that this river of raw speech contains "organizations and genres that you can discover and prune into shape."[10] His idea is that speech—how we naturally express ourselves—is the key to good writing and that as we learn to listen to ourselves, we can gather "valuable linguistic resources" from that "careless speech."[11]

Essayist Patricia Hampl writes, "The right voice can reveal what it's like to be thinking."[12] To re-create thinking on the page is a goal for writers in all genres, as that twisting mind path is part of what makes writing feel alive. This also points us to a method: we have to watch ourselves and listen to ourselves in order to hear and catch those voices and thoughts. In many ways this sets us a deeper and larger goal of noticing those voices that we might not want to hear and of accepting a more varied version of ourselves than the one we might see as our one goal, singular voice, or ideal.

The good news is that the voices are still there, waiting to be listened to. Voices continue to flow and combine. Voice is made up of the words you like and the words that hurt you and that you reclaimed and the way you in particular put words together to try to describe the indescribable. Voice includes techniques and craft elements, including the ones you loved so much—or were exposed to over and over—that you adopted them into your manner of speaking and writing. Voices are made up of styles, but they have a much deeper source.

Voice is more than the icing on the cake of meaning. With its musical changes, its pauses, its circling back, and its emphasis, voices exist to help us absorb meaning. Elbow writes, "When readers hear a voice in a piece of writing, they are more often drawn to read it—and that audible voice often makes the words easier to understand."[13] Phrasing, rhythm, and repetition allow us to feel and absorb meaning from sounds and words.

Voice (to pile on a bunch of metaphors in a very "incorrect" way) is the seed or nutrient that makes ideas and insights gel. It's the yolk that nourishes and grows whatever writing chicken will be roaming around out there in the world. Voice isn't a spice you add in after you're done cooking a dish. Voice is the ground where the crops are grown to make the bread. Elbow argues that writers need to be supported in reconnecting to the source of their expression, which is language and thought itself.[14]

You might have noticed that the voice I'm using right now is not a "normal" textbook voice. Instead, it's more of my speaking voice, and specifically the direct way I talk in the classroom, using shorter words and phrases and more images and some terrible mixed metaphors and similes. I have some confidence in this odd choice only because I have heard myself teaching over a number of years, and this voice has been honed as my body and voice and expression developed in conversation with other writers. This voice was a collective project, edited by many young people who sat and either smiled at me or pulled up their hoodies and put their heads on their desks, and my language changed in the direction of their engagement, in response to what worked. Naming it as my teaching voice gives me confidence in it and helps me pay attention to its qualities and then helps me inquire into where it comes from and what its lineage is.

Voice work can help us write better and also learn about ourselves, inhabit ourselves more fully, figure out what to write and how to write it—and it can fuel writing in any genre in which you like to work. After I began to get comfortable with using a range of voices when I sat down to the keyboard, I also began to be tempted by wilder voice options. I wanted to try everything we're told not to do with voice. What if you let your sixth grade voice write your quarterly earnings report? What if your research paper started with a full-on rant? What were some more rules about voice and genre that I could break?

Getting comfortable with voice—with *voices*—led to me feeling comfortable with my voices for the first time. And once I got comfortable with my voices, I began to think about the hard stuff, the ways in which my voice had been shaped and narrowed and cookie cut. And then I began to push against all those limits, to ask what voices I was allowed to use and what voices I wanted to claim as my own.

BEGINNING YOUR LIST OF VOICES

I'm hoping that as I share my wide range of voices and some writing exercises, these will invite your own range of voices to come to the surface and play. I encourage you to make a list of the voices you discover.

You can even use the back pages of this book or the inside cover of a journal or a separate document. When I'm stuck in one voice, I often forget about the other options, but when I go back to my list, it frees me up to see how many different ways I might tell a story and how many different questions I might ask myself.

In the field of literary nonfiction, essayist Phillip Lopate describes using a "double perspective" to start a conversation between past and present versions of himself.[15] A narrator or speaker can look back and reflect, telling a story about a past experience. Writers can explore and name multiple versions of themselves at different points in time and experiment with the voices associated with those selves. The art of writing in a child's perspective, using the diction and point of view of that child, is one example in which a writer's voice changes with age (more on that in chapter 5). This is also definitely present in fiction and nonfiction, the ability for a persona or character to look back, to say "now I think" and "once I thought."

Pat Schneider, in *Writing Alone and with Others*, talks about writers having three categories of voices: an "original voice" of childhood, a "primary voice" used in our present everyday life, and many "acquired voices." She describes the primary voice as "the natural unselfconscious way we talk to the people we most love and with whom we are most comfortable," one that has "taken on color and texture from every place we have lived, everyone with whom we have lived, and all that we have experienced." It has "traces of our original voice" and "the colors, the rhythms, the peculiar intonations of your own generation."[16] Peter Elbow describes this as the "home voice," which he says is a necessary ingredient for becoming comfortable with the act of writing itself.[17]

To access home voice and other voices, Elbow helped to popularize the practice of short bursts of "freewriting" in which writers spill words on a page in a timed burst for five minutes or longer, not worrying about correctness or form or any other requirements. That practice will also be used quite a bit in this book. Schneider's *Writing Alone and with Others* describes the freewrite as having begun with authors Dorothea Brand and Brenda Ueland in the 1930s, then spread by Elbow, and then used with still wider popularity by writing teachers Natalie Goldberg and Julia Cameron.[18]

Freewriting has a lineage that connects to gesture drawing in art and to the artistic movements of surrealism and Dadaism, which focus on process and the act of creation. And even before those movements, writers were discovering this technique on their own. Charles Darwin described how he stumbled on this technique in his 1887 autobiography, finding that writing worked best when he would "scribble in a vile hand whole pages as quickly as I possibly can, contracting half the words; and then correct deliberately. Sentences thus scribbled down are often better than I could write deliberately."[19]

Those first scribbles aren't the finished product, but you can take your wild and authentic and causal expression, your freewrites and your sketches, and trace within them your own complex lineage, asking yourself about all the influences that formed the way you express yourself. Then you can consciously decide to feed and grow certain voices, to analyze and understand them, to study them to see what makes them tick, and to use them to not only enliven your writing but also to create new genres and styles and forms.

You can play dress-up with your voice, with the voices of others, and in that process of changing and enjoying and performing, you can become good at "voicing,", at making the sounds and inhabiting the voices, at sensing your own voices, and at tuning into and appreciating and nurturing the voices of others. You can change your voices as much as you can change your life, and even more. Your voices can wonder about lives you haven't lived yet.

TRY THIS

1. To start our exploration, make a list of the voices you use in your everyday life. The voice I use to tell my son to get up in the morning is not the same as the voice I use to write emails to my department chair. Include your various social media voices, if you have them, and voices you use to talk to your pets and neighbors, maybe even the voice you use to argue with the evening news. Think about an

average day and all the voices you use to communicate in your present-day life. Aim for at least ten on that list. Feel free to give them names.

2. Now choose one voice from that list and write for five minutes using that voice. What does your Text Message L O L Hahahaha Woman have to tell you about your life? What is Work Email Woman afraid of? What does I Love My Doggy voice think about work? Take a voice and let it comment on anything besides what it normally focuses on. Give it free rein. This might feel odd. Don't worry about making any of these brainstorming exercises leap off the page to become finished pieces of writing. Instead, you're building an inventory of all the tones and sounds and stances you have to work with, including many that we dismiss because their output or points of view are not seen as important. But they can all be of use, and they are all parts of you and how you see the world.

3. To sharpen your voice-catching muscles, try to pay attention to your expressions as you go about your day. How do you answer a question? With a "Sure thing" or a "Yeah" or an "I'm sorry?" Jot down some of the words and phrases that come out of your mouth as accurately as you can. How you speak is connected to how you write and who you are.

Listen for yourself during three times in which you speak this week. Maybe even record yourself. Write down exactly what you hear. The important thing is see it as an exercise not in in finding errors but in really paying attention to the beautiful flow of living language of which you are a part.

Look at an old piece of writing. What figures of speech, grammatical constructions, words, and habits of language do you see? Do these connect to a voice you can name?

If there is an area of a current writing project you are having particular difficulty with, try to rewrite that section as simply as possible, using your speaking voice. This does not have to be language that will go in your final draft, but it can help you see where you are tripping over your own language or covering up interesting points with needlessly complicated words.

2 *The Voice Lineage*

We use the word *voice* to stand for an entire spectrum of actions, qualities, and objects associated with expression. Imagine studying a book of matches, a flame, the heat from the flame, and a pile of ashes and describing them all as "fire."

Philip Roth writes that voice "begins around the back of the knees and reaches well above the head."[1] To me voice begins even farther back than that—with an itch in the mind, an impulse in the body, a leaf blowing on the family tree. And then a voice goes out into the world, and it gets heard, and whoever is around to absorb it takes in all the elements, from word choice to tone to pauses to volume, and then shapes the voice in response as expression continues. My main focus is on giving you a wider range of material to ignite. If the sources of voice are exercised and expanded, you're going to sound a lot different and feel more empowered to make those choices yourself.

Kids understand voice play. When I wrote my first stories and poems as a child, I heard a voice in my head suggesting the next word. I knew from endless games of pretend with friends how to don a scary Dracula voice or the voice of an imagined walrus. My voice was the way I liked to tell stories, with tricks borrowed from other people, with storytelling phrasing that was an amalgam of "Once upon a time" of *Grimm's Fairy Tales* and "A long time ago in a galaxy far, far away" from *Star Wars*.

Kids take on voices boldly, using outside voices when they are supposed to be napping. And then, as they grow up, they learn to be quiet.

You wouldn't believe how many times I have had to cut the phrase "I think" from this book. Almost every sentence begins, inside me, with an "I think." This is like a tiny little diving board for me, space to venture a theory, to say that I'm speaking from my own experience—and that you, my reader, shouldn't be mad at me because I'm not trying to start a fight. *Hey, I might be wrong here, but I think . . . though I'm not sure.*

I've published seven books, and yet in some ways I'm less confident in what I know than when I was eight. And that is one of the many ways that life shapes our writing. I'm imagining my "I think" has something to do with gender, something to do with being a midwesterner, something to do with being an essayist positing guesses and asking questions.

Peter Elbow describes voice as being composed of three strands: "audible voice," or what the author's writing sounds like; "dramatic voice," or what kind of speaker or writer is implied; and "one's own voice," or the relationship between the speaker of a text and the real author.[2] Ideally, I think that writers can become aware of all three strands, and the awareness gives us more options.

In composition studies there was an explosion of interest in helping writers find their voice in the 1970s, followed by a movement against this approach, as the concept was seen as both too vague and too focused on an individual essence rather than social and historical forces that shape an author or text.[3] Elbow responded to these critics by saying that voice is complicated and can be both about the self and about society; voice is about freedom to explore as well as careful and focused editing and shaping. We can analyze a text as a text, we can analyze how a speaker sounds and what their ethos or persona or reputation is in a text, and we can still talk about voice. After forty years of discussion in the field of teaching writing, Elbow still says that talking about voice "can help people enjoy writing more." And I agree with him.

Talking about voice gives us permission to examine the urge to express that begins as a tickle in the mind and can help put the focus on what it feels like to write and speak, what it feels like to hear oneself speaking or see oneself writing, and to shape and revise. And that comfort or knowledge of voice builds confidence, which I think then subtly allows us to stretch out a bit and explore.

Writers play. We put on masks for satire, we don character for fiction, and we slip into intellectual and social roles or make them up as we go along. And play is serious, productive work. Part of why writing my book about pain was so liberating was because Pain Woman surprised me, taking on characteristics I hadn't seen in myself or had been too afraid to inhabit. And then she paved the way for changes in how I acted in my real life. Elbow writes that this play, including "role-playing and irony and make-believe," helps us to access "possible or temporary selves or dimensions of the protean self that are important and useful but unavailable to conscious thinking and feeling."[4]

As we move beyond childhood, we get more complicated, as do the roles we are asked to play. We are asked to be polite when we don't feel like it. We are asked to be quiet when we want to yell and to restrain ourselves when we want to cry or throw a book. Or we are called to be a loud voice, to lead or defend, when we're tired or scared and don't feel like we have it in us. We grow up, and we begin to reckon with authority, first at the level of the rules and then later through experience, with the complex ways a word or action might affect us. We have responsibilities that require us to bring certain elements of our personalities to the fore, and we are forced to develop separate masks and selves and voices to manage these different roles.

In school we practice the genres and forms needed to demonstrate learning and that will be useful in our future work. We summarize and analyze and take positions. Expressive writing usually disappears sometime in grade school, and that's when, for many kids, writing becomes the enemy. I think it's no accident that reading drops off for some kids around that time too.

The good news is that even if this happened to you, your palette of voices is still inside you, constantly growing and accruing detail, as experiences and other voices and reading shape you. We switch among a few voices we need to navigate through the day, and we try out new voices all the time on our friends, in jokes, in emails, and on social media. The internet is a cornucopia of voices, as is most comedy. Our various masks and roles grow some of our voices, and voice can be found in connection with literary terms such as *persona*, *form*, and *genre*. As a way to get into discussion of voice, let's explore a little about where we can find it and what it does.

PERSONA

Historically, the notion of voice comes to us through the writings of Greek and Roman philosophers of antiquity like Aristotle, who analyzed drama and rhetoric. The word *persona* has its origins in Roman drama, as an actual mask that was used to amplify one's voice. These were oral cultures in which voices debated live in the public square.

The word *mask* implies that there is a real being behind it and that the mask itself is a kind of disguise. A persona is said to be a role, which also implies that there is an element of fictionality and performance to what is being expressed. Instead of persona, I am using the idea of a range of voices, so we avoid the dualistic conundrum about "real" and "false" selves.

Personae can be helpful as a way to think of clusters of voices. I've been watching more stand-up comedy lately, both as stress relief but also as a kind of craft study. Comedy exists in an interesting state between fiction and nonfiction. Robin Williams onstage was not the entire range of Robin Williams who existed when he got up in the morning and brushed his teeth. Audience members who tuned in to his show or bought tickets to one of his performances understood the rules of the game. They understood that Williams wrote his act using his comedic persona as a lens that seems to magnify certain personality traits and even twist experiences to make them funny. Comedy is a fun house mirror version of reality.

Tickets to his performance of persona were sold under the "genre" heading of comedy on a ticket website. Williams wouldn't necessarily be brushing his teeth onstage or sitting down to watch television or having a serious conversation with a family member. While those all fall under the umbrella of "Robin Williams the person," they don't necessarily fall under the umbrella of the "Robin Williams comedy persona," unless he decided to include them by making jokes about them. Stand-up comics take observations of themselves and others in real life and amp them up to create their comedic personae.

If you had bought a ticket to see Robin Williams perform, you would have a very general idea of what you might see: Robin Williams doing something related to what he had done in the past under the general umbrella of comedy. Robin might have decided to mess with you a bit—maybe start off serious and sad—but eventually, he'd bust right into what he did best, including being funny and thought provoking and zany.

Whenever we write, we offer a certain slice of reality: either the fictional world we are writing about or the world of our present and past or some shadowland merger of the two. If I'm writing a memoir about health insurance, for example, I would select experiences that intersected with that topic and would leave out, for example, the fact that I once knocked over a mannequin in a dress shop because I sat on a display while my mom was looking at clothes. (I'm saving that moment for my chaos memoir.)

My nonfiction persona, which you can also call the "narrator," shifts slightly with each book, but each rendition overlaps. The persona promises the reader a certain version of my life, as filtered through a certain consciousness. Persona is a huge box that can include one or more voices, and I would describe it in nonfiction as the character of the narrator.

In fiction and poetry a persona is a character that the author speaks through. I'd like to make a distinction between persona, or character, and voice. In Lisa Ko's novel *The Leavers*, which is about immigration, imprisonment, and loss, many stressful things happen to the main characters, a mother and a son. You might think that the characters' individual personae, lines of dialogue, and points of view form the voice. But what's fascinating about this novel—and what makes the magic of resonance happen in literature more generally—is that Ko manages to infuse the book with narrating voices that distill not only tragedy but the recalcitrance, stubbornness, hope, humor, and life force of a child and then a teen boy. He describes a couch in an apartment that he and his mother shared with others: "Deming saw worlds in its patterns, stared at the colors until he got cross-eyed and the flowers took on different shapes, fish tank, candies, treetops in October, and he envisioned himself underwater, swimming against the surface of the fabric."[5] The character isn't always speaking in that mood, but Ko's narrator keeps in contact with that range of voices as a life force to anchor the story.

Often, without even realizing it, a writer chooses a palette of voices that express or first kindled their interest in the topic or the story. I've read a really funny and warm statistics textbook and a reverent and spiritual book about plant genetics, so authors are definitely not limited to the voices that seem closest to the expected sound of their topic.

My everyday expressing self is quite a bit wilder even than the voice I'm using to speak to you now. Yours is too. Elbow writes that when we write, we edit out a lot of what makes our text messages and tweets and emails funny and engaging: exclamation points, the mic drop dry humor of omitting punctuation, shouty caps, and emojis. And never mind our speaking voices and our expressions![6] What I love about Elbow is that he asks questions no one else asks, such as: Why do we assume that "good writing" is writing that strips out all the fun stuff? Many of us get nervous performing this "hush up" act of our true selves on the page, and we think we're not "good writers" because we don't know the rules for conforming.[7]

This doesn't mean that everything should be a tweet or a text or that we should stop teaching formal communication in business writing. But it would help to be a little more clear-sighted about our options.

Robin Williams was a master of voices, and he could put his brain into anything. He could pretend to be a toaster. It probably seems, with any comedian you might love, that their hilarious voices emerge as fully formed brilliance from pockets in their minds. But I guarantee that they've put in work and hours to locate the whispers of those voices and then to amp them up and make them effective. Hints of voices can come up in our lives and imaginations, but we have to choose to grow and develop them. The poet Sandra Beasley describes how writers develop voices, using craft choices in the categories of "Point of View, Tense-Aspect-Mood, Image, Sound, Structure, and Diction. Every word on the page contributes to these decisions."[8]

As we make conscious choices about words and style, we can also name and flesh out the voices we have to choose from. Capturing a voice, one of our voices, on the page is about listening to ourselves and then transcribing that music. Listening to our inner voices and catching them is a skill. Whether it's writing with voice or doing stand-up comedy or playing soccer, hours of practice build the ability and awareness to use these range of skills well.

I have a certain "teaching voice" that comes out of my overall persona. I know that when I start talking, I will often spill coffee on myself and be momentarily disorganized (chaos and enthusiasm, always). At the same time, getting in "teaching mode" means that I move my body in certain ways that are an exaggeration of my regular movements, like punctuation. I speak with more pauses, and my voice has more modulation. I use my hands very actively to gesture; I make more eye contact; I have energy; I elicit laughs and poke fun at myself. I want my students to be engaged.

In writing and in living, different voices have different goals and focuses and worldviews. Voice, while it has beautiful range, is recognizable by its sound, its cadence, its rhythm, and also by the types of things that voice is likely to say and the questions it is likely to ask. A voice can change throughout a piece of writing, but the types of changes that the voice can make have to be organic, dependent on what that voice has brought to the reader, what images arise, and what has been developed in the piece.

Recently, when I was teaching a weekend seminar on voice to creative writers at a former convent turned into a retreat center in the hills of Connecticut, I wrote this on the easel flip chart:

$$\text{Voice} = \frac{(audience + place + time) \times (emotion\ or\ idea + hope + goal)}{\text{all the past voices}}$$

The idea I wanted to explore in that made-up math is that our voices form a kind of goo that carry their history, which I've represented in this formula as "all the past voices." A writer experiences, tunes into, or follows a voice, and a reader connects with that voice on the page. So, the more voices we read or listen to carefully, the more our own voice options expand.

For example, if I'm drawing back into my personal life to excavate a voice, I might discover punk rock girl. But then later, knowing her voice, I might notice her cropping up in places outside a concert or a demonstration. Or I might delve into her a bit and find out that a shading of her voice that's more accurate is "nerdy punk rock girl who doesn't want to drink seven beers because she still wants to read when she gets home." And then later I'd notice that library girl wants to say something.

TONE

Tone and mood are two ways to describe how the writing feels, but we often give a piece of writing less credit for its emotional range than it deserves. So we'll say, "You sound angry in this piece of writing." Then the writer thinks: *Oh, no—I'm angry. I didn't mean to come off that way! I'm sorry! Let me dial it back!*

Or "This piece sounds thoughtful and sorrowful." *Oh no, I didn't mean to bring you down!*

Tone is a very imprecise way of talking about writing, and I recommend not thinking about it when you're writing your first draft. Tone is easily changed from sentence to sentence with a few word choices, so I banish thinking about it until after a piece of work is done. Tone is often more useful in analyzing a particular paragraph or section of a larger of work, because tone is also fluid.

Good writing is going to make a reader feel a whole palette or painting full of emotions, ideally in combinations that no one has invented before. A piece of writing may feel stiff if a writer hasn't yet explored the range of tones available within their chosen voice. And one piece of writing can make three different readers feel three different things, which is great. You will think and feel a range of things in an average hour, so your tone in writing will have range to reflect that.

If we try to aim for a consistent tone in a piece of writing, we are going to create bricks of words instead of living strings of sentences that might spawn other fascinating sentences. You can edit with tone in mind, but tone comes from voice. Tone is one note that voice produces.

The Russian theorist Mikhail Bakhtin described "intonation" as "the point where language intersects with life." Bakhtin also believed in and wrote a lot about the fact that a piece of writing could have "many voices" even when written by a single author; he coined the term *heteroglossia* to describe this phenomenon (in music this is connected to the term *polyphony*). Whereas we sometimes use the word *tone* to describe a singular "emotion" summoned by a piece of writing, intonation is the sound of the sentences and of the emotions and associations that each sentence carries.[9]

GENRE

Genre is another important tool we have to talk about writing. It's a basic question: what are you writing? Sometimes you'll have a writing task for which the genre and form are already decided, like a report or a set of instructions. But sometimes—often—writers noodle around with an idea, unsure whether the tickle in their ribcage is meant to be an editorial or a novel.

Some writers and scholars talk about genre as if it's the *only* thing that matters and that there's a formula for writing well: look at what everyone else has done and do that, then you will be able to persuade an audience and write a good text. Unfortunately, distinguishing a genre by its rules and separating modes of writing can freeze natural discovery processes and creativity and even restrict a writer's ability to use their own experience as a resource.

Voice is actually the thing that creates genre. People long ago ran into problems with trading grain, for example, and a conversation transpired (not historically accurate):

"Hey friend, please trade me some grain for some goats."

"Okay, I'll take that pile of grain for these four goats."

(Scooping and transporting of grain commences.)

Later:

"Thank you! Here are your two goats for that lovely grain."

"Two goats!? You said four goats."

"Did not!"

(Tearing of hair and gnashing of teeth commences.)

"Fine! I am going to take this %$@#$ stick, and we are going to agree that I am making four lines on this hunk of clay to record how many goats I'm going to get for my grain!"

In my joke history, the lines on the hunk of clay were very orderly, omitting the ancient forms of swearing and fighting and gnashing of teeth, and voilà! The genre of accounting was created, along with the form of an invoice or contract. The voice and the need, passion, and human experience—whatever it actually looked like—created this genre as a way to solve a problem and capture expression.

Voice—if it's a living thing—is always pushing at the edges of genre, swinging from the boundaries like a jungle gym. The limitation of genre can give voices a place to play. If we feel something, voice is what guides us to get the mess onto the page. When we follow a voice and listen to what it's telling us, we can then figure out what genre might be most appropriate for the task.

Understanding genre conventions is like a ticket to get in the door to that genre, but voice directs us to genre and form. Starting to write in a genre or form can call forth a standardized or expected voice, which is often very helpful to get started. Voice comes far before genre, however. It allows us to write in a way that "feels like us" even when we're writing a report, giving us the option to express things that feel true. Each voice reveals different truths; voices may reveal truths that contradict one another. The voices we practice become stronger, so that we essentially make ourselves up over time. Voice determines what we absorb from the world as well as what we say and what genres seem appropriate to say it.

Form is a specific thing inside a larger, looser category of genre. A form has certain requirements, decided not by the Form Gods but, instead, by what people have done in the past, over and over. Notches on sticks, business letters, résumés, book reports, academic papers, short stories: these are forms, and they each have an expected voice that goes with them.

Jonathan Swift's "A Modest Proposal" recommended a method for cooking and eating Irish children. It was written as a satire (the genre), in a letter to the editor (form), but it had a serious point about economics and colonialism and English rule of Ireland. It relied for its humor on the tension between the content and the form of the letter to the editor or editorial. It's a brilliant send-up of form and voice.

Brenda Miller and Susan Paola use the term *hermit crab essay* in *Tell It Slant*, a guide to creative nonfiction writing, to describe an essay that lives inside an unexpected form it has adopted as a home. You can do this in fiction and poetry too; I've seen a short story in the form of a shopping list. If you take some content and put it into a form that's unexpected, that electric tension between an unexpected voice and the voice summoned by the form creates all sorts of interesting effects for a writer and a reader. In all genres we have so many fun ways to play with form, from sonnets to one-act plays to book reviews . . . wheeeeeee! Put a meditation about your relationship with your dad into a "how-to" and the results can be fascinating because the form channels a certain expected voice, so it asks you for content that the traditional essay doesn't specify.

The composer Johann Sebastian Bach wrote preludes and fugues in each of twenty-four keys, according to David Bayles and Ted Orland, who explain that "working within the self-imposed discipline of a particular form eases the prospect of having to reinvent yourself with each new piece."[10]

Form is a great way to bring out a voice, but voice and form are not the same thing. A form is a container that can give us the freedom to speak with more authority than we feel, and that boost in authority can allow us to tap into a voice that we might, up until now, not have felt like we had the right to occupy. For example: I love a numbered list when I'm angry. A numbered list makes me outline my points and makes me feel as though I'm not screaming. It helps me to think clearly and also gives me the illusion that I'm being very calm and logical and convincing (even though anyone who's received a numbered list from me knows that I am yelling through gritted teeth).

As another example, I had a lot of feelings about my old car, a Nissan Sentra we named Dentra because of its many scrapes and dings from past accidents. When it could no longer be driven on the highway, we sold it to a teenager in my town so he could use it for parts. For some reason I decided to take the love for my old car and to put it in the form of an ode to a fallen sea captain.

Ideals and rules of a form are essential to show developing writers what good writing looks like and to reveal the possibilities for expression used by writers with different goals, voices, and audiences. Yet each piece of writing, presented as an ideal, invites the type of imitation that focuses on a list of necessary qualities and criteria for that ideal while often implicitly excluding invention or transgression.

So, there are two ways of building writing skills, and they're not mutually exclusive, but they *are* different. One is to fill in forms with content. But the other way is to start with voice—the one that feels connected to your existence and your body. You can write first the way you speak and then, as Elbow says, be pragmatic and edit to "get rid of most of the voice problems for readers" by fitting your voice-generated writing within the form. Elbow shares the benefit of the second way as it builds over time: "When I use the voice or voices that I experience as mine . . . for exploratory and private and early draft writing and try them out on myself and others—listening to them and in appreciating them—these voices tend to get richer and develop. For example, an insecure voice tends to become more confident. Gradually I find I have more flexibility of voice—more voices that feel like me."[11]

TRY THIS

1. Experiment with form and voice from both directions. First, write a standard letter to the editor about a cause you care about, arguing for a specific policy change. Next, start with a rant about something that makes you upset and turn that into a letter to the editor during a second or third draft. What's different in content and voice between the two? How did both feel to write?

2. Think about or look at a favorite book in any genre. Apart from the plot or the content, how would you describe the voices that the narrator uses to speak to the reader? I'm very spatially oriented—I see concepts as two- and three-dimensional shapes—so I might describe a voice, first, as deep and heavy, large, bright, or taking up a lot of space and then home in more deliberately on what I mean. There's no correct way to describe voice. The important thing is that as you read and think about voice, your awareness of your own options expands.

AUDIENCE

Audience is who we are talking to, and rhetoric since the time of Aristotle has focused on how our idea of our audience affects what is said or written, why we are telling something to this particular audience, and what is our goal. Choosing a form helps to shape our sense of audience. When we write a letter to the editor, we're speaking to people who are likely to read letters to the editor of the local or national publication we are writing to.

Mikhail Bakhtin describes how our sense of audience shapes our voice. If I step up to a podium in a convention hall filled with gun owners, I am going to phrase my campaign for total disarmament a little differently than if I were at a nonviolent hippie gathering in the woods. In the first case I might be either more defensive and argumentative, or I might try a different voice to get around what I perceive to be the hostility of the audience. In the second example I would feel more confident in what Bakhtin calls the "choral support" of my voice, and I'd sound very different. I would be looser, more relaxed, and my voice—and specifically what Bakhtin calls my intonation—would range more freely.[12]

Sometimes, though, we think about audience way too early in the writing process, and that hostile audience peering over our shoulder freezes up the writing. The biggest challenge in a writing task can be that hovering audience. A useful trick is to tell that crowd to leave until you're ready to take the stage.

Early in the creative writing process, the only intended audience should be ourselves as we figure out what we want to say and as we play with language and discover what we think. All communication is motivated, but not every communication is an argument. Some communications are merely jottings, thoughts, or unformed blobs or sighs. Our feeling-thinking river of voices is often winding, and we're not sure what we're doing, or perhaps we're contradicting ourselves. And that is *great*. That's where our thoughts, our ideas, come from.

However, we don't talk about that river. And because we don't talk about the river and because we study finished, edited pieces of impressive writing, it's very logical for developing writers to look at those examples and feel like they are, by comparison, bad writers.

Imagine showing kids endless videos of soccer games in which Lionel Messi is making perfect shots on goal and then telling them not to have fun playing a soccer game and instead grading them on how close they come to Messi's form. Everyone would hate soccer.

Poets Tony Hoagland and Kay Cosgrove describe voice as "warmth and élan, humor, intelligence, and wildness."[13] If we think too much about audience when we start to form ideas, that warmth can freeze, and that wildness can run fleeing into the woods.

ETHOS

Ethos is a rhetorical term used by Aristotle to describe how the author comes across to the reader, including whether the author is or seems trustworthy and how that affects our judgment of the person's argument. Basically, ethos is the social media of rhetoric, that sense of how you look to other people.

The confusing thing for writers is that the term *voice* is sometimes also used as a way to describe the ethos or persona of the writer. To me, voice is bigger than ethos and contains it as one of its elements.

A voice has the feeling of a live person, and this voice can also be crafted and abused. Political candidates with authentic-sounding voices have transfixed many voters, and this resonance seems, for many people, more important than any political platform or goal.[14] A voice can be transfixing and powerful. Whether it is authentic or a mixture of authenticity and manipulation, its power is more than a conscious crafting of ethos as an appeal. Voice can be woven from strands that the writer or speaker isn't even aware of.

The lesson from political campaigns is that relying on voice is powerful—so powerful, sadly, that its relationship to fact is often secondary or nonexistent. Voice is a life force that can be used for good or evil; it is as subtle and complex as art and story. As communicators, we ignore voice at our peril, and once we appreciate it, we can use it to draw forth resonant and necessary writing and speaking.

For writers voice is more about listening to the words and rhythms inside us and less about crafting the image of a reliable person you want to sound like or be like. Voice is an exploration of complex authenticity. Poet and essayist Claudia Rankine's book *Just Us: An American Conversation*, for example, weaves multiple forms of poetry and prose, and the text rings true as she meditates on her reality as a Black woman because she's searching and pushing at the edges, questioning and lamenting, breathing and pacing her reflections. She morphs before the reader's eyes, shifting from poetic line to prose and then into paragraphs of cited research. Her voices include pointed anger but also a larger voice that seeks connection, a generous voice that invites engagement, peeling back layers and layers, asking for "Black women and white women to face each other's angers without denial or immobilization or silence or guilt"; she describes this way of coming together as "a heretical and generative idea."[15] Her control of voice is virtuosic, not because it's consistent but because the weaving together of voices is so subtle and allows ample room to move and think. In your own reading, listen for the woven voices that emanate from the page, then ask yourself what within you is responding.

GOOOOOOOAL!

When we start talking about a goal for writing, our minds easily go to persuasion: to convince, to argue a point. (Or we might assume that Messi has scored a goal.)

Most student writers encounter writing in school as the act of having to choose a thesis and support it with evidence, but they are often also asked to put on a false voice, a mask developed before they discover complex standpoints they feel passionately about and before they know themselves. Persuasive writing is often framed as a kind of battle in which a writer has to "hook" a reader, bash the reader over the head with evidence, dispatch counterevidence with swipes of a blade, and restate one's main point like a final body blow. William Zeiger describes assignments like the argumentative research paper as documents with a goal of wrestling a resistant audience into submission with a voice of "intrusive rigidity."[16] When writers come into my college-level creative nonfiction classroom, they often tell me that they had no idea that the personal essay—with its range of voices, its research and humor and personal experience and questioning—existed. They've been taught that the only way to speak and think correctly is to deploy a particular and narrowed form in a disembodied voice.

The practice of persuasion has been allowed to devour real, warm, living voices that don't always have persuading to do. In areas of our culture focused on buying and selling and reducing everything to dollars and cents, every communication is assumed to be persuasion: a seller and a buyer, a candidate and a voter. The audience isn't an audience anymore. It's a target. The unfortunate downside is that when persuasion is abused or overdone, people tune out. And when the same genres and forms are used over and over, our range of voices—and our thinking—is impoverished. So often, we use text to divide and not to connect.

Yes, we need to understand these tricks, and we need media savvy to understand the rhetorical attacks and manipulations being rained down upon us at every turn. The vital deployment and analysis of persuasion allows us to take part in community debates and in conversations inside or outside of our workplaces.

But communication and writing are not all about persuasion. They are not all battles. In fact, we can breathe a little freer—and understand why communication is beautiful and nuanced—when we give ourselves the freedom to *not* persuade. I believe we are turning children and young adults away from writing by teaching only persuasive writing in a culture in which persuasion has become our default and facts aren't respected on their own, in which they are only seen as ammunition in an argument whose end goal is deception.

Most stories and poems don't exist to persuade but to explore ideas and consequences. And much of nonfiction provided a space for personal meditation and reflection or to help an author draw together notes or records for the purpose of further examination. The practice of journaling and also journalism are both records of asking questions, reviewing experiences, and seeking answers. Research in most academic disciplines presents the evolution of a researcher's questions over time. A diary involves a call-and-response between the data presented by the world and the writer's reaction to what is observed or noticed. Many theorists in the field of rhetoric and composition have highlighted the degree to which writing is a question-asking and recursive discipline. As a writer commits a sentence to paper, that writer learns and reveals what is unknown or half-formed.

Thinking about voice *first* gives us another way into writing, a relational view in which we get in touch with voices to see what they might want to say and who might want to listen. Brenda Ueland writes about this act of discovery in her classic book *If You Want to Write*: "At last I understood that writing was this: an impulse to share with other people a feeling or truth that I myself had. Not to preach to them, but to give it to them if they cared to hear it."[17]

Voices can form this sense of connection between reader and writer. When the writer or narrator feels like a friend and displays the signals and pauses and humanity of a person speaking, the text builds up "an environment of companionable warmth" and "an atmosphere of connectedness, of relationally."[18] A relationship is established between speaker and audience when we imagine this choral support.

This choral support can be especially vital if a writer comes from a community or perspective that is often denigrated or dismissed. In her framework for an anti-racist writing workshop, Felicia Rose Chavez recommends "a pedagogy of deep listening—to one's self, to one's workshop leader, and to every member of the collective—ensuring equal access to voice."[19]

Writers can discover a wide range of voices—beyond voices intending to deceive, to woo, and to wrestle the audience into submission—so that they can hear or sense themselves as they choose to communicate. Stephen Peter Healey recommends that writers look at a wide range of samples "without needing to choose one approach as a stable identity," which he sees as a way to "gain access to many different voices."[20]

Our voices each have truths to offer, and some of the best writing comes from merging voices, braiding them, and letting them run free. One of the most brilliant and complex examples of this approach is the satirical essay by Adriana Páramo entitled "The Wetbacks Are Coming," in her book *Looking for Esperanza*, which relays the author's quest to talk with a migrant farmworker who lost a child crossing the U.S.-Mexico border. An immigrant Latina herself, Páramo uses the inflammatory and pejorative word in the essay's title to inhabit a voice that *seems* to be speaking for an anti-immigrant perspective. But then, before the reader knows it, she infuses the immigrants with superhero qualities, then turns the assumed audience on its heads, poking at an unaware U.S. citizen, "you," who does not understand where her strawberries have come from or who has picked them, with the reader in on the joke:

Build a wall of inextinguishable fire, set up posts along the border with venom-spitting dragons, rotate lethal formations of blood sucking bats, position angry cherubs along the fence and train them to release their arrows south-bound, send armies of engineered fireflies to illuminate the perimeter, dig bottomless trenches. Take your pick. But remember, these wetbacks are willful, hungry, thirsty, desperate, and are the descendants of Mayan kings and Aztec princesses who practiced human sacrifice. And you'll see all of this in their faces as they cross the border. Again. And again.[21]

Her vision shifts from dehumanizing anonymity into raw power; a set of directions for how to repel immigrants ends up short-circuiting to reveal history and strength. And the piece quivers with voices.

ALL TOGETHER NOW

Here's a messy, sprawling, extended metaphor to give you a visual: genre is a big container, say a room in a house that's usually devoted to a specific purpose. One room is for cooking, one for sleeping, and so on. Forms are little containers inside each of these large containers. You may have a saucepan in the kitchen, and you have a container for jewelry on your bedside table.

Voice is whatever in the universe might go into these containers: the silver earrings and the apples and nuts and fuel for your body and the books on the shelves. Or the bowling ball on the bookshelf and the piñata over your bed—whatever makes you happy. The lovely thing about voice is that it comes first, and it can go in any container you want to put it in. Voice is the reason that these containers exist, and voice is so powerful that it can bust right through the sides of a container. If the saucepan has a crack, you pour the soup into another pot. And if you keep adding to the soup, you change it into a gravy or a casserole, and then it needs another container altogether.

A voice can shift throughout a book to create a structure and experience for the reader. The tone would change from page to page or even from sentence to sentence. The persona would likely be consistent, but it wouldn't have to be; maybe something that happened to the narrator would change the person. The ethos would be a specific subset of qualities that would help a reader make a decision about how to feel about that speaker, and we might argue that the most effective way to convey the complexity of a real person would be to weave the most complex fabric of voices.

My writing projects in various genres are intimately connected. The impulse for one approach or topic comes out of a problem raised in another genre. An insight that emerges in a commentary piece provides a new insight into pedagogy, and a work of memoir will require research and persuasive or exploratory writing. I draw from my own writing process to explain the cycle of writing from inspiration to final product, and I call it a cycle because a final product will naturally lead to the next source of inspiration.

TRY THIS

Exploring voices can help us understand and connect to facets of ourselves and others. Getting comfortable with the range of voices that I inhabit has given me, somehow, more compassion toward myself. If you are working with a fictional character or a persona in a poem, you could also do the exercises here for that character, instead of yourself, understanding that the source of the voices that emerge might be connected to something in you.

1. Walker Gibson writes, "We are all made up of all the selves we act out, all day long and every day." What are the voices that speak through you in an average day? I use several voices a lot in everyday life:

Writer-encourager-wowee-excited woman (often with lots of mentions of "dude" and "awesome")
Pain woman
Twitter random tangent woman
Soapboxer of justice (have you read this incredibly disturbing article?)

Mom to a teen: active listening and then not reacting too strongly
Customer
Responsible employee
Smart-ass
Focused thinker kinda-academic researcher
Exhausta-girl
Tornado of anxiety and doom

What are yours? Can you write just one sentence or phrase in one of these voices? You might even look through emails or posts on social media or text messages to see how one of these voices sounds. Keep these voices in a big list that you'll add to as you work through this book.

2. Take five minutes and write in one of these voices.
3. Listening for other people's voices and voice techniques will also help with your ability to hear voices in general. Think about a person who you are close to and whose voice you hear regularly. How do they say "good morning" or "goodbye"? How do they start a story or try to make you laugh? What words do they use to pause or interrupt themselves? What words do they use when they're surprised or disappointed? What figures of speech do they use regularly? How do they show doubt and confidence?
4. Try a day or two of active listening to or engaging with speech or expression. Whenever you have the chance—in a meeting, in a restaurant, in a class, on social media, on a bus—jot down exact phrases that you encounter. You don't have to catch everything, but the habit of collecting live expression is a huge gift to your own writing—and is also very surprising and enjoyable, once you get the hang of it.
5. Try a day or two of listening to yourself again. What words irritate you? What words, phrases, and expressions do you love and use all the time? When other people imitate you, what do they sound like?

3 *Voices Live in the Body*

Our speaking and signing voices emanate from the body. And reading was also once "voicing," as people spoke aloud as they read, even to themselves, and some still do. Reading silently is a more recent skill, and studies show that many of us still engage the nerves and muscles in our throats when we read.[1] I often catch myself misspelling words based on what they sound like, such as *made* for *maid*, and when I encounter a difficult passage in reading or writing, I often read it aloud under my breath to parse its meaning. My writing and my speech both sound different when I feel in tune with my body versus when I'm holding my breath and writing from my head.

Jill Hackett describes voices as being located in different parts of the body, which may be a helpful visual: "We have three voice centers: the voice from our head (the rational voice: ideas strike us and set off thoughts and plans), the voice from our hearts (the emotive voice: feelings, memories, longings, and passions), and our body voice (language of the gut, hunches, intuition)."[2]

Writing from the voice of the body, however, is probably not so simple. We live in a culture in which bodies are edited and critiqued, so hardly anyone has an unproblematic relationship with their body. Health problems such as chronic pain make it easy to want to detach from the body, and trauma also makes people want to "leave" their bodies and dissociate. The Western dualistic framework of body versus mind implies that our bodies don't play a role in intellectual work.

Often when I'm writing, I end a paragraph or long sentence and realize that I've been holding my breath or breathing very shallowly. Sometimes when I write, I hunch at the computer like a troll, curling my spine into a shape that would get me immediately banished from any self-respecting yoga class.

I'm not a paragon of body awareness, so I'm not going to tell you that disembodied writing is bad. I've done so much judging of myself that I do better when I'm more neutral about it, when I view my range of voices as colors on a palette. Some are connected physically, and some are more "heady."

I don't feel like I live in a state of active body loathing, but I have a lot of body privilege to thank for that. I "fit" roughly into people's expectations for a cis white woman, and I usually pass as abled even with my invisible disabilities. But I have absorbed the cultural messages of constant imperfection: *you are a home-improvement project that is not quite working.*

I'm prone to aggression toward what is and tend to grab on tightly and try to wrestle my experience into a version of how I *think* it should be. Maybe writing from the body—as it really is—is an especially dicey game for writers who always know that the sentence could be better, that the backspace or delete key are ever ready.

Chronic pain has made me even less willing to sort through the range of physical sensations and signals I get from the old meat carriage, but in general I'd rather be reading, in my head, away. I often use writing as the purest form of escape from my body. I'm not advocating any kind of body hatred, as lived experience is really all we have. But I think disconnection from our bodies affects the power and range of our voices.

Still, I suppose hunching in front of a keyboard and burrowing into the alphabet is my form of chain-smoking. I like it. It makes a complicated world into a simple one in which I have control. Like smoking or eating a bag of chips or watching television or playing a video game, writing is my way to reduce the inputs and control the outputs and let me be in charge. We humans have engineered thousands of ways to make the complicated world a little simpler, but it seems that each of them has a different cost. And I've been rewarded for this particular form of leaving my body; I've made a career of living in my head and on the screen.

Relaxing and being in my body, just letting things happen, is overwhelming by comparison. There are all these signals from my body, some of them about pain, some of them about past and present feelings, and like many people, I get panicked because there's a tug-of-war happening: leave; stay; leave; stay.

Ultimately, when I commit to being present and breathing, it's not so bad at all. It's just a different set of sensory inputs, and then, after a few minutes, the experience gets kind of nice and fulfilling and lives up to all those annoyingly positive things that people say about reality. Still, I've got an out-of-body habit to fight against. Maybe you do too.

Like many people, I have come upon some of my writing techniques by accident. That's how I learned to take a walk or stretch when I'm stuck. I'm sure this wasn't planned as a way to write, but I do like to take walks for stress relief, pleasure, and exercise.

I noticed that once my body started moving in a rhythm of steps, once I straightened out and altered my breathing and got some oxygen flowing to my brain, ideas started emerging. Sometimes they were the seeds of new essays, and other times I would start out on a walk with a thorny structural problem to consider. I knew that after an hour, I'd return home with one foothold, one idea, one alternate way in.

Many, many writers—from Friedrich Nietzsche to Ernest Hemingway to Brenda Ueland—describe walking, or getting away from the keyboard in whatever form that takes for you, as a key to generating ideas. When the body is engaged in a new way, the brain's neurons fire a little differently, and new thoughts and connections emerge. At an even deeper level, some neurologists argue that the very act of complex thinking is built on gestures, which are spatial ways of representing reality in our heads. As Barbara Tversky writes, "Spatial thinking is the foundation of abstract thought." She documents experiments in which people, prohibited from gesturing with their hands, literally couldn't form ideas.[3] And movement, of course, makes gesture happen. Part of the magic of moving in rhythm is that it gives us a baseline with which to *feel* the rhythm of sentences. The most basic units of measuring time in our bodies are our breath and our heartbeat.

Virginia Woolf, master of language and masterful observer of the human condition, writes: "Style is a very simple matter: it is all *rhythm*. Once you get that, you can't use the wrong words. . . . Now this is very profound, what rhythm is, and goes far deeper than words. A sight, an emotion, creates this wave in the mind, long before it makes words to fit it; and in writing . . . one has to recapture this, and set this working . . . and then, as it breaks and tumbles in the mind, it makes words to fit it."[4]

Rhythm is the way the body thinks, from our heartbeat to the way we respond to and create movement through dance, sports, or rituals. We respond to language and music because we sense them with our whole selves. Different bodies make different rhythms, sounds, and voices. And the same body can make a range of voices if it alters its posture, stance, or emotions.

BREATHING

My own disconnection from my body and my breath was a difficult knot to undo. But once I starting focusing on my body, my breath began to recover. I started having panic attacks in my twenties, and since that time, I've wrestled with what it means to pay attention to my breathing without strangling myself or hyperventilating.

When I started to try to meditate, I was given the instruction to watch the breath. The only problem was that I had a hard time feeling the difference between "watch" and "crush." I thought too much about breathing, and then before I knew it, I was lightheaded, and I forgot what a normal breath feels like. How can a person not know how to breathe?

I asked a question about this at a meditation instruction event, and the teacher furrowed his brow and said, "Well, there's some self-consciousness at the very beginning, I suppose, but that goes away."

At that point I'd been meditating for four years, and now, years later, the challenge has improved a little but hasn't vanished.

Instead, I discovered a secret work-around that helped me. I watched my breathing in my peripheral vision and focused, instead, on various constellations of muscles in my shoulders, asking them to relax. Then both my breathing and my muscles loosened, neither of them fully in the glare of my watchful eye. I then asked another meditation teacher about this, and she told me that paying attention to the body is fine. A lot of meditators apparently do this. She helped me relax by telling me that I could do whatever worked to keep myself focused.

I learned, once I got this trick down, that the shape of my body affects the voices and rhythms in my head. When I am able to relax and take a few breaths, to feel the tightness in my hips and shoulder and stop wrestling and resisting, the music and hum in my head changes.

This is not good or bad; it is just another tool. I notice, too, that when I'm tense and holding my breath, I'm more likely to write super-long breathless sentences that never stop and that loop in a thousand interesting curlicue ways. When I'm breathing, I relax. My sentences do too. They get simpler and more direct.

TRY THIS

1. Try watching your breath or your body—whatever works for you. Is there a writing voice you can connect with, and how does it change as you watch? Try writing a sentence or two about how you are feeling in your physical body right now.

2. Many meditators use a technique called "body scanning" to help them relax muscle groups and to connect to their physical selves. To do this, you can start at your scalp and work down, or start at a problem point (for me, my shoulders). The goal, rather than to struggle against those tense muscles, is to just *investigate* the actual sensations. Amazingly, when you stop fighting against them, they begin to loosen in response to this attention. Try writing about some of those knotted parts of your body, maybe by making a list and trying for metaphors that describe those sensations. Do

you notice, as you attend to different parts of your body, how the sensations shift and change?

BODY, TRAUMA, AND STORY

I recently read an excellent book entitled *The Body Keeps the Score: Brain, Mind, and Body in the Healing of Trauma* by Bessel van der Kolk. It's about trauma and post-traumatic stress disorder and the ways in which those experiences can trigger dissociation from one's body. Van der Kolk explores therapeutic options for forging a stronger connection between one's mind and one's body after trauma. This is important to me because my anxiety will periodically get triggered by something, and then—whoosh—it's hard to breath and to stay physically present.

Van der Kolk writes: "Our sense of agency, how much we feel in control, is defined by our relationship with our bodies and its rhythms: Our waking and sleeping and how we eat, sit, and walk define the contours of our days. In order to find our voice, we have to be *in* our bodies—able to breathe fully and able to access our inner sensations. This is the opposite of dissociation, of being 'out of body' and making yourself disappear."[5] He's talking here about voice as a sense of self and personal agency. Being grounded in our bodies helps us know ourselves and hear our own important stories. But again, don't worry about the dualism of "in" or "out" of body, and don't judge yourself if this seems like a huge task based on your experiences and background. You might find power in listening to your body for a minute at a time and work from there, or put this technique aside entirely if you are not in a place where you can investigate this.

Some voices are doorways or fulcrums. We use them to access things we can't get to another way. Some voices we use only in conversations with ourselves. Some voices are bad habits, and others bring in a breath of fresh air or a reminder of what sustains us. A list of possible voices that grows and grows can give a sense of wealth and abundance and can let you take up space on the page.

Sonja Livingston is a nonfiction writer whose work often channels various voices. I use her essay "Thumb-Sucking Girl" in many of my writing classes because it is such a powerful channel for a version of the author's life from when she was a child.[6] It begins:

> Look at me.
>
> At me, over here.
>
> Look and shake your head all you want. At my uneven bangs, these broken-down shoes, my momma, all us kids, and all our belongings shoved into just one car. Whisper and sigh all you want because I have something better than good clothes and a permanent address. I've got my thumb. My right thumb to be precise—and the soft pink underside of its arch.

With just a handful of short sentences, Livingston conjures a bold childhood voice that we can assume was key to her own audacious survival. Despite the evidence of family turmoil and displacement, she demands that the reader look right at her and then says that her thumb is the anchor to her comfort, in a moment when it's clear she doesn't have much else to rely on. We can also see the threading of her adult voice and its advanced vocabulary in these lines, leaving traces of the guidance and distance needed to turn back to this child voice.

The poet and physician William Carlos Williams wrote that poetry channels voices of "the past, the depths of our very beings . . . the deeper portions of the personality speaking, the middle brain, the nerves, the glands, the very muscles and bones of the body itself speaking."[7] If we let the body speak, we might not even know yet what voices we are channeling; they might be new and surprise us with their secrets or their confidence.

TRY THIS

1. Try to put yourself into the mindset of the kid you used to be. It might help to first pick an age, think about what you liked to do at that age or what were your favorite things or moments of comfort and joy, then write from that point of view. Children are often bold, physical, and a little feral. What was your wild voice like, and what would it say to the reader?

2. Now try another age, five years ahead or before the first one. What happens to the voice?

THE BODY POLITIC

As an adult, one of the first ways I tried to write about my body was to tell my story as it intersected with the long-standing national health insurance crisis in the United States. In *Cover Me: A Health Insurance Memoir* I pushed against my tendency to intellectualize the issue and instead described what was happening to me physically:

> By age thirty-three I had yelled into a megaphone for universal healthcare on the steps of the Ohio statehouse. I had enrolled my baby son in the state program for low-income families. I had seen my picture in the newspaper and heard my voice on the radio yelling about healthcare. By age thirty-three I had already been sent to collections several times for medical debt. I worried about money, which sent cortisol and other stress hormones coursing through my body, triggering the fight or flight response that proclaimed an emergency and then subtly wore me down with the effort of staying on physical alert. By age thirty-three I had lived through eleven gaps in healthcare coverage. During each, I wore a groove of worry in my frontal lobe that seemed directly connected to my lymph nodes, white blood cells, and serotonin levels.

By using cues to the physical body, with active physical verbs like *yelled*, *heard*, and *lived through* and by repeatedly mentioning organs and bodily fluids triggered by anxiety and other external events, I tried to remind the reader that the body is both physical and epistemological, that there's a connection between our cells and the meanings we make of the world.

One of the effects of more embodied writing, for me, is that I slow down. You can almost feel a heartbeat of regular rhythm in those sentences and observations with the parallel structure I used, the repetition of the same introductory phrase *by age thirty-three* and then a simple subject-verb construction.

That book is partially an attempt to argue that our body as an instrument of knowing has been physically and psychically shaped by our access to affordable health care, including the very physical existence of the mind itself. I ask readers to consider the extent of the invasion of corporate health care into our very selves.

TRY THIS

1. What political issue or community has shaped your physical or mental existence? This could be anything from the debate about high-impact sports and concussions to air pollution and environmental racism as they connect to asthma. Consider a body part that has been affected and try to write in the voice of that body part. (As one example, I got COVID-19 in early 2020, and my lungs could write a whole rant or lament about that. Hmmmm, maybe they need to.)

VOICE AND PAIN

As luck would have it, a further challenge in writing about the body emerged, deepening my embodied tale. In my late thirties I developed joint pain and fatigue that would eventually announce itself as rheumatoid arthritis. I knew I had to write about it if I was to ever understand where I was and how I was going to navigate through it. I vented in my journal. I was so sad that I thought maybe I should write a book on happiness and my quest to intellectually hunt it down and hold onto it, but that didn't work.

I would lay on my bed trying to find calm, and I would listen to Buddhist podcasts. Over and over again I heard the simple yet profound guidance that change is inevitable and that the suffering we are experiencing in one moment will shift in the next into something slightly different.

I watched the pain in my body, and the Buddhists knew what they were talking about. I could almost, with practice, watch the pain move around my body, surging and rolling like the surf. That guidance, plus instructions from teachers about sitting and watching my experience, helped me descend into my own body and become curious about what my experience with pain was actually like.

I had to let go of what I wanted my body to feel like, though every day I had many moments of frustration and wanting things to be different than what they were. Eventually, I realized that I had to put this lively experience into words rather than wrestle it into intellectual submission. Up until that point, I had thought about "writing the body" as a kind of fieldwork, writing "about" the body instead of letting go and letting words come up from physical experience.

The notes in my journals got weirder and weirder. Instead of showing or telling, I started to watch and listen. I tried to capture the internal experience of pain in colors and space metaphors. As I wrote, I watched how snippets of poetry, personae, humor, wild metaphor, and experiments with form crept into my nonfiction. I let myself write nonfiction in a range of voices that were all mine but that were me at various points in the kaleidoscope of pain and autoimmune disease as it intersected all the details of my life and identities.

In that simple directness, I found that I was saying what I actually meant without apology or qualification. Because of the pain, I used all my energy and focus to make the sentences when I could.

Before pain, I used to swig coffee and think very quickly, typing to match the speed of thought. After pain moved in, I couldn't get access to that voice and way of thinking on most days. But if I relaxed and leaned more on intuition and less on speed, the paragraphs still emerged, but they were different. Then I had to ask myself whether that speedy writer had churned out my best writing or whether that writing merely *felt* good because it was the first process I knew, the process that made me feel smart and productive because the paragraphs and pages piled up. Was the text better because there was more of it?

My essay collection on chronic pain turned out to be a big voice experiment.

I had interpreted "Pain Woman" to be my brain on pain, but I think her directness emerged from being forced to stay with my physical being. Pain had scattered and blasted my focus. I had a narrower window in which to write, so her sentences were simpler and more direct. There is a breath between them. The music of the words sounds completely different. But there is still the music of words.

FELT SENSE

Psychologist Carol Gilligan writes, "Speaking and listening are forms of psychic breathing." To me this quotation means that communication is natural and necessary for survival. I like her pairing of speaking and listening, which implies that listening is as important as speech, that they are the in-breath and out-breath.

After pain emerged, I found the voices of pain by pausing to *listen*. Listening—waiting for someone else to speak—can be uncomfortable because we don't know what will emerge. Many people, myself included, have to fight the urge to interrupt, to fidget and get distracted, to fill the space with words and thoughts.

Sondra Perl describes this process in her innovative discussion of writing with "felt sense," an idea that came from the philosopher and psychologist Eugene Gendlin. Gendlin considered felt sense to be a kind of preverbal intuition in the body, like that gut feeling when you know you're forgetting to do something but you don't yet remember what it was. Rather than a thought, Gendlin described felt sense as "a single (though often puzzling and very complex) bodily feeling."[8] A felt sense has to be attended to as it develops, and the "body-sense of meaning" will eventually deliver its contents or its insight.

Gendlin used the symbol . . . . . as a way to stand for that bodily intuition that needed to come to fruition.[9] I don't know about you, but for me this completely describes part of what it feels to be human. Sometimes I have a nagging sense that there's *something* that my brain or body are trying to figure out, or I have a gut feeling about an impending decision but I don't know, intellectually, why I feel that way.

Perl and other scholars of the writing process used the idea of felt sense in the 1970s to develop techniques and workshops with timed exercises that encouraged writers to pursue this sensation. One of Perl's most important insights is that the experience of a . . . . . can feel "murky" and that the fuzziness of the experience can be translated as a kind of edgy, itchy, physical discomfort or unease. We might want to move or pace or walk or eat or stretch. Perl's writing exercises help writers focus on that feeling as a tool rather than a sign that something is wrong.

Often people who think they "can't write" or "are bad writers" are unsure about what writing *feels* like to other writers. Felt sense to me often feels unsettling, but giving it a name helps me see it as generative, as the thin edge of something good or important to come. When we imagine a professional writer at work, we might at first imagine someone who sits down at a keyboard and begins pounding away to express a torrent of language, rather than someone who puts her head in her hands and sighs with agony. Developing writers often look inside themselves for the words and encounter pauses, silences, painful chunks of undigested experiences, and itchy felt senses as they write, and they judge all of these things, as I have. It's easy to assume that these weird feelings are anomalies rather than central parts of the process.

Felt sense, for me, is very connected to the body, and sometimes when I'm wrestling with a nagging felt sense about a piece of writing, I need time away from a document. I think this is partly why so many writers are devoted to walking, which gives the body a chance to bestow a felt sense with rhythm and a space to let that felt sense unfold. Other writers garden or clean or cook or make art or exercise or meditate, engaging in any non-writing physical activity to give space for those felt senses to breathe.

Here's a bit of writing I found in a journal that describes my own devotion to walking the roadsides in my small town when I was younger: "I bend over to pick up a rusted circle of metal fringed with gears, some old part that looks like a rusted version of a kid's drawing of the sun. It feels cold in my hand, and I put it in my pocket. Standing in the alley, I am my sixteen-year-old self, my twenty-year-old self. It's cold. I'm in a quiet, worn-out-looking alley near a brick wall with faded white paint, picking something up off the ground."

To me roadside scavenging feels like writing. Brenda Ueland describes writing as an activity that should involve frequent pauses and a slow, relaxed pace because, as she puts it, "the creative power" isn't "nervous or effortful."[10] The imagination, she writes, "needs moodling—long, inefficient, happy idling, dawdling and puttering."[11]

Ueland also needed walks to help her think. "After a few minutes of unpleasant mental vacancy," she writes, "the creative thoughts begin to come. And these thoughts are at first bound to be depressing, because the first thing they say is: what a senseless thing life is with nothing but talk, meals, reading, uninteresting work and listing to the radio. But that is just the beginning. It is just where your imagination is leading you to see how life can be better."[12]

Connecting to the body can be verbal, or it can be preverbal, that felt sense that comes as an idea emerges. In that space of potential and lively interface between being and becoming, inward attention is focused not on forming an argument for an audience but on being alive. To reduce my tendency to aggressively edit and judge my own experience, to dissociate, and to alienate myself from my own life, my narration and argumentation have to alternate with a silence that allows me to receive that living sensation. Like Gilligan's description of "psychic breathing," this is a process that alternates between absorbing and releasing.

Voice grows from that living thrum and exists in the space before we formulate argument. Voices are flowers that grow out of the earth of your body, out of what happens to your body and your spirit and your soul. Voices are performance, are ethos, pathos, logos. But voices are not arguments. Voices are what can be used to shape an argument, but they are also the source of an argument. Voices are sound, rhythm, movement, and silence.

Our felt senses come from a changeable and changing body shaped by experiences. Life writes itself into us. My voice changes radically in different settings, and my posture expresses an interrelationship with what I feel comfortable saying in those settings. Habitual posture shapes voice, and experience in the world shapes both voice and posture. Voices have muscles. If my "wondering and questioning" voice is nervous or out of practice, I might feel more comfortable turning to a funny, self-depreciating voice.

Tova Mirvis, who wrote a memoir, *The Book of Separation*, on leaving an Orthodox Jewish community, struggled with physical symptoms of constricted vocal cords as she was trying to write the book. In an essay she describes her struggle: "I had an ever-present awareness that there were things that couldn't be said. The words allowed and forbidden, appropriate and inappropriate, nice and not nice battled inside me."[13]

She began to work with a voice therapist, who gave her pronunciation exercises and also encouraged her, over time, to speak about a "bodily sense of constriction, my own life closing around me too tightly." She discussed the slow decision to leave her community, and as she spoke, she realized she "stood with my arms crossed tightly in front of me, my nails digging into the skin of my arms as though I needed to hold myself intact."

Mirvis eventually wrote her book, after the speech therapist told her that her voice is her identity. She realized that the "voice of my book was where I would live most plainly."

Our range of voices needs to be respected, including the hesitant ones because they are so changeable and tentative at first. They come well before considerations like genre, goal, and audience.

There's a popular textbook of composition entitled *Everything's an Argument*. By "argument," the book's author, Andrea Lunsford, offers a helpful lens through which to analyze reality for beginning writers: everything we see is a kind of text that includes values, point of view, and choices. Once we figure out our argument, according to this framework, we can think about who we are talking to and what we want to have happen with our words. I used Lunsford's books for years as I began teaching.[14] At the same time, I wrestled with the idea of creative writing as an argument as I watched my own composition process.

What I began to see was that thinking too soon about "argument" puts the focus on a text's audience and goal. This line of thinking doesn't always flatten felt sense, but sometimes it can make that felt sense harder to access. In our rush to persuade, to figure out what we're arguing for and against, to conform to audience expectations, to fall in line with the way others express themselves in well-established genres, we lose touch with the wild inventiveness of writing. And as we lose that wildness, we may also lose our writing's power, because inventive text often *works* better than cookie-cutter text.

Watching my own process, I see that as a writer, my concerns about audience and goals emerge as I shape a piece of writing toward a form that can be shared with the world. But introducing audience too early can feel like editing before I've written anything, which can shut down invention, play, and discovery.

I have found my voices and agency constricted when I tried to edit what I wanted to say and when my thoughts about audience crept in and overwhelmed my ability to listen to myself, in that space before anything is an argument.

Sometimes, a . . . . . is an argument. But it can also remain a sense of unease for days. It can turn out to be a personal revelation not meant to be shared. It can be a decision or an *X* on a treasure map that says, "Dig here."

The "Writing with Voice" workshop that I taught came out of a felt sense, after years of teaching and writing, that I needed to dig further into the topic. I'd been circling around it and had given quite a few talks that connected to voice. I had also been mulling over, as many writers do, what voice *means* and how writers come to be detached from their voices.

As I thought about the topic of voice, I began to see that at various points in my writing life, I've battled with my own voices: wanting them to be different, distrusting them, judging them as not smart enough or annoying or wrong. I began to think about voice and identity and what it means to feel entitled to listen to one's voices. I drew an odd diagram that attempted to sum up for myself my own relationship to voice in writing over time. It was kind of a timeline that represented my voice journey.

When I began writing as a kid, I had understood writing as voice, but then through writing classes in college and graduate school, I'd been wooed away from voice and toward scene as the essential building block of writing. I still had voice, but in some ways I was trying to flatten it out with more action, more of a novelistic discipline in the vein of "show, don't tell. Telling is all about voice," it seemed, and part of my training as a writer involved distrusting telling. Still later, long after graduate school, I began to read more about the essay and saw how telling and asking could be wonderful. Then I fell in love with structure, and then finally, I returned to voice. It took me a long time, decades, to gather an understanding of how important voice is and to gain confidence that my voice itself carries meaning.

I had to accept that my voice—as it was—was inextricably connected to what I was writing about. I could edit it, but I couldn't edit myself out of my writing. Thomas Merton writes about acceptance as active awareness: "Finally I am coming to the conclusion that my highest ambition is to be what I already am. That I will never fulfill my obligation to surpass myself unless I first accept myself—and, if I accept myself fully in the right way, I will already have surpassed myself. For it is the unaccepted self that stands in the way—and will continue to do so as long as it is not accepted. When it has been accepted, it is my own stepping-stone to what is above me."[15]

That weekend workshop on voice was scheduled at a difficult time in the semester: I was too exhausted, and I didn't feel like I had a handle on what I was going to teach. Snow blanketed the hills, and the clouds and the forecast promised icy sleet. As I drove the winding road toward the former convent, my Doom voice echoed in my head: how was I going to offer these people something that would be worth a whole weekend of their lives? Weirdly, I had done something very uncharacteristic for me: I didn't overplan. Maybe out of exhaustion, I just kind of winged it. I developed a framework that felt right, one that forms the basis of this book, but didn't fill in many of the blanks.

Fifteen writers gathered at tables in an old farmhouse. First, we wrote in our traditional voices, the ones that we turned to for everyday writing, and then we stretched into our "head" voices of worry and to-do and regrets and the repeated concerns that seem to flop over and over in our minds like wet laundry in a dryer.

Then I gave a few odd prompts that focused on the body, and as people read and shared, they had the same experience I did: we found that the writing that came from our organs or our skeletons—whatever we summoned, using a kind of Magic 8 Ball of biology—was more confident, deeply rooted, and calm than what came from our "head" voices. Our writing as we shared it seemed to thrum at a different level than the mind. We enjoyed these voices, even when the body had something hard to say.

TRY THIS

1. Describe your life story from the point of view of one of your organs.
2. Ask a voice based in a specific body part to speak. If your hands had a voice, how would it sound?
3. Speaking for a body part, write something starting with "I remember . . ." Then try "I am tired of . . ." and "I am longing for . . ."
4. In a story and in a scene of a moment of high tension or surprise, write about the physical sensations in your body.
5. What do you like to do to relax after a long day? (This might sound prosaic, but in the workshop this prompt brought up details involving physical comfort that were surprisingly moving.)
6. What have you been told about your body that isn't true? How would your body respond to those falsehoods?
7. Where does strength reside in your body?

4   *Mind Is the Source of Voice*

"At first I thought this, but then I reconsidered."

The story of a changing mind—anyone doing battle with themselves—pulls me right into a text. This is the experience of being alive: tossing and turning, shifting and struggling each day to make decisions, wrestling with what I don't know, reframing what I thought was true. It's comforting, I suppose, to fall into the grooves of another person's turbulent mind and to find how much it feels like my own, even if the circumstances are different. We all struggle with not having the full picture.

The essayist Phillip Lopate describes the task of writing literary nonfiction as the attempt to capture "the mind at work."[1] The energy of changing one's mind, reconsidering, and reacting to new information creates a lively internal narrative in any genre. In essence the mind wrestling with itself is an internal scene: the action, drama, main character, and quest are all there, and we never even have to leave our chair.

A side benefit of this internal drama is that it engages the reader and snaps with life. Peter Elbow notes that a text gets a boost of energy from the story of thinking or speaking. He quotes the literary theorist Stanley Fish, who says that this energy isn't at the surface but is a deep wellspring and hunger because "the mind needs to investigate its own activities."[2]

This is so striking. How else to explain the deep sense of relief in writing, in journaling, in meditating, in talking with a friend about a difficult problem, in prayer? Reflection—seeing the image of the mind and considering it—is the font of wisdom in process, even if we don't know where we are going. It is an inner voice.

TRY THIS

1. Start a freewrite with "What I am wrestling with is . . ."
2. Create a change-of-thought narrative with "Once I thought . . . but now I think . . ." or "My friends think . . . but I have come to believe . . ." Notice how it feels to connect with those shifting felt senses.

OFFICIAL VOICE

We are often taught writing in a way that implies we must focus and battle to subdue the disparate voices in our head. This school of thought says that to create clarity for a reader, we should winnow out the conflicting voices, the unsure voices, and the distracted voices. Sometimes we channel "official voice" first, as if that voice is the key to writing, and then we seem surprised when that super-persuasive salesperson voice—which can be so hard to whip ourselves into inhabiting—has nothing to say.

One of the unexpected pleasures of writing a book on pain was that I simply didn't have the option to channel "official essay voice" or "academic voice" all the time. Often I would look into my head and find not a palette or range of voices but, instead, a slow slug of a voice or only the barest hint of a thrum of life. What do you do when you want to make a painting and all you've got is peanut butter?

The "creative constraint" is an idea that expresses an experience long known to artists, writers, scientists, and anyone else who has to make do with limited materials or information, a short time window, or maybe a single color of paint.[3] When you're forced to work within a narrow set of rules—think about the tight rhyming framework of a sonnet—the brain comes up with inventive solutions that it might never have encountered otherwise. This is why writing prompts can get us to unexpected places and why people like puzzles. In fact, this is what the brain does best: figure out how to get the tasty piece of fruit hanging far up in the tree with only a piece of rope and a rock.

So how does this relate to voice?

I found great inspiration from having to work with a tiny narrow window of voice, which initially seemed to be so limiting. All it could say, at first, was "ouch."

We assume that a certain official voice matching the genre of our finished work has to generates our ideas. That's not true at all. In fact, really any voice can be used to excavate insights and truths that can get translated, eventually, into the voice required for a certain form.

Writer and teacher Jill Hackett writes that we tend to have a voice we use that feels most comfortable, our "primary, favored voice center," but, she continues, "any of the voice centers can lead to effective communication."[4]

Maybe you are feeling "blocked" because all you can hear in your head is a lazy "I-wanna-chill-and-nap" voice. Fine. What does that voice say about your writing project? I want to take a nap but I'm at work, and sleepy me is talking to you in a way that is cutting through the convolutions of my more academic ideas. Or a sleepy voice is whispering three words, and those three slow words are very important.

When I learned to listen to my various voices, razor-sharp caffeinated me could take a break. And I learned that sleepy me and pain me had insights that were fine and usable as well.

FIRST, LISTEN

Nancy Sommers, a writer and teacher of writing, describes how various voices have come to her: "On the waves of life . . . when I least expect them, when I am receptive enough to listen to their voices. They come when I am open. . . . These voices bring up bits of everything we've read and seen, sifting our experience like waves sift sand at the shore. This is subtle motion, and students are often not trained to catch it, instead mouthing the words of others, allowing sources to speak through them unquestioned, unexamined."[5] Sometimes we have to do a little listening to tune into those internal voices.

TRY THIS

Plan a two-part writing exercise with a timer. You'll be sitting quietly with your eyes closed for two minutes and then writing for about five minutes.

1. As you get ready to sit for two minutes, imagine setting aside a tiny portion of your mind as a "watcher" who is going to keep a running list of topics that come up as you sit.

   You don't have to force yourself to think of anything. Instead, you can just watch the way your mind jumps from one topic to the next. It might take ten or fifteen seconds for you to get oriented to the quiet, and you might first be distracted by to-do lists or noises in the room. All of this is fine. After a little bit of practice, you'll be able hold the play of thoughts lightly and still let them go where they will.

2. After your timer goes off, write for five minutes about everything you were thinking about. You can jot down a list or phrases that occurred to you or linger on one topic.

CHANGE YOUR MIND, CHANGE MINE

George Orwell was a master of nonfiction and fiction, and he took rhetoric and stood it on its head by using his *real* voices rather than sliding into fake voices evoked by established forms. Scholar Richard Filloy describes how Orwell began essays modestly, plodding from one everyday observation to the next, swerving from sentence to sentence with "individual thoughts and feelings which were then adjusted, altered, even abandoned, to fit political principles." Orwell's primary nonfiction voice was plainspoken and yet sharp as a diamond, anchoring the reader's experience, offering the thoughts of "the person struggling with social justice and political necessity." As the narrator works through various ideas, "the narrator's character thus becomes the chief means of persuasion."[6]

In the essay "A Hanging," Orwell relates an experience during a time in his life when he was stationed in Burma (now Myanmar) as a representative of the colonial government. He was already more and more opposed to the colonialism of the British Empire, and in the essay he tracks a more subtle shift, a moment when intellectual positions become physical convictions.[7]

He describes walking as part of a crowd toward the gallows with a man sentenced to death, and the restrained prisoner alters his step slightly to avoid a puddle. Orwell writes: "It is curious, but till that moment I had never realized what it means to destroy a healthy, conscious man. When I saw the prisoner step aside to avoid the puddle, I saw the mystery, the unspeakable wrongness, of cutting a life short when it is in full tide."

Orwell is admitting something both ghastly and mundane: the way that we can hold various political positions and yet not really grasp or understand their implications. His plainspoken voice admits in simple language that his entire life up until that moment had been the "before," in which he didn't have a gut-level belief about capital punishment. He then has a moment of revelation about "the unspeakable wrongness" of the act. Because he was also devoted to fiction, and to concrete detail, the detail of the puddle is the pivot point for his insight.

This would seem to be the opposite of persuasive writing. He's showing a moment when his beliefs were in flux and he was transfixed by a reflection, not an argument or a major event. But weirdly, this makes a reader trust him *more* because he's willing to share both his own lack of awareness and a moment of vivid transformation. Before that instant with the puddle, his mind and beliefs had been incredibly muddy.

What Orwell shares with the reader is an internal experience, a mind action triggered by a detail. It is persuasive, even though he does not provide a barrage of statistics that might cause the reader's eyes to glaze over. Instead, he invites the reader to stop and see the scene, to feel it with him. Orwell is working through vulnerability and identification, using personal experience as evidence, and his voice shows the narrator to be reasonable, thoughtful, approachable, and most important, self-critical.

Our thoughts and even our beliefs are complex and sometimes contradictory, which is good news, especially in an era in which people have been reduced to battling sound bites. We are complex, and complexity contains untapped possibility.

Returning to essayist Patricia Hampl's insight about how certain voices "reveal what it's like to be thinking," we can call to mind what thinking feels like: internal and shifting.[8] These thinking voices are very personal, and their authority and confidence emerge from the brave task of revealing our contradictions.

TRY THIS

1. What is the voice that lets you be honest enough to reveal the shifting sea of beliefs and thoughts inside you? You might try summoning this voice by starting a freewrite with the phrase "To be honest, I don't know what I think about . . ." And then delve into a difficult issue.
2. You might try Orwell's technique of pinning down a moment when your beliefs either changed or crystallized.

VOICE CHORUS

This morning my teenage son sat eating his breakfast and said that he was going to quit school, that he had too much work and was going to fail every subject. He wasn't saying this while hyperventilating or crying; he was saying it to vent a bit of emotion. He was maybe also trying to get a reaction from me as he watched a video on his phone.

My first response was to feel a shot of adrenaline, then to realize that I was catastrophizing right along with him: what will we do if he fails all subjects? Then I told myself that he had to figure this out for himself. *Then* I listened to that voice and realized it sounded familiar.

It's me. I do this too. I did it first, probably at many points within his range of hearing, so it's pretty likely he picked up this voice and cognitive habit from me.

This is my Doom voice, which speaks pretty loudly in my head. My husband has come to be a very skillful navigator of the Doom. When I break it out, he chuckles sympathetically and asks, "Is this Tired Doom or Pain Doom?" He doesn't argue with me, and he reassures me while also letting me know I'm in the Doom.

Naming a voice can be great because, like an awareness of physical sensation, this voice will pass. It's a weird phase in my work process too. I often imagine a worst-case scenario so that I can get it out of the way and start working.

Certain voices help us talk ourselves through the day, and others help us keep a lid on reactions we can't share. Because these internal voices are usually very familiar, we might assume that they have little literary or expressive value. But if we put them on the page, it's quite likely that they will resonate with readers and help us see things about ourselves.

What are the range of real voices that get you through the day? I have an impulse to panic or worry about things, and then I have another voice that talks me through that panic and helps me focus on the next task and reminds me that things are *fine*. I have a third, unimpressed high schooler voice that rolls her eyes and says "Whatever," in effect refusing to be scared by my own Doom or external pressures. In effect, my day is a conversation between those two or three voices. Do you have two or more voices whose conversation determines your mindset?

Watching the mind at work and then artfully re-creating that change on the page can result in some great writing. And this "watching the mind" often includes watching the body. A felt sense can happen anywhere, which is why the phrase *gut feeling* is so vivid. Its description of intuition is borne out by research that reveals myriad neurons in our digestive organs. You might try locating the various voices by thinking about what they connect to in your body.

This is also the magic that animates great fiction and poetry. For example, in Eugenia Kim's novel *The Calligrapher's Daughter*, we get to see a character's mind and body change in reaction to minute actions of other characters in this scene in which a character is receiving a marriage proposal: "My throat caught, a small gaspy breath. I looked at the jewel. I looked at him, and saw he was unsure of my response, his eyes deep, serious, open to me and yes, loving. It shocked me, the unjudging wanting I saw, and I felt my body flood with unexpected relief, gratitude, and acceptance. My eyes filled, and I nodded."[9]

As we begin writing in any genre, it makes sense that we would envision our characters or narrators as rough sketches embodying a single emotional stance or point of view. But their voices and experiences shift from minute to minute in reaction to the world, and capturing these changes on the page is magic. What Kim does here, too, feels so real because the character's body reacts before her mind does, feeling the emotions that her mind then interprets.

TRY THIS

1. Take five minutes and add to your list of voices by writing a list of those internal voices that help you get through the day but that don't get to "speak" much. One of mine is definitely "swears a blue streak," and another is "high school study hall eye roller." I don't know what forms those voices will work in or what they will produce, but they're mine, and they undergird the more formal writing voices I use.

2. Write for five minutes in one of those voices. You might notice that one voice shifts into another as you write, which is fine, or that the voices are in dialogue with bodily and external sensations. You can also write about what triggered the voice shift. Do you have two voices that tend to spar with each other or a third voice that mediates?

STREAM OF CONSCIOUSNESS

If you watch your mind, you learn quickly that it's less a "stream" of consciousness and more of a tidal wave, a brackish wetland, or a single drop in the process of evaporation. The name implies that the writing about this stream should be just as easy as turning on a faucet or dipping a cup into the voice river. As with other supposedly "natural" things, like love and persistence, there's nothing automatic about it, and it's hard work.

A great example of this is Phillip Lopate's essay "My Drawer," which is honestly about a guy opening his junk drawer and sorting through the stuff that's inside, including random stuff he's saved for no clear reason mixed with deeply personal mementos.[10] That's *it*. The action is the narrator reacting to items in a drawer, showing his consciousness as it is triggered by the physical world in a continuous loop.

Lopate sorts the objects into groups, asking himself why he keeps these things, coming up with theories and then disagreeing with the theories, listening to his rational and semi-rational internal voices, making random associations, and casting back into his memory in order to see what comes up from his past about each object. It's a whole theory of junk drawers. Plus, it's funny and sweet, and many readers connect with the experience of having such repositories.

Part of what makes Lopate's essay so riveting, despite the lack of external tension or action, is his attention to and pursuit of these movements of mind in a narrative arc. And those movements, as he catches them, might also feel very familiar to the reader.

A few paragraphs into the essay, Lopate describes a group of small gifts he keeps in the drawer. Then he asks himself, "Why not follow logic and chuck them?" He listens to a voice and finds a sort of ominous whisper that believes, in whispery parentheses: "(If you throw away a gift, something terrible will happen: the wastebasket will explode, or you'll never get another.)"[11] This sentence focuses on his mind's subterranean movements, and I get a very complex empathy not only for Lopate but also a reminder of the sweet, vulnerable children we humans remain even as adults, the irrational nature of our hopes and fears and the searching for meaning and order.

He moves from front to back of the drawer, and at the end of the essay, he reveals a memento of a lost love, which reminds him of "all that is never lost." This is not his thesis. It is a point he arrived at after the mental wandering and physical action of examining these objects and watching his mind, all as forms of research. I have such a drawer, too, and I get a shock of recognition as Lopate unpacks my life merely by following the train of his own thoughts.

You might imagine the internal action of a mind as running, relaxing, walking, strolling, or moving with varying speeds as a body moves in concert or in conflict with that mind. The mind and body are in conversation, watching each other, in relationship. Each mind has its own habits of movement, its own gait and speed and tendencies. It is that very churn of voices that marks our existence. Capturing that movement in words invites the reader to deeply relate with their own internal churn.

In an interview Lopate describes the human thought process as "incredibly random and vagrant."[12] For a fantastic view of internal dialogue in fiction, you can also check out Raven Leilani's novel *Luster*. As her main character, Edie, is getting ready for a first date, she tells herself, "*You are a desirable woman. You are not a dozen gerbils in a skin casing.*"[13] The humor, the attempt to remake oneself, and yet the reach to a chaotic image all resonate so deeply with me throughout that book. This private image and the voice that brought it forth make her character so distinctive, a sign that the voices inside the character are alive and complex.

Writers can't actually transcribe the bursts of electrical and chemical energy that represent thought, but they can dip into the experience of the push and pull of consciousness, the moods that pass like clouds, and try to describe our daily experience. As writers pay attention and narrate their thoughts, a kind of sense, depth, structure, and insight emerges that might not be produced through the normal living of a day with a human mind. Observing and noting the churn allow that insight about possible patterns to come to the surface.

SHOW . . . AND TELL AND TELL

One of the most common guidelines in creative writing workshops is the command "Show, don't tell." This aphorism was originally offered as a corrective to the beginning writers' tendency to write in abstraction and overview, to explain the action without descending into the details. Over time, though, it has come to feel like a law handed down from stone tablets to writers sitting in coffee shops around the world.

In reaction to this, many writing teachers have adopted the guide of "show *and* tell" because it seems to encourage a wider range of natural voices and fewer attempts to write in the clipped modernistic style of Ernest Hemingway. (Hemingway is fine, but he already wrote his books.)

Watching the mind and describing the active play of thoughts seem to be a gray area between showing and telling, giving us another reason why the binary is overly simplistic. Showing the mind at work has all the activity and conflict and surprise of a tennis match or dance performance. The action is captured via a narrator, who you might think of as the announcer of that tennis match.

Sometimes the two voices playing together are the voices of the present and the past. Lopate describes that reflection as the Voice of Experience. The Voice of Innocence is a person going through an experience as it happens, without the benefit of hindsight or the ability, yet, to reflect back on it from a distance in time.[14] Writer Vivian Gornick writes about this duality at length in her excellent book *The Situation and the Story*. Portraying the action of a mind at work is gripping because we are all struggling with partial information, with lack of clarity, with searches for meaning.

In the essay "My Drawer," Lopate doesn't limit himself to two voices, the Voice of Innocence and the Voice of Experience. He's braiding several. In effect, he's using everything that comes up. He uses voices that sound smart, or "essayish," a voice of Innocence to relay scenes when he was given certain objects, as well as a voice of gut-level magical fear, providing a depth that gives the reader new insight into being human. Much like my German grandfather would use "all the cow" for various meat products he made from his butchering, I have tried to listen to all the voices, including those that I wasn't expecting, the voices that didn't seem like they'd write well. Those voices revealed things I couldn't find in any other way.

And you can use this twining of voices in many more genres than you might think. Writer and teacher Ken Macrorie offered his student writers the "I-Search paper" as a way to make a narrative experience of a research paper. He advised writers to tell the "story of the research" both as a way to gain clarity for themselves about their conclusions and their decision making and also as a way to increase tension by creating story.[15] In the field of creative nonfiction and literary journalism, this is emphasized practically through the subfield of immersion journalism, which is a combination of research and lived experience in conversation with a complex narrator.

PLAYING FAVORITES

When you're sifting through the voices in your mind, it's natural to favor one that's most familiar or that sounds like a best version of yourself. Even if you're not writing for an external audience, there's a tendency to want to make a slightly more put-together, ethical, and smart-sounding version of ourselves, polishing up the edges a bit for our future readers, rather than Leilani's "dozen gerbils in a skin casing."

In *The Memoir and the Memoirist* Thomas Larson writes about the search for an "authentic self" in writing that can prompt us to delve deeply and reflect, to "tell the story of how mask and self have been intertwined."[16] Even though "the core self can never be found," each moment of conversation with our past selves and various voices lets us create the record of a grand and continuing conversation.

Most of us feel a certain pressure to adopt or maintain certain voices depending on our social identities and relationships. Renee Rutledge writes about questioning, as a Filipino writer, whether her work was political enough. She worried whether her writing was helping to channel and release "voices that have been suppressed throughout history." Sometimes our sense of responsibility toward those historic or choral voices can end up shutting down our writing. Her writing led her to conclude that her voice would guide her to "write about the things I want to, the things that bring me joy or pain or reflect my deepest curiosities. Because they matter to me, issues of history and suppression and identity will come up organically. When I write from this place of authenticity, I represent myself—and my people—best."[17]

For me the authentic self is kind of a cloud of electrons endlessly in orbit, in constant motion, but I get too hung up when I hold too tightly to the idea of authenticity. When my writing "sounds like me," I'm listening to as many of my voices as possible, including the gut feelings and the wayward phrases, the strange ideas, Rutledge's "myself—and my people," the quotations and words that my brain tucks away from my reading, bits of songs on the radio, and I am trying to capture the interplay among all these different voices.

TRY THIS

1. Describe the environment inside your head right now. If it were a setting and we could see it, what would it look like? What voices are lounging around the living room? Are any of them arguing with each other?

2. Think about a conversation you've had recently with a friend or family member. Describe the voice that you inhabited in that conversation. What are the patterns of voice you fall into when you talk with different people, and do any of them represent internal voices, or are they more shaped by external contexts?

3. Do you have a voice you use to encourage or discourage yourself? A "coach" voice? Is this modeled on anyone from your past?

5   *Time and Place Grow Voices*

Occasionally, someone will send me a video clip of myself speaking or reading or maybe a link to an audio interview. I can hardly ever bring myself to watch or listen to these. Like many people, my first instinct is to cringe when I hear the sound of my own recorded voice, never mind seeing my goofy facial expressions and wild hand gestures on a video clip.

The first thing that makes me wince is something I'd be hard-pressed to weed out: the actual sound of my vowels. Though my mom is from Germany and my dad is German by way of rural Arkansas, I grew up surrounded by a weird intersection of two sound communities. One is the rough Chicago accent that is shared in different forms by people in the Rust Belt, the industrial swath of former steel mills that stretches from Pittsburgh through Illinois along the Great Lakes. This area is probably inflected with the Eastern European sounds of the immigrants who worked in the mills and mines, and there's something Polish and Germanic about the sound. If you've seen old 1980s *Saturday Night Live* clips, there's a series of sketches in which two Chicago characters talk about the city's football team, "Da Bears" (If you want to hear this, search "Da Bears SNL" in YouTube.) I've got a little of that.

The second layer of my speech is a nasal midwestern twang that almost comes more out of my nose than my mouth. The vowels can sound a little honky, and yet as you go farther south in the Midwest, into southern Illinois, those vowels get longer and get more of a southern feeling to them. This is the rural Midwest, settled up north by

Scandinavian immigrants that give Minnesota and the Dakotas their quasi-Canadian sound, and as you go south, the landscape is layered with people who came up from the South and from Appalachia.

While some places on the earth come with accents that charm, like a British accent or a southern drawl, almost nobody besides other midwesterners says to me, "Oh I love your accent!" Or "Gosh, I could just listen to you talk all day."

Putting the sounds of our background into our writing, rather than stripping them out, can help a reader connect with our writing. bell hooks writes that she offers personal details, including where she comes from, as "a welcoming gesture, offering the reader a sense of who I am, a sense of location."[1] I like the idea of a voice as a welcome, the way in which we might smile and say a little about ourselves when we are introduced to someone for the first time.

TRY THIS

1. Do you have a voice that sounds like the place or places where you are from? In what situations does that voice come out?
2. Write about your accent, if you perceive yourself to have one, and about whether others have reacted to it in positive or negative ways. What do you love about the sound of that voice?

YOUR ANIMAL AND ITS PLACES

The link between place and communication isn't an accident. *Ethos* today refers to "the character of the speaker," but before Aristotle's time, it was translated as "the places where animals are usually found."[2] An animal was observed to have certain characteristics and habits, and we, too, have our habits, which can be observed by anyone who seeks to learn more about us.

I wasn't self-conscious about how I sounded when I was growing up. If anything, I received feedback from my peers in school that I sounded too fancy and upwardly mobile, with too much nerdy book learning leaking out of my mouth and vocabulary. In the region and town I come from, fancy vocabulary will get you slapped with "What, you think you're better than us?"

Another voice discomfort began when I went away to college. I would meet someone new, open my mouth, and people would react physically, looking up and tossing their shoulders back with a little surprise, and ask where I was from. Sometimes out of nowhere, even now, people ask, "Are you from near Chicago?" I also became aware that, far from sounding "fancy," my skills in oral expression were a little awkward as I began to meet people whose upbringing was different than mine. After college I moved to Boston and started thinking about social class, mulling over which sound environments and speech patterns felt comfortable and which were not and why that was.

Today I'm a professor at a private East Coast college in Connecticut, yet I have a hang-up that I sound dumb when I talk in formal or academic settings or to audiences of readers and writers. I much prefer written communication because I feel as though I have more control, and I feel less intelligent and less "quick" when trying to put my thoughts into sounds. Growing up, I did not have many in-depth face-to-face conversations; all my development of complex argumentative skill took place on the page, so my expressive abilities developed where I could draft and redraft to make my sentences sound sharp.

I've been a professor for over twenty years—receiving daily additional external recognition that my voice "matters" and is "smart"—and yet I still struggle with this self-consciousness about how I sound.

Voice isn't merely a container to convey and deliver meaning. Instead, it shapes what is said. Voice *is* meaning. You can take a sentence and strip away all the style and voice to reduce it to a certain level of information in machine code, but voice conveys a wealth of background with great efficiency, including a "welcome" to the reader and so much about the speaker on a subconscious level. If we were to add an appendix to that line of machine code with everything that voice conveys, I bet it would be a book-length document.

Pauses allow us to pick up hesitancy and get ready for emphasis. Even grammar—say, choosing a passive verb over an active or using a collective "we" pronoun instead of an "I"—reveals the conceptual world in which the speaker operates. A voice is the particular thumbprint that an individual puts on their lived communication in a moment in time.

TRY THIS

1. Has social class or home community affected your voice in any way, or has exposure to multiple classes given you new voices to use?

2. Write about a place that's significant to you. It can be a general place, a country from which your family emigrated, an area or a state, or a place as small as a neighborhood. Imagine yourself there: what do you see, and how does this place make you feel? Notice how the image of this place affects your speech and how you see the world.

3. Did you grow up in a home or homes where multiple languages were spoken? Add to your list of voices based on your ethnicity, race, region, and background and the overlap among them.

VOLUME

My volume control is a little wonky. I grew up in a loud house; both sides of my family come from working-class German communities and somehow passed down a motherlode of strong throat muscles. My true laugh bursts without warning, scaling rapidly up the register. I laugh often, and I fear I've turned my vocal cords into little body builders who don't know their own strength. My howl has even allowed others to locate me in the midst of forests and through cinder block walls of school buildings. In the wild I would be the first to be eaten by a sharp-eared mountain lion. Or maybe my howling could serve to round up a clan, like a whale call echoing through fathoms of water.

A few years ago, as I was working on editing an audio recording of an interview for a podcast, I saw the sound waves of my laugh. The squiggles pitched and dipped wildly like the ocean at hurricane strength and then blasted through the top and bottom of the sound graph. A joke from a guest speaker made me laugh and ruined four seconds of the recording. Using a sound editing program, I clicked on the graph, trying to shave off the tops and bottoms of the sound waves. I pulled and nudged down the sound wave, cutting again and again.

I had tried to edit the laugh in other ways earlier in my life. In high school I was called Woody Woodpecker or Machine Gun, so I tried to restrain the laugh by shutting my lips tight and keeping the sound inside. But my lungs pumped their full force to spite me, and the bodily spasm of contained humor created a vacuum effect, a sort of rapid schnuffling of air from my nostrils—quiet but far weirder than the laugh I'd been trying to disguise. People started to make fun of my silent fits of hyperventilation, so I gave up and went back to the sonic attack.

TRY THIS

1. Your best voice could very well be the exact voice that has elicited cringes, the "too much" voice that you were taught to loathe. Do you have a voice that comes out occasionally that you wish you could control? What does it do, and how does it sound? What would that voice sound like if it could run free? What is the root of that voice's strength?

2. How does your laugh sound to you? Does that laugh connect to a voice? Try writing in the voice of your laughter or try to describe that sound.

3. What voices are your loudest? Try to write in the loudest voice and then in the quietest. What settings or moods help those voices emerge?

VOCABULARY AND ERA

One of the enduring features of my voice is the deep grooves dug into my brain from the United States in the 1980s; for better or worse, I sound like an extra from the movie *Bill and Ted's Excellent Adventure*. When I'm excited or happy or feeling any strong emotion, here's how

I sound: "Dude, that is so awesome!" Some people are able to let these pieces of their former voices go and move with the decades, but sometimes our eras and histories get lodged into particular words or phrases.

Another piece of language flotsam that crops up in my verbal communication is the placeholder syllable *like*. I've tried, in bursts of self-improvement, to weed this out, but the resulting sentences were filled with weird pauses as I gathered what I was going to say next. Pausing to try to root out the *likes* often made me lose my train of thought!

I believe I use *like* because I am trying in each pause to gather certainty about what I'm going to say next, but that same *like* followed by an extended pause can signal to my conversation partner that I'm struggling to say something difficult and therefore that they should home in on the next syllables and give me extra assurance that I've been heard.

Placeholder syllables are exactly that—ways to help us keep track and figure out where we're going. These might vary from region to region or person to person. Now that I live on the East Coast, I am often struck by the placeholders *okay* and *know what I mean?* which seem to be particular markers of working-class background here but aren't used as often in the Midwest. These words and phrases might be so common that it takes extra listening, or maybe even recording and transcribing a conversation, to catch.

TRY THIS

1. How has the decade, generation, or era you grew up in influenced your writing or speaking voice? Write a list of phrases or sounds that, for whatever reason, seem lodged in your speech like fossils. If you aren't able to hear them in your own speech, can you notice them in the speech of family members or friends?
2. Listen for the figures of speech in the way an older person communicates. What kinds of pauses do you hear and where? What specific words and phrases catch your attention?
3. If you write fiction, you can think about how each of your characters has a specific history encoded in his or her voice. If you try

eavesdropping in a public place and transcribing exactly what you hear, you'll learn so much about the variety of rhythms and vocabulary that might go into each of your characters.

VOICE PRINTS

The voices you speak and write with each have their own fingerprint. Think about a particular voice you use, and maybe analyze a piece of your own writing that you feel sounds like you. What would be a sentence you would say to someone to tell them a piece of bad news? What are words you overuse, and what are words that irritate you? What are words you love?

Listening to yourself or another speaker, try to analyze how often a thought is interrupted. Do the waves of thought regularly get chopped up with questions or asides, or do the sentences move on to completion? This is also a fascinating thing to observe in real human conversation. We interrupt each other and ourselves and leave sentences unfinished far more often than you might guess, weaving together a cloud of phrases as we speak.

Try to identify if there are patterns in rhythm and pacing in a piece of your own writing. Is it a rush of words or a slow, steady progression? Do the sentences quickly state their subjects, or do they work in a gradual and circular way toward figuring out meaning? How formal or informal is the voice, how confident or hesitant?

VOICE INFLUENCES

Unlike my speaking voice, my voice on the page got a ton of support. As a white kid in a safe farm town not far from a major city, I was identified early for gifted classes. As a result of my test scores, my teachers' expectations were always high. It was always assumed I would go to college. I was listened to, and mentors responded to my written communication with support and praise.

Then I was given a column in my small-town Illinois newspaper, the *New Lenox Community Reporter*. Before the internet (yep, this was in the 1980s, or as my college students now like to call it, the "late twentieth century") it was a wild and rare experience for a preteen to have readers and an audience. Sure, when I proposed vegetables for the school lunch line or uniforms, a group of boys threatened to beat me up, but even that let me know that writing was power, making me both more afraid and bolder. Encouragement and support help grow and make a place for voices. Voices broaden and strengthen and proliferate when they are heard, responded to, and encouraged, and they wither in self-protection and hunger when they aren't listened to. Or if they're ignored and dismissed, they learn to explode and boom to make some space.

It's a little strange that the voice in my sixth grade column still sounds, over three decades later, like me to my own ears. That thread of "me" is what I believe many writers and theorists describe as the singular voice, though the sound of the writing was composed of a few strands that I was trying to grow and others I wanted to discard.

One of those voices is a quality that others who read me have described as "plainspoken," or direct without too many abstractions, which I credit to my region and class. I wrote about things I thought should be different and that could be fixed in our town: more nutritious school lunches and bike paths and things like that. What gave me the right, as a kid, to think I could recommend changes to a town? The presence or absence of entitlement—having opinions and assuming that someone would listen—is an important element of how we express ourselves. I am white, and I therefore have a huge degree of "voice privilege." I also sound "acceptable" to those in positions of power, but I've also been afraid of them, and parts of my voice have been very— too—accommodating and placating as a result.

One of the ways I began to play with voices was by absorbing them from books. When I was in grade school, I would read anything I found lying around. My mom was a big reader, and she loved science fiction and also checked out nonfiction library books by women, the "helpful hints" type such as *Hints by Heloise*, about managing a house-hold, and Jean Kerr's humorous books about raising kids and running a household, including *Please Don't Eat the Daisies*. I was also very influenced by public service announcements that ran on television between cartoons in the 1970s, usually little environmental spots about not wasting electricity or not littering.

My problem-solving mode was formed first by Heloise, who seemed so smart and let me believe that there were other ways of doing normal tasks, along with the humor of Erma Bombeck, and a dash of the kids' mystery series *Encyclopedia Brown*. I borrowed the idea that problems could be investigated and patterns could be changed, even if Heloise didn't inspire me to clean my room.

Then the PSAs let me know that there were problems in the world that had practical solutions. Jean Kerr let me know that you could tell stories about your life, even embarrassing or funny ones, and that you could let readers into your life and somehow the honesty made everything better.

Add in a dose of investigative reporting from the news show *20/20*, which spiced up my voice with the desire to engage in public issues. My writing style was borrowed straight from Heloise plus Erma plus cartoon infomercials and *20/20* host Geraldo Rivera, and that foundation (probably with other influences I'm not even aware of) formed my voice base.

Many writing teachers these days focus on genre: if you practice writing a recipe, you can write a recipe. My experience tells me that voice both births genre and grows the ability to cross genres. I wasn't borrowing Heloise's style to write household hints; I was using an amalgam of voices from different genres to blend into a strong braided thing that gave me the confidence to propose solutions with some humor. I wasn't obsessed with audience. I had a goal: think outside the box. That was it. Getting into print emboldened me; the idea of journalism with the personal voice of Erma Bombeck's memoirs helped me work into the personal essay, even though I hadn't studied the personal essay at all.

TRY THIS

1. Are there books, television shows, web shows, or memes that have stayed lodged in your voice or that you used for a time and discarded?

2. Who are writers whose style has stuck with you, whose music you still hear in your head? How do they influence your own writing?
3. What influences helped you feel heard? What convinced you it was better to say as little as possible in certain settings?

CHILDHOOD VOICES

Getting to know your own voices lets you see what you're working with, what you're made of, and why you express yourself the way you do. This can help you make more conscious choices on the page. Writers and teachers Linda Trichter Metcalf and Tobin Simon write: "To be a writer, and especially to write out of your own life, you must be imaginative about what it's like to be *you*. It is not enough to spill words, even intriguing or provocative words, onto the page. Writers have to penetrate experience."[3] Listening for our own voices and the influences that shapes them can also provide us with greater confidence in using our voices in person and on the page. Our voices can also tell us things about ourselves that we'd rather not hear or that delight us, perhaps things that we have never appreciated about ourselves and our communities.

Pat Schneider, in *Writing Alone and with Others*, describes the voice of childhood as an "original voice," and Peter Elbow describes it as one of our "mother tongues." Schneider talks about the long process of learning to value the voice she grew up with in the Ozarks, a voice with accents, sentence structures, and pronunciations that teachers and other writers tried to edit out as not sounding professional enough. "We have too often been trained to distrust our original voices," Schneider writes.[4] She quotes novelist Amy Tan, whose essay "Mother Tongue" is about writing stories "using all the Englishes I grew up with," including the mix of Chinese and English spoken by her mother, which to Tan's ears was not "broken English" but contained "her passion, her intent, her imagery, the rhythms of her speech and the nature of her thoughts."[5]

Award-winning fiction writer Jacqueline Woodson writes:

> People tend to block out what was unpleasant about their childhoods, but I don't . . . I never left the mind of a young person, and I remember

who I was and what I wanted as a child. I remember how I spoke so when I write I pay attention to cadence and what's left unsaid. Along with memory, authors writing for young people need to know and care about the world their characters live in so they can see the meaning in young people's dialogue no matter how staccato or hesitant it is, or how few words they use. There's no magic formula for that.[6]

Reading young adult literature is a great way to recapture the voice of childhood, and many writers who focus on adult audiences also choose to narrate some or all of a book from a child's perspective. It can be a challenge to "drop into" a kid voice and get it right the first time, so it's better to work up to it, to think about yourself at different ages, and to try to write from a child's or teen's voice using moments that evoke emotion, both positive and negative. Children aren't simple beings, and a child or teen's voice has as much if not more emotional range and expression than that of most adults, as we explored in chapter 3.

At one point when I was stuck with a draft of a memoir, I wrote a version in my preteen voice, the narrator wanting to solve the world's problems and not yet having encountered the full weight of sexism and other forces that wanted to still my voices. I then tried to rewrite the book with more confidence and energy than my previous drafts had contained.

TRY THIS

1. What was your most confident voice from childhood? Your most frightened?
2. What were some of the voices you used as a teen? Since this is such a period of growth and change, you might even have been trying on multiple voices in each of your preteen and teen years, searching for what felt right.

CAUTION: VOICES AT WORK

An additional layer of voices came with each of my first jobs. After years of inhabiting the voices of the student and the playground, learning our various "work voices" is often a shocking and limiting transition. So, it's important to add significant jobs to your voice list. My voice as a Pizza Hut waitress brought out a certain side of my personality, and I also grew into it, gradually allowing myself to inhabit the script of "And would you like an order of breadsticks with that Double Cheese Pepperoni?"

Work can often feel like a kind of pantomime, with a required voice we must maintain in bursts or throughout the day, one that suppresses a wide range of emotions and reactions. At the same time, a work voice can ask us to rise to a challenge, to inhabit a version of ourselves, or to defend ourselves against large forces and manipulative supervisors. We are asked to become new roles before we are ready, and then we pull together a voice that functions to meet the need.

Sometimes I have had my voice critiqued at work or watched as others' voices were critiqued, according to strict guidelines that were often very different for people of different classes, races and ethnicities, and genders or sexual preferences. People of color, especially women, as well as workers of all backgrounds are often expected to signal flexibility, "niceness," and subservience in subtle ways with our voices, and over time these voices infect the others and can trickle into our personalities or be diverted to a voice of resentment or resistance to that forced voice. A demand that one be subservient at work can lead to being less able to switch gears and articulate one's "true" self at home. A tough pose at work can lead to silence in life or maybe be used as a tool to re-form other voices. I initially experienced great discomfort when someone judged me as being ready to step into the voice of a teacher, a public speaker, or a community organizer. I learned those voices by absorbing the voices of others, and I also learned through experience and practice how to adapt those voices to fit me.

One of the ways I excavate voices is to think about the intersection of life experience and reflection at different moments in my life. What version of me could speak if she were given space on the page, and what would she say? I would go so far as to say that each era of everyone's life has a potential voice attached to it; each habitual mood generates a voice. My voice as a junior high mathlete is very different than my voice when I was struggling to get out of a difficult marriage. I am inhabited by all the voices of my former selves, or at least the ones I have given space to. Writing with voices gives us room to let these "I"'s out to pasture, let them wander and weave themselves together.

TRY THIS

1. To make a voice timeline, you can take a large sheet of paper and draw a horizontal or vertical line to mark time moving forward. Start with your birth and end with your age now. Mark significant events along the way and ask yourself whether there are voices associated with those events. Label voices in the gaps between those significant events and with specific jobs and roles and activities you've been a part of.

2. Note significant voices across your life's timeline, and feel free to draw or use symbols or write on the timeline. Can you channel yourself at age sixteen talking to yourself? Talking to a friend? How about you at age twenty-five?

3. Here are some more ideas to explore some of the voices inside you—feel free to write into any resonant voices as they come up:
   - you with a best friend in grade school;
   - you during the moment in your childhood when you felt most confident and least confident;
   - you swooning in love;
   - your voice during a breakup with a crush or significant other;
   - your voice during any class you remember in grade school or high school;
   - you first understanding or grappling with a complex problem from the world of adults;
   - you on what made you most sad, such as during a time of loss;
   - you doing chores or working;
   - you describing parents, relatives, or siblings at a specific age.

6   *Voices of Challenge and Change*

We all receive subtle and overt messages that some of our voices are more acceptable than others. Many voices are lost because they are associated with painful moments in our lives or because the voices received small or large helpings of criticism. Some categories of voices are devalued before any words are uttered at all. If you come from a disenfranchised community, nation, social identity, or racial or ethnic background, the voices you grew up with and the voices in your community may be viewed by people outside your community as being inadequate, less intelligent, inappropriate, or less "articulate" than others. This might either sabotage your confidence in your voices, or you may channel defiance or find refuge in the voices that give you power.

Peter Elbow writes: "Voicelessness may stem from not getting enough respect and support. After all, it is hard to speak if you feel you will not be taken seriously." Philosopher and literary theorist Mikhail Bakhtin wrote about how our intonation changes if we don't have "choral support," or the attention of a supportive audience.[1]

This is a conundrum that many have experienced: first, you live through experiences that separate you from a powerful, empowered voice, then you're told the voice that comes from that experience is inadequate. For those who live at the intersection of multiple forms of oppression, such as queer women of color, "coming to voice requires tremendous courage," writes Hackett. Such writers "are already standing apart. To take another step more, to go on record, requires courage and fire."[2]

Shame—when we feel that something about our very selves is not right, when we internalize the bad treatment we've received—can shut down a voice completely. It can be provoked through mistreatment or trauma, and it can be triggered long after that mistreatment by a variety of experiences. And it can affect our voices. Poet and writer Maya Angelou stopped speaking for five years after being sexually assaulted as a child. The wonderful news for all of us is that she found her way back to words and then forged her way onward to the page, into advocacy and activism, and graced the world with her bright, deep, unique voices.

No matter what community we come from, the process of weeding out voices and selves starts young. A writer might have been teased at one point in their lives, and as a result that whole era and all its voices might have been packed away and marked as unacceptable in one's mind. Brenda Ueland writes: "Families are great murderers of the creative impulse, particularly husbands. Older brothers sneer at younger brothers and kill it. There is that American pastime known as 'kidding'—with the result that everyone is ashamed and hang-dog about showing the slightest enthusiasm or passion or sincere feeling about anything."[3]

Were you made fun of as a kid? I was a nerd, an overenthusiastic dork—and that was okay up until seventh grade. Before then, I'd been sort of insulated within a little pod of other nerdy kids. In seventh grade I became aware of the criticism that would shape the next decade of my life, jabs leveled at my appearance and at my behavior. I should add that I was not a pariah, just a normal kid navigating junior high with a good range of friends and social supports.

That was also the age in which many people experience intense scrutiny about their changing bodies. That scrutiny and attention in and of itself created a new internal voice, which whispered: "Freeze. Don't react or you'll just make it worse. Don't give them any more ammunition." I don't think it's an accident that that transition to junior high was marked by a rash of mental health crises within my extended peer group, and that was the point at which I started to struggle with depression. Yes, it was hormones as well as a greater awareness of the world's issues, but it was also pressure and judgment and thus, an over-awareness of a hostile audience during a particular era and in a place.

There is a sliver of me that goes to the page to vent and process these feelings and a sliver of this girl who still freezes, who can't put a response into a quick comeback, who looks down and away, still inside me. Such experiences—even if they seem tiny—stay with us and affect the range of voices we feel comfortable using today.

I slowly began to understand the way these experiences affected my voices in adulthood. Then I tried to reach back and write from the sixth grade voice because she had a lot of great qualities, including confidence and enthusiasm.

TRY THIS

1. Which of your qualities, traits, or characteristics became targets for teasing, bullying, microaggressions, or intimidation and violence? Find a voice to describe the person you were in that moment.
2. Reach back before that treatment entered your consciousness, if you can. What was the voice that was blissfully unaware of such a possibility?
3. What is the voice that comes out of you after you've been mocked or made fun of? How has that formed a part of who you are?
4. Try to hear those critical voices and write for five minutes in response to those voices. Can you name the voice that speaks back to that experience? Is there a voice that wants to shout in response?

THE VOICE SAVERS

Many communities, particularly if they are the target of systematic repression, have built institutions that save voices, that amplify the community's cadences and rhythm and unique language, that allow members to bask in the unique gift that is voice. Churches, community institutions, art and music groups, and social and political movements have all offered shelter for voices to come together and be strengthened, supporting a range of vibrant expression and theorizing about existence and self that have been unsupported or actively targeted. Finding activities and places where one's voices matter, where voices can get choral support, may be vital to the ongoing development of self. When human beings are able to throw themselves into something they love, they often find a community speaking a language that quickly becomes their own, and the conversations within that community help anchor and broaden a sense of self, belonging, and agency. Language and conversation bring us and our voices into being and into conversation and connection with others.

There are also internal and quiet tactics we adopt to save our own voices. Philosopher bell hooks writes in the book *Remembered Rapture* about diaries as "crucial to women's development of a counter-hegemonic experience of creativity within patriarchal culture." She describes diary writing as "subversive autobiography" that "emerges as a narrative of resistance, as writing that enables us to experience both self-discovery and self-recovery."[4]

When I was in grade school, poetry became an important way for me to process my reactions to the world. Writing poems allowed me to capture half-feelings, wisps of insights, and experiences that felt too insubstantial to assert anywhere in my outer world. As I worked on a poem, I became more and more aware of a new voice, one that had a quiet authority, was still able to ask questions, and one that could slow the world down to try to capture insights in language. Poems helped me understand that I had something to say, that I needed space to pursue my thoughts, even if they were vague or tentative. Although I would later publish some poetry, the true conversation—and the shock of recognition—was in reading a poem as I worked on it and seeing something *there*, having the conversation with myself, and then working on growing that voice.

When I was in second grade, we pushed all of our desks out to the edges of the classroom for music class. Mr. Romano came in and led us in an activity to help us feel rhythm in our bodies. We stomped and clapped in time to a song about a bear in his lair.

Bear-lair.

That feeling in my body awakened a poem; the bear came to life on the page as the beginning of stanzas about leaves falling in autumn. I borrowed freely, writing it down because it pleased me, because it was an appreciation of the delicious feeling of rhythm and rhyme. But the writing was as natural as singing a song to myself on the playground, which I did all the time. No big deal.

I gave the poem to my teacher because she was supportive and friendly. Then she laminated it! This was a big deal in the 1970s; we didn't have the internet, so we laminated everything. Then the laminated poem was put up in the front entranceway to the school. I sent a copy to my Aunt Rosy in Arkansas, and she submitted it to her local newspaper, and it got published.

I am writing in my second grade voice; can you hear it? That voice and that person had received a shocking signal from the world: an audience, a completely unexpected jolt of support, and a real change in identity. Without those external signals, and without the support of music class in second grade, I am not sure whether I would have continued to listen to the songs inside my head.

In high school I began to get very interested in social issues. In the 1980s the Cold War threatened nuclear annihilation. The evening news presented many social problems in voices that made the world seem chaotic and sad or angry, focusing on shots of yelling and conflict, cutting away to maps slashed with arrows and graphics with numbers of stockpiled missiles.

During that time in my life, the public library's section of new books was my source of oxygen and connection, before email and social media. I read the books in their slick library covers about nuclear war, about environmentalism and social movements, written by authors who were people, who had voices and histories and who cared and were using their own lives and actions to try to change things. Those voices showed me the voice of the researcher and activist I might become. Those voices had footnotes and observations and passion. They cared, and they acted, and maybe I could summon that voice too.

TRY THIS

1. Try to make a list of voices from your past that were your safe voices, the ones that let you claim authority and love what you loved, even if it was only in your head or among peers. What voices kindled interest in the things you care about? Write in one or two of these voices for five minutes.

2. Were you drawn to any new activity or interest because of the voice you heard from others? What was attractive about those voices and the space they created? Was there a "felt sense" in you that responded?

TRAUMA AND VOICE

Normal life can wear away at our voices, eroding them and shifting them. A traumatic experience can have a massive and sudden impact on one's voices and ability to use them. Sometimes a new voice is necessary to navigate a new reality in the aftermath of trauma or major stress. Such voices—which can, if we're lucky, emerge with resounding clarity and depth—might be forged by the need to use every tool at one's disposal to remake one's life.

Author and writing coach Jill Hackett writes, "If one has been through a crisis—creative or personal, that crisis can be used in service of strengthening voice. And clarifying voice."[5]

After getting out of a difficult relationship at one point in my life, I began receiving a long barrage of messages from my ex, which wore away at me and made me afraid for my safety. In a moment of hopelessness, I had an experience I captured in an essay:

> I curled into the couch like a ball of used Kleenex.
>
> *I can't do this anymore. I'd do anything to make this end.*
>
> The thought faded, but the poison aftertaste made me stop. I raised my torso upright in the silent living room, sensing a new level

of danger. . . . I reached for the phone book and flipped through tissue-thin pages.

The next morning I contacted an advocacy agency to help me navigate the events surrounding that breakup. My turning point was not in the suffering itself. Instead, I realized something was wrong when I witnessed the depth of despair in my own internal voice, a voice of hopelessness that scared me. When I listened to that voice, I knew I was in danger, and I acted.

My writing about this experience is still not published; it has taken a long time to get right, and it's complicated because the story touches many other lives. But I wrote throughout these years, trying to understand what was happening in my life and to my voice. I journaled, I talked, I wrote emails to friends, and as the months passed and I navigated to safety, I kept trying to write about this experience.

Creative writers often get hung up on the debate about whether writing is therapy. Some writers worry that other writers or readers don't understand the difference between literature and journaling and want to stress that writing well is not a guarantee when writing about a difficult subject—and that combining the two is difficult. What they mean, I think, is that an author's suffering—or torment or substance abuse or mental illness—is not the key ingredients in good literature. And writing a book isn't a healing process, as a rule. It's often quite frustrating, and it has different goals. People who have lived through trauma are often dismissed or discounted, especially if they are socially marginalized in any way, so it is doubly dismissive to assume that good writing about difficult life experiences is "easy," like opening a vein right onto the page. That's never how good writing works. But other writers seem, in their insistence in this issue, to want to separate themselves from the mass of people who are writing trauma but not writing in an artful way, as if it's an embarrassing crowd to have to sit with in the lunchroom.

I believe some of the anxiety responds to a lingering judgment or assumption that those who live through traumatic events are damaged in some way. Living through a difficulty doesn't inherently create a good story; writing about something traumatic in a way that invites the reader into the experience and adds reflection and meaning is extremely challenging. There is more trauma than we can process in everyone's lives, and a small percentage of people who have lived through trauma are writing books about it. A tiny fraction of that small group has published books about their trauma, but many of them share it in an accessible and beautiful way.

Carmen Giménez Smith writes in her poem "Parts of an Autobiography," which is in the form of a numbered list, "59. The writing is not the catharsis. The decision to excavate is the catharsis. The transformation from dreadfulness to art is the catharsis, but the art is the art." I'm very much drawn to her transformation of a simple binary into a series of steps, then her decision to locate that sense of catharsis or release and change in the writer's decisions and commitment.[6] Later in the same poem, she writes, "86. I want pathos, bathos, and sinking in the viscosity of feeling. If I can make something lovely of my broken crockery, then I shall."[7]

As we work to summon our full range of voices, our "broken crockery" voices—closely associated with difficulty, horror, or violence—may start as shattered whispers. In drafting and writing, in discovery, we put the fear about "Is it good? Is it art?" to one side. Art gets made in the revision (and re-re-revision). But we can't revise or make art without the raw material of our broken crockery, and that requires space for the voices that we might judge to be least artful, least pretty, least acceptable.

I believe strongly in writing as a therapeutic exercise, and clinical studies seem to back up the popular practice, finding that "written emotional expression promotes integration and understanding of the event while reducing negative emotions associated with it."[8] Yet I believe with equal intensity that writing teachers are not therapists or healers. Writing teachers share skills to aid writing, but most are not trained to offer skills for living, which is more the domain of therapists and healers.

And still: I'd be lying if I claimed that writing wasn't a key to my own sanity. Composing fiction and nonfiction has helped me to better understand myself, other people, and the world. The page is my refuge, a guarantee that for at least an hour a day, I can explore an endless alternate universe in which I listen to myself. Through this activity I am part of my own choral support. My current life includes writing as a cornerstone, and I get very edgy when I can't do it. We do not often tout such benefits of writing, and we certainly don't advertise our profession as one to keep a person sane, because I'm not sure what our success rate is.

One theory about writing as a way to heal is that timing is everything: if stories are shared too early in the healing process, or with skewed expectations or to a hostile audience, the sharing can even be damaging. Writing for an audience of one—the writer—can grant freedom to explore the riskiest of truths and questions. In *Writing as a Way of Healing* Louise DeSalvo writes, "I believe that it is our responsibility to ourselves and to our work to control the conditions whereby we share our work so that we do not foreclose our need to tell our story."[9]

DeSalvo urges writers to become aware of their own readiness to share with an audience. Sharing too soon can shut down the positive effects of writing to explore as we drown out our barely formed views with a cacophony of other voices. Exposing experience to an uncareful audience can lead one to feel misunderstood or worse, which can blunt the desire to connect through language.

But I have also had the opposite experience: working very hard on essays about trauma, sharing them and getting rejected and editing, sharing with writing groups, editing, submitting, getting them edited, and then finally publication. The aftermath, especially when I wrote about physical pain and its effects, was and continues to be both confusing and amazing. Strangers with pain have told me that they can see themselves in my words. I have reduced both my isolation and the isolation of others by acknowledging shared experience.

Vivian Gornick reflects on what she loves about certain essays: "It wasn't their confessing voices I was responding to, it was their truth-speaking personae. By which I mean that organic wholeness of being in a narrator that the reader experiences as reliable; the one we can trust will take us on a journey, make the piece arrive, bring us out into a clearing where the sense of things is larger than it was before."[10]

In other words, it's not what you tell; it's *how* you tell it.

Gornick's closing phrase, "the sense of things is larger than it was before," is devilishly vague, yet it captures the essence of our responsibility toward our possible audiences. If suffering is everywhere, then art is a wise conversation about suffering. Art takes suffering and, with that raw material, nonetheless makes us slightly more inclined to stay alive, even with the horrors that life can bring. And how we define and summon wisdom is up to us.

If we are working to share something difficult with an audience, the goal is to give something, to reveal something true won from that difficulty, to enhance communion and communication. We all experience trauma and heartbreak. Writing and reading about it should help somehow to lighten our load, to witness and record, to make sense of it or see it in a new light. Insight can come as we listen to our voices.

TRY THIS

1. Write for five minutes about a time when your own voice signaled danger. Can you give that voice a name? You can also try to write in that voice, but be attuned to your own inner signal of discomfort and feel free to skip or stop at any point.

2. List the voices that you have inhabited at moments of difficulty. What would one of those voices have to say to you today? If there's a very loud voice offering opinions and judgments about an experience, can you put it aside and listen to another voice that might be only a whisper? What do you have to say to one of those voices from your present vantage point?

3. Sometimes two voices have very different takes on the same experience, and the resonance between them captures a clue to the meaning of the experience. Try to write about an event you've experienced as a dialogue between two voices. Sometimes that's a conversation between "now" and "then," but sometimes it's a

different pairing, maybe "hope" and "cynicism" or "the good daughter" and the "hell-raiser."

JUDGING TRAUMA

I was sitting in the audience at a panel at a writing conference in the early 2000s when a male panelist made a crack about "another incest memoir." I'm pretty sure a writer could not say that today, after the #MeToo movement, but this was a common occurrence even ten years ago.

As about half the audience chuckled, a fire seemed to ignite deep in my intestines that was not at all pleasant. I was nauseous. How far would I get in the world of writing, I wondered, if I were to stand at a podium and scoff at "another fly-fishing memoir" or "another baseball memoir" or "another memoir with a touching moment in which a grown son shaves his ailing father's face in the hospital." Those moments have all produced great literature, but we don't dismiss the raw content that birthed them.

Sometimes writers get signals—even before they begin to write—that their subjects don't matter. Writing about *some* kinds of trauma is scary because the writers of these kinds of trauma are subject to a great deal of criticism and even stigma, no matter how much they may have achieved beauty and depth with their work. Those who happen to have experienced trauma are often seen as "brave" if they are not part of a socially oppressed group. Sometimes, blame filters down the social hierarchy, and those who are marginalized are also asked why they didn't do more to avoid the trauma or why they are cashing in on the trauma or even told "how lucky" they are to have difficult subject matter to write about. I remember reading about a woman who got a six-figure book deal based on the blog she wrote about the sandwiches she made for her husband, yet such writers are rarely accused of mercenary instincts, maybe because it's easier to pick on the folks who are taking the biggest risks. Memoirs about trauma by people from oppressed groups are often accused of "oversharing," but no one is accused of oversharing when someone goes on too long about their home repair project, the amount they drank last weekend, or their favorite sports team.

Literature about soldiers' experiences reveals trauma of all sorts. However, if we put these same brave soldiers back in the United States, fighting for mental health care for their post-traumatic stress disorder and unable to work or function at home, these stories may be seen as "depressing" and maybe not even "sellable." The soldier persona is "brave" when abroad with a gun, but at home in the waiting room of a clinic, that soldier's story falls outside the narrow definition of acceptable or brave, maybe because it calls on the reader to act or to challenge surface assumptions.

Our subject matter tells us nothing about how that subject will be written, and books—as well as people—should not be judged based on content. I'll read a memoir about a person struggling with addiction because I'm curious about how that person survived. I've read an amazing memoir about a guy (Steve Almond) who did road trips to chocolate factories, and I've read a great essay about a guy (Ander Monson) who visited a bunch of car washes in suburban Detroit.

What's vitally important is that we study, as a culture, precisely these memoirs in order to learn how humans survive the trauma enacted by our violent world as well as the systems that made that violence happen. While those who live through traumatic stories still face stigma, these stories have also helped readers learn and break silence and have been used by activists as foundations for social movements. Telling stories through social media as a public act, to say "me too," reasserts the humanity of those who survived and reduces stigma, allowing others to reduce their shame and to share. The recent move toward trauma-informed care and trauma-informed education also sounds a hopeful note for an era in which *all* of our stories may share shelf space and be witnessed.

THE HOSTILE AUDIENCE

It's no accident that in this cultural context, developing writers are asked to imagine a hostile, or at least skeptical, audience. Voices often wither or change when they are harshly critiqued or subjected to an overly critical gaze. Student writers tackling research papers are typically told to assume that their audience needs convincing, so they grow a defensive voice with an argumentative streak, ready to whip out counterarguments and gain an edge by collecting only evidence to support their own points.

In asking writers to write with this voice, writing instructors pass on the alienating idea that a false self is necessary for writing and communication. Voice is seen as a trick that writers perform on command rather than an expression of real interest or feeling. This, I think, is a quiet tragedy, one taken from the origins of composition instruction, when such classes were used to prepare a legion of stenographers and office workers whose sole job was to parrot the voice of their employer.

The hostile audience in a writer's head—the one that is ready to sneer at any assertion the writer may make on the page—is the face of writer's block. Sitting right next to that hostile reader is another peach: a reader that is completely indifferent, that couldn't care less what a writer says, that has to be "hooked" with a catchy point. I do not want to sit near either of these horrible people at a party. So why are we taught to write for them?

Imagine, too, a writer who has been tormented or bullied, who carries sources of shame and embarrassment that are regularly triggered by the world. Putting this writer alone on the page, under the gaze of this hostile sneering audience, could trigger the writer's self-critical voices internalized from outer torment. Imagine hearing this in your head as you sit down to write: "No one cares."

It makes me angry that this is how we teach writing.

Claire Vaye Watkins wrote an excellent essay, "On Pandering," in which she examines her own tendency in past work to write with the internalized criticism of various white men peering over her shoulders: "I have been reenacting in my artmaking the undying pastime of my girlhood: watching boys, emulating them, trying to catch the attention of the ones who have no idea I exist."[11]

Persona and voice are so complicated because they are shaped by our sense of, and experience of, self in the context of others and the world.

We receive critiques on our writing and on our non-writing voices, and these critiques stick and can reemerge consciously or unconsciously to shape our future voices either as we write against or toward that criticism. Both the story and the voice are evaluated by readers who decide whether a story is "relatable" or not. Often, the sense of what's relatable has to do with reinforcing power structures and judgments that keep those structures in place.

This can even shape the structure of how we tell our stories, what we tell and what we don't. I "grew up" as a writer during the beginning stages of creative nonfiction in higher education, before it was a genre that was taught in many MFA programs. Because fiction was the foundational prose in workshops, many writers in all genres receive the classic fiction adage of "show, don't tell" as part of their training, as mentioned in chapter 4.

However, as a nonfiction writer attempting to write my own reality, it was the "don't tell" that tripped me up and stalled my voice. The advice at the time coming from agents and editors, especially for women's memoir, was to make it "more exciting" by developing a strong narrative, with strong scenes that would draw readers in like a movie.

I tried very hard to squash my telling voice out of one of my books, thinking that if I had a strong enough narrative through line, it would be a stronger book. I focused as much as I could on *action*. Strangely, my focus on scene ended up producing what I now think of as my weakest book because I didn't give myself the space to talk directly to the reader. In a way I assumed the reader wouldn't care what I had to say. I imagined a reader who was judgmental and easily bored, and I had to amuse that reader with scenes, to entertain and entice with details.

This is not to argue against writing for readers or imagining a reader's needs as one writes. But there's a slight but important internal shift between writing with a reader in mind and writing defensively, protecting one's story against a certain barbed line of criticism.

It took a lot of reading and writing, long after I had completed my MFA, for me to really understand the essay, to understand that I had a voice and that the voice itself was the engine for books and shorter pieces. In many ways I returned to my grade school columnist voice and that confidence, though I've never been able to reinhabit her completely.

A voice can take on or reject the culturally accepted mainstream values of a generation or a subpopulation, and writers may consciously or unconsciously edit voices so as to not be too "offensive," too "radical," too "angry." Finally, the way we tell our stories takes on the values of our era, our communities, and our background. In the United States we have an ideology of continuous improvement, so readers may expect a tale that fits within a narrative of a happy ending, in which a character makes mistakes, learns lessons, and earns something in the end, having emerged changed. Whether these progressions happen in reality is a matter open to interpretation. All of these storylines, however, and these cultural stances form the ground upon which a voice will stand. An awareness of possible choices with regard to voice may empower you to choose, for the right projects, a voice that is seen as an outsider.

TRY THIS

1. Who are the voices judging your writing? Give them names and describe what they say. Where do those voices come from? What biases do these critical voices have?

2. Write for five minutes from a voice that you use and that annoys you. For me it's my "clipped and stressed" voice; I get snippy when I am feeling certain kinds of time pressure and am overwhelmed. Dig into the vocabulary, sentence structure, and rhythm of this voice. At any point you can feel free to transition to writing about this voice and what it means.

3. Sometimes a voice I encounter in the world gets my hackles up—and not even because the speaker necessarily means harm. Maybe it's just because the voice reminds me of something I experienced or something negative I believe about myself. Make a list of five of those "sticky" voices. Now, for each one, describe the subtext voice you hear; what's sticky or challenging about that voice? For each voice, write your response, either your knee-jerk defensive response or your more reflective response.

Rhetoric, at its source, has provided a series of fine and useful tools and analytic frameworks, but these tools have in places become a parody of their original function.

Yes, a helping of concern for the reader's time is a very helpful strategy. Being conscious of conveying some insight to the reader is important, one that French sixteenth-century essayist Michel de Montaigne employed by using some measure of modesty to introduce his work: "I am myself the subject of my book; it is not reasonable to expect you to waste your leisure on a matter so frivolous and empty."[12]

This was rhetoric, common courtesy, and an understanding of context. Montaigne was pioneering a new form, a version of the personal essay. Although it was not unheard of for a man of his social class to write, it was a little odd for him to write about himself. But he had enough self-regard and choral support, as a French nobleman who had retired in his forties, to set himself up in a stone tower and explore his mind on the page.

As much as it's nice to approach the reader with a little humility, there's no need to grovel and flinch before our audiences. There's also no need in any setting to write for a hostile audience before you're ready. In fact, sometimes the words only come when we feel a sense of shelter on the page. John McPhee, an acknowledged master of the form of nonfiction, with over forty books to his name and regular articles and essays in the *New Yorker* since the 1970s, has said that every book he wrote, in a first draft, began with the words "Dear Mother."[13]

If one has a good relationship with one's mom, such an imagined audience might open one's heart in the presence of a kind and benevolent audience. And you don't have to choose your mom. Choose anyone in your life who listens well, who encourages. And if you haven't encountered that in real life, imagine that person. Make them up. Envisioning support gives the writer time to wander, to explore, and to develop one's ideas under the warmth and encouragement of a reader who is interested in what the writer has to say.

I often write to my mom in my head, and that imagined audience cues me to cut down on the jargon and to imbue my sentences with the care and joy that my own mom exhibits as she goes about her day. Imagine having care instead of hostility toward a reader; you might be more likely to create a text that a reader would enjoy.

TRY THIS

1. Try McPhee's technique to home in on what matters most about a subject you want to write about. Think of a person who adores you, and start a five-minute freewrite as a letter to that person.

2. Another way into this feeling is to start a writing prompt with "What I really want to say is . . ." What I like about this prompt, and why it works, is that is cues the writer to focus on what's most essential, and that invitation to clarity ends up benefiting the audience without making audience an obsession.

PIRATE-ROGUE VOICES

The imagined audience is an inevitable part of most (but not all) writing. Often the imagined audience is shaped by the form we choose or the form provided by a teacher or the person signing our paychecks. We then internalize the teacher or mentor as an audience, and part of what we consciously or unconsciously hear in our heads is that imagined reader's reaction to our sentences as words unfurl on the page.

When we realize we're being watched or listened to, often our first instinct is to sit up straighter or smile, to make ourselves look good, or maybe to get defensive. But a writer can also be blocked by this sense of judgment and performance.

Janet Burroway writes: "The version of yourself that you choose to reveal is part of your meaning. No matter how earnest your attempt to tell 'exactly what happened,' 'the author' is always a partial or slightly idealized you, writing from a frame of mind more focused and consistent—and probably more virtuous—than any person ever possessed."[14] We are always editing ourselves and our voices for others in social situations. Our public voices and their awareness of scrutiny can, sometimes, hide the real messy selves and voices that are more accurate and that get us through our days and our rough patches.

An awareness of your imagined audience can give you much more voice power. What if you wrote to an audience of pirates, cheering on your saucy irreverence and every moment in which you bucked the system?

Mistakes and misadventures and poor choices and dilemmas can be some of our biggest sources of growth. The act of catching myself in a mistake is couched in a quest for meaning, which gives that mistake a purpose. For a while people were doing "Talk like a Pirate Day." I don't know why that emerged or where it went, but it was weird and funny. How much would we learn if we listened to those pirates?

TRY THIS

1. Write to an imagined audience of pirates, proving what a badass you are. Start with: "Fellow pirates, I celebrate my most glorious reckless adventures!" Or choose any other rogue figure that speaks to your soul.

2. What's the voice you use to make yourself feel and seem virtuous? That voice—and we all use it—is one among many. Take that voice and write in it for five minutes, maybe amping it up to an extreme, so you can see what moves and phrases signal this voice.

3. What's the voice you use when you are embarrassed? When you're worried you've done something wrong? When you're angry?

4. Write to an imaged audience at a Failure Conference, devoted to those who understand and celebrate massive mistakes, the experts of error and wayward choices.

VULNERABILITY AND REFLECTION

I encourage my writing students to take back the "I" and explore it on the page. They struggle at first because their own selves have often been judged as completely irrelevant to the texts they have been asked to produce. The things they most love and wonder about have been deemed extraneous to the writing process.

I ask them to tell stories about their lives and also to write about the times when they were challenged, when they were not their best selves, when they made mistakes. I ask them to reflect, to show their vulnerable selves when they were unsure—and then to wonder about what those moments mean. This mulling is what our brains do as we lie in bed at night wondering about our futures, thinking about our pasts, and asking questions about reality and other people.

Yet the strength to put these vulnerable ideas onto the page is a muscle that has been, in most cases, atrophied through lack of use and challenge or through lack of space to relax and grow. Often those who are able to be vulnerable are those who've had the safety to let their guard down and receive choral support. It's heartening to see this ability come to life, even when it's a huge risk, and to watch writers delve into questions. They learn that this exploration is what makes any experience on the page accessible, whether or not the reader has shared in the experience. Because we all have doubts and questions, we always have something to say.

Once these writers understand that they care about each other, and if the classroom workshop has been structured to encourage a benevolent audience, their writing begins to sing and leap. This generous audience gives critiques and asks very direct questions—the toughest questions—but asks those questions in the service of making the writing stronger. Writers thrive because the workshop is a generative space for experimentation.

And Aristotle would be fine with that because it produces rhetorically sound writing that appeals to readers.

Often when writers are pursuing something challenging in writing, they will allude to it and then pull back. Metcalf and Simon have developed a check-in system in their book *Writing the Mind Alive* to challenge this tendency. Their system of "proprioceptive writing" helps writers engage in conversation with themselves by grounding the body in a certain routine. One of their exercises recommends a five-minute freewrite, followed by "the Proprioceptive Question" of lifting a few words from that freewrite and filling them in the blank of this sentence:

"What do I mean by_____?" This approach allows a writer to delve into unarticulated thoughts. You can also follow up a freewrite with "What thoughts were heard but not written?"[15]

Imagine, with your own careful observation of the unsaid, making the world a little bigger for a reader who also carries the unsaid.

TRY THIS

1. What is a secret you carry? What's something you've done that you wish you hadn't? What's the thing that people will judge you about? Or what is a tiny secret that others might think is funny? What voices emerge to tell these stories?

2. Name five voices you would never bring out in public or who don't usually get a chance to unfurl on the page. Maybe these are voices you or others have judged in the past. Take five minutes and let one of these voices speak.

3. Try the prompts offered by Metcalf and Simon to follow one of these freewrites with that Proprioceptive Question: "What do I mean by _____?" What thoughts whispered in your head but you didn't write down?

7   *Detail Is the Seed of Voice*

"Show, don't tell" is outmoded advice because of the *don't*, but the act of showing is, to me, an invitation to see, enjoy, and understand the world. Showing in writing is an encouragement toward observation and detail. Showing requires me to absorb the world, to understand my life anew, and concreteness and specificity are why I write. These details bring writing and the world alive, and they activate voices.

Let's start with the place you're in right now. Even if it is a nondescript classroom in a building made of cinder blocks and concrete, the range of possible details to describe in that room is quite possibly infinite. You can zoom in to an ant-sized view of a particular brick, or you can zoom out to talk about the geometric shape of the room or move out even farther to describe your location, its political and geological history. You could describe the rock miles beneath your feet to the earth's mantle or the gases and clouds miles up in the atmosphere. You could describe the sound of the air conditioner whooshing in the vents, or you could describe the afternoon light filtering through the window. You could spend a long time trying to capture the exact shade of industrial gray used to paint the cinder blocks.

In the room where I'm sitting (my dining room), I can choose some details out of these infinite possibilities and, with my voice and perspective, select a bouquet to present. The choice of which details to share is an act of vision and voice.

In the mood I'm in this morning, I gravitate toward a ceramic container for cream or milk shaped like an reddish orange cow that I bought at a garage sale. Its mouth, which forms the spout, is perpetually open in the longest moo ever. One shelf above the cow is a papier-mâché puffin that is looking a little ragged from the time our cat hunted and tackled it. How I describe these and other objects could be spun toward capturing my lack of a unifying design sense; my penchant for rescuing things from garage sales, clearance bins, and thrift stores; the fact that I like animals; or the fact that housekeeping is not my strong suit.

On the shelf below the cow is a picture of me and my husband at our wedding. I am wearing jeans, and my son and the family dog sit in front of us in a prefab flower arch in the office of the local justice of the peace. So, I could pick out the details in this ramshackle but fun room that tell the story of our family. The more I look at the stuff here, and the more I describe it, the more I see all the possible stories this room could tell.

DETAILS GIVE LIFE

We sometimes need to write our voices into being. A few semesters ago, my creative writing workshop was scheduled to discuss two essays written by undergraduate students who had each chosen a topic from their own lives. One of the two students was firmly convinced that she was a "good writer" and one was firmly convinced she was a "bad writer." Both essays happened to struggle with getting specific, so after a few minutes of discussion, I transitioned to what I call "furniture moving." I stopped the workshop and began to list on the whiteboard the questions that other students had about the first essay.

Then I started to draw—a series of rough circles, boxes, and arrows; maybe a few stick figure people, some words—in diagrams that represent a timeline or major themes and events. Then we as a class began to use the diagram to search for places where the writers could expand their essays. The target here is detail: asking the author to give us more texture and real-life data to in order to locate scenes and details. Once the students in a workshop understand that asking questions about details brings the event to life before us, we all get energized. The questions are a collective and joyful pursuit, even if the subject matter is difficult: *What did your parents do during the big fight? Did they see you sneaking out of the apartment? Do you remember the color of the carpet or the lighting? What did you take when you left? What scenes are missing? What did your mom do the minute she saw you? What did her face look like?*

I urge the workshop on and praise the questions as well as the answers. *What exactly did your parents say, and what do you remember about your father's face? How did it feel? What details do you remember about the furniture? What else was happening in your life at the time?*

Though I use this approach with creative nonfiction, the exercise can also be used to draw out the fictional world of a scene or story. This activity turns a "struggling" piece of writing into a fertile plot of land upon which the next draft can grow strong. The writers are emboldened because they are the experts, and they see that their memories and imagination are full of all the richness they need. They learn that there really is so much to work with, so many details to be pulled in to show this moment in a new and vivid way.

The workshop supportively calls upon the writer to share the details of what exactly happened in the writer's past or mind's eye. As we uncover the chronology and the sensory information as a group, the conversation becomes increasingly lively and animated by the pleasure of helping a writer to resee an event and understand it in new ways. Instead of workshopping the text, we discuss the richness of detail and meaning that the writer has to work with.

I began doing this so-called furniture moving in classes more than a decade ago, out of need. I'm a visual person, and I draw diagrams to see structures in writing because it helps me to understand my own options for revision. My sketches were, at first, a little self-conscious, but then I saw they were helpful to students, and these drawings got more and more elaborate. Writers would take pictures of the whiteboard diagram, or if I'd drawn it on easel paper, they would ask if they could take the diagram home. It was something we'd made together, using the student text and our collaborative spontaneous questions.

During one semester I had a teaching assistant who had worked as a therapist and was therefore a keen observer of group dynamics. After a class with the diagrams, her own face was aglow as we debriefed.

"Did you see their bodies, the way they lit up when we started talking about scenes and detail?" she asked. She had seen an anxious writer smile and relax.

Writers at any stage of the writing process may not see where there's potential for diving into the details. Often the most important potential scenes are hidden because we don't think our lives are interesting and we don't remember the scenes or because we're seeing large actions in our mind's eye and not getting to the texture of life. Once we learn to see the scenes and how to bring them out more fully by asking questions, both the details and the voices come alive.

One peer asked a writer how she felt in the moment we were examining and excavating a piece she had written. She replied that the experience had allowed her to put herself there, in a scene that she had dismissed. She sorted through the feelings and memories in her body, and then she was able to remember her mixed emotions during that moment in her life and what had caused them. That was how she found the best and most complex voice for her essay: by realizing that the simple voice she'd chosen didn't match the complexity of her experience.

In her essay "The Site of Memory," Pulitzer- and Nobel Prize–winning writer Toni Morrison writes that image—often derived from memory, even in fiction—provides a touchstone "to yield up a kind of truth." She describes image not as a "symbol" or hidden meaning but simply "a picture and the feelings that accompany the picture."[1]

Morrison gives an example of an image of corn on the cob in her memory that summons something she wants to pursue in writing: "I'm trying to write a particular kind of scene, and I see corn on the cob. To 'see' corn on the cob doesn't mean that it suddenly hovers; it only means that it keeps coming back. And in trying to figure out 'What is all this corn doing?' I discover what it is doing. I see the house where I grew up in Lorain, Ohio." As she pursues and writes about this persistent image, she also sees the people that inhabit that powerful memory. What's important, too, is that this process works for all genres. Morrison is using the image from her real life as a generative seed for her fiction.

Morrison writes that the people around the image "are my access to me; they are my entrance to my own interior life." Her research starts in that image. She describes how this process works: "All water has a perfect memory and is forever trying to get back to where it was. Writers are like that: remembering where we were, what valley we ran through, what the banks were like, the light that was there and the route back to our original place. It is emotional memory—what the nerves and the skin remember as well as how it appeared. And a rush of imagination is our 'flooding.'"[2]

As our bodies ground us in the world, our actions and observations tell us about and show us our relationship with the world and with others. Observing past and present scenes and details from our lives reveals a wealth of information about ourselves, including our preferences, decisions, and stances that we may have ignored or forgotten about as well as the nature of the events, large and small, that happened around us and to us.

Writers often go to the details to unearth the feelings, the experiences, and then the voices that can serve as guides for a scene. We "show" to let the reader experience our little slice of the world, and the act of providing detail is like a flashlight's beam, revealing to the writer more about their topic and its related emotions and associations. Details evoke a voice through memory or imagination, and they can help a writer get in touch with various selves and voices.

TRY THIS

1. Write a list of five "memory triggers," objects that hold a great deal of significance in your memory. Choose one and try to describe the object and then the world around the object, the person or people it is connected to, and the string of emotions that this cloud

of an image evokes. That cloud of words and phrases is bound to evoke strands that emerge outward in a rich web of associations, so you can write in the form of phrases, questions, and even single words if that helps you capture what Morrison describes as the "flooding" that the image evokes.

2. Write for five minutes, in any direction, on the story around that memory trigger or what you see and feel about it now. What voice is associated with that memory trigger? Is there more than one voice that emerges?

THE LIFE OF THE MIND

In writing, *mimesis* is a word that means, basically, representation of life. As writers present details, they trigger moments that *feel alive* in a reader's head. Mimesis is what happens when you open a book, get lost in the story, and look up to find that hours have passed. You weren't just reading; you were living that story.

Research into neuroscience and the discovery of mirror neurons has highlighted the ways in which our brains, upon encountering a representation of action in another, mimic that action within our own brains and bodies. We essentially experience the action, with all the neurons firing, so that our body thinks it's raising an arm to sip from a cup or a foot to kick a ball. A second set of internal commands stops us from moving our bodies, but inside we are still mimicking the actions of others as we see them. Isn't that lovely?

The mirroring—and thus the social bonding—impulse is hard-wired within our biology. In philosophy, long before the discovery of mirror neurons, the German philosopher Edmund Husserl defined *Einfühlung* as "feeling into," a process of connecting with the lives of others as an urge toward empathy or connection.[3] We have the opportunity to understand another's position when we imagine walking a mile in that person's shoes. Sadly, reading doesn't guarantee that we'll feel greater empathy, but it presents an opportunity to try.

Bringing together these ideas in neuroscience and philosophy helps illuminate the ways in which reading a series of lived details allows us to mimic the lives of others internally and thus connect with them. When a writer delves with commitment into details and images, real or imagined, a voice often emerges, one full of greater humanity and complexity. Summoning detail and scene—calling it up from the depths of your memory and imagination—is a way to immerse yourself in an image and thus a way to summon a specific voice.

In *Still Life with Oysters and Lemon*, the poet and writer Mark Doty writes, "When we describe the world we come closer to saying what we are."[4] The more specific we can be, the more we get the chance to hear, and be, ourselves.

CONSUMED BY "THINGINESS"

Our eyes and minds grow their own clichés and habits of taking in the world, so we routinely miss certain categories of detail. And systems of power and biases further train us to see what isn't there and to ignore evidence that doesn't fit with our worldviews. Our training as writers is a kind of exercise of taking in sensory information that moves beyond those clichés and habits—trying bit by bit to see more of the world than we might otherwise be inclined to. Writing, for me, is often a vague grasping toward a sensory cliché and then letting it go, instead looking to see what is the next real piece of sensory information beyond the habits that block specificity.

George Orwell's life as a writer was all about the details. Barry Gewen, in a review of a volume of Orwell's diaries for the *New York Times Book Review*, described Orwell as "consumed by the thinginess of life," with a vision focused on "heavy coins, stamp collecting, dart games, an irrational spelling system" of his home country of England. Detail for Orwell was more than decoration; it was, instead, directly connected to his politics. Gewen writes that Orwell knew that abstractions "were the enemy of the powerless. They destroyed the diverse particulars of everyday life and necessarily culminated in some type of inhumanity, killing people for the sake of the idea."[5] Orwell explicitly describes the connection between clear concrete writing and political ideals in the essay "Politics and the English Language." In it he made clear that when we pay attention to the particulars, we see people, impacts, complexity, and effects, rather than abstractions.

James Baldwin was another writer whose commitment to honesty and observation began with the world as he saw it. Baldwin describes the writer's task as being "to describe things which other people are too busy to describe."[6] The act of taking in detail includes, as it did for Orwell, the ability to absorb painful and complex realities, as Baldwin's attempt to really *see* his father in the essay "Notes of a Native Son" and understand better what living as a Black man in the Jim Crow United States had done to him.[7]

When we describe, we surrender a luminous warm object to the reader without being completely aware of its meaning or its implications. Rather than using objects as plot mechanisms or symbols, we reveal them as snapshots of complexity. We can let objects also be mysterious characters. If you can surrender the idea that you know what an object means, you can begin to see what else it might reveal to benefit your writing.

Vladimir Nabokov, author of *Speak, Memory*, among many other well-known works, advises writers to "caress the divine details."[8] A detail can emerge clearly from our memory or present-day experience, glowing with specificity, like Morrison's corn on the cob. Getting in touch with voice and spirit is about honestly examining the details in a life.

As writers, we can work to train ourselves to be open to the details of the world. Franz Kafka recommends a quiet discipline for writers that will produce a kind of rapture: "Stay at your table and listen. Don't even listen, just wait. Don't even wait, be completely alone and quiet. The world will offer itself to you to be unmasked; it can't do otherwise; in raptures it will writhe before you."[9] In Kafka's lovely image of the writhing world, the "you" is performing a discipline that often does not get noticed as work: quietly waiting for the world as it unfurls.

TRY THIS

1. In his book *Zen in the Art of Writing*, Ray Bradbury recommends making a list of details or simply nouns you might want to write

about someday or things you observe. Give yourself five or ten minutes to make the list. Once the details begin accumulating, you'll see how much you have, and you can come back to it to add new entries.

2. The poet Linda Gregg writes that many beginning poets struggle to collect detail: "I have my students keep a journal in which they must write, very briefly, six things they have seen each day—not beautiful or remarkable things, just things."[10] This might seem easy, yet you will be surprised at how much discipline it takes to collect even three things a day. Try this for a week. This "finding" is an important habit of narrating and naming specifically what you can collect through any of your senses. This is how we learn to be open to the world.

3. Sit in front of an object and try to describe its color in your notebook. Don't just name the color; describe it deeply, comparing its color to other objects. Or listen to a moment and describe the sound. Or use whatever sense feels particularly rich or available to you.

STARTING WITH THE DETAILS

As writers, we collect images and work with objects on a symbolic level. But an object's message can run toward cliché by relying on easy or familiar correlations and associations. The objects we choose in our writing will evoke clichés unless we excavate their complexity. Even if we write surrealistic fiction or works of magical realism that take place on other worlds, we must watch our own world to populate our writing with enlivening details.

When we are driving in the car or chatting at a party, our minds can be awake, collecting and analyzing the slightest detail. We see the green on the trees and challenge ourselves to push against not only habitual ways of describing that color green or the movement of the leaves but also against tired ways of taking in that tree, instead seeing the web of details that surrounds and contains it.

This is a kind of surrender. The world offers a daunting array of beauty and pain and complexity, presenting a challenge that always pushes against our abilities. So, avoiding cliché in our writing is about much more than skimming to cut out phrases like *my love is a red rose*. Your writing can confront, on a minute-to-minute basis, the idea that you have not yet fully learned to absorb the world.

Some details do present themselves with a clatter, like a bright-pink plastic skeleton that fell one night at 10:30 p.m. from my lime-green bookshelf to the wood floor in my dining room: clatter-thump. My pulse raced, and I reached for my notebook to collect the random smatter of reality around the skeleton's disassembled limbs.

The skeleton fell as I was sleepily reading Renata Adler's collected nonfiction about the Watergate scandal. I wrote about how it might have fallen: my son in those months was in the habit of dribbling a basketball through the house, and my husband, Cliff, and I were in the habit of yelling at him to stop, so the vibrations from each dribble had probably jarred the skeleton millimeter by millimeter from its perch up on the shelf beside a Lucite paperweight containing soil from Graceland (a gag gift from a dear friend) and a plastic glow-in-the-dark Virgin Mary.

I squatted to scoop up the pieces, observing that my joy at this skeleton's mysterious intrusion had shattered a kind of helpless Watergate mood. My husband later said the skeleton had probably jumped to its death because it was sad about where it had ended up, which made me laugh. We mulled over what his name would be, which devolved into more jokes. In a way this tiny moment could be used to reveal the entirety of our history and relationship or my relationship to unconventional rescued decorations or both. And it could capture my relationship with my son, who in those years loved Halloween decorations, so we would buy them on clearance after trick-or-treating, which connected to the clearance rack habit I'd been devoted to since before he was born.

VOICES USE DETAILS

Virginia Woolf exhorts writers to "examine an ordinary mind on an ordinary day."[11] This interface between details presented by a day and the mind interacting with those details leads us back to voice.

A single concrete detail in a writing workshop from years ago stayed with me as an honest expression of social class. A poet in a writing workshop said, in describing her current situation, that she was financially secure enough to go to the grocery store and not worry about what she put into her cart. In particular, she said, she could buy fancy ingredients and cooking oils without checking the price tags with anxiety. Because I've had a similar experience with living on both sides of this financial line, her concrete observation struck me right in the chest that night, and even today I can't walk past the fancy truffle oil in its embossed bottle without feeling a specific flutter of a complicated thread that runs through my life.

In a similar way my voice and my view on life changes when I say the phrase *duct tape*. That humble bit of fix-it hardware evokes a time in my life when the Dollar Store was an important part of how I got by. One day my local Dollar Store offered a clearance bin full of bags of colored electrical and duct tape, and I bought one, a wealth of strange material that stayed with me for years as I moved here and there. I used those rolls to mend things but also to weave odd covers for homemade books and journals I sewed together.

The voice that might come out from that time in my life is not what one might assume from the outside, not all gloom and want. The voice summoned by *duct tape* comes with a kind of straightening of my spine, a kind of focus, and an intense commitment to wring joy from wherever I can find it. I respect that version of myself. She's important, as is what she has to say. Her voice has a sadness to it, due to losses I experienced during that time, but also the dignity of having figured things out for myself, marking it as a period of critical growth. Describing her from the outside, I might resort first to jokes that lean on the ramshackle nature of my living, but once I think of duct tape, a scrappy dignity emerges.

The eras in our lives are attached to voices, and these voices can be triggered and explored through humble objects. In the writing class I led on voice, a woman wrote about a fond memory from her childhood in which she spent time with her mother, who was a painter. The writer described being in the warm glow of her mother's patient work, and then she described the feeling of what it is like to paint—the attention to color and shape, light and dark—that made me feel as though I had never before observed light gracing a bowl of fruit. Getting to feel the experience of painting helped me resee the world.

Every action we perform in contact with concrete objects triggers its own voice and its own vision.

TRY THIS

1. Do you have a voice attached to an era that you can evoke through a single concrete object? Write about that object first as you might see it from the viewpoint of today, and then write about the object using the voice it triggers. Try this again for another noun on the list generated by Bradbury's exercise.

2. Think about something you like to do—and maybe even go and do this activity as a way to research and observe. What's the voice in your head as you do this? How does this favorite action channel itself into a worldview? How might that voice describe the action in a how-to?

3. Describe someone significant to you. Describe why they are important to you. Describe them doing an activity they enjoy with lots of attention to detail.

MANAGING VOICE AND SCENE

In fiction and nonfiction, putting details together into a narrative—pressing the "play" button on the video—creates momentum. A scene asks, "And then what?" In narrative writing generally, across genres, the writer often instinctively wants the action to unspool and reveal itself. When I began to write scenes in both fiction and nonfiction, I found myself distracted by the momentum of action and plot. Narrative has its own logic, and I found myself searching for the meaning of the story through the arc of action, racing all the way to the end for some kind of closure presented by each scene's final move.

But we can also resist that narrative pull. A writer has an amazing power to stop time. In temporarily lingering on a detail of a scene or using a moment in a scene to leap to reflection or flashback or association, the writer can build a web of meaning that allows the reader to enjoy a temporary freedom from the bondage of forward motion. These pauses in scene allow a narrator a breath to reflect and allow voice to fully bloom.

When I was focused on writing a memoir that worked primarily with narrative, using the scenes in my life as building blocks, the "what happened" didn't reveal everything I wanted to say. In fact, my simple what-happened story was like a lot of lives in which characters bumbled around making mistakes. When I tell my story as a series of actions, the reader might ask: "Why is she dating that guy? Oh no, why did she do *that?*" My life as an action movie delivers very little inherent meaning. When I tended to make choices that fell along culturally prescribed tracks, my actions were easy to judge, unless I also included an internal monologue to humanize myself and draw out the meaning, which is delivered through a mostly internal voice as it tries to make sense of the world.

I did no mountain climbing and no fighting of wolves during the plot of a memoir-in-progress. I married someone and had a baby, and there were struggles. In my drafts of writing to describe that era, I would often summon a critical voice. I imagined how a hostile anonymous reader might judge me, and I wrote defensively against that imagined judgment. In other words, without excavating the voice of the woman in those moments during a few difficult years, I turned my story of the past into a list of regrettable actions. I can't expect the reader to come to a complex understanding of the character in those scenes if, as the writer, I am not able to get inside those scenes and that character myself. And—crucially—if my story is evaluated based only on its actions, relying on the cultural tropes around it for meaning, it dehumanizes me.

And yet . . . who was that woman? When I summon her through the details, I first see my computer, an old Macintosh laptop that I had propped up on a white plastic dish rack because my neck hurt to peer downward into the screen. I see a nursing pillow with blue-and-white stripes that I bought from a secondhand store. I see the bins of board books that my son joyfully flipped through and patted with his soft little hands. I hear a woman who in her deep joy and deep confusion and deep anger was full-on wringing what she could out of this life with its mix of difficulty and abundance.

She was fierce. And when I began to listen to her voice and to plumb what she was angry at, I began to see her as a character. From the outside she made mistakes, and she made mistakes from the inside, too, but her voice itself—in my journals, in the notes and essays I wrote—was on fire with perspective and meaning and opinion and hope and fear.

In thinking about voice, I went back to read some of my writing from that time. I was surprised at how funny this woman was. And then I remembered a small scene, not something that I'd mark as a key dramatic action: I had made an appointment for an eye exam after I finally scored a job that offered health insurance. As I browsed the racks of eyeglass frames, I said to myself, "Give me the frames for a woman who might leave her husband." The detail of what those frames looked like—the tiniest hint of a cat's-eye swoop at the temple, the flash of turquoise inside the arms of the frames—was a signal to myself of what I was contemplating, what wouldn't appear externally in my life until years later.

My friend Jenny noticed the glasses and admired them, and then she said something to me that has stayed with me, the way a true friend can see who you really are. "It started there," she said. In a concrete way Jenny meant that my penchant for wilder and wilder eyeglasses began with that choice, but in knowing me, she saw I had reached a turning point, a signal to myself to move beyond the modest minimum of self-denial, like a flower turning toward the sun.

TRY THIS

1. Freewrite about a moment in the previous few weeks that seems to be weighted with intense emotion. Maybe it's the most interesting, most conflict-ridden, confusing, or joyful moment. Record

any detail you can remember: color, light, smell, texture, object, weight, temperature, sound.

2. Now write that moment as a scene, even if the action is very small. Include your internal actions and reflections. How would you describe the voice that emerges, in its point of view, mood, and intonation?

3. Describe what you're wearing right now: just the facts, with extreme detail.

4. Now write a description from these observations that connects these details to who you are as a character, letting the audience get closer to your character by understanding the emotions, choices, past experiences, and any other influences that led him or her to wear this particular outfit.

8   *Embodied Voices, Racialized Lives*

The framework of race is a construct ingrained in our minds and in society, particularly in structures of power. It's both true that race doesn't exist on an essential biological level and that it definitely exists as a social and systemic reality that has shaped underlying social structures and enforced inequalities. It makes sense, then, that this looming presence would also deeply shape the ways that we see reality and the ways we listen to others and express ourselves. No matter who we are, our ethnic and racial backgrounds can be sources of rich inspiration and important questions, if we choose to pay attention.

In the anthology *The Racial Imaginary: Writers on Race in the Life of the Mind*, edited by award-winning poet and essayist Claudia Rankine, with Beth Loffreda and Max King Cap, the poet Charles Bernstein calls attention to the implications of the very languages we speak and write: "And there are all the languages, the ones lost on the prairie and on the high plains, wiped out systematically. . . . And the ones retained, the resistant strains that bubble up through our speech like sparks of light; the voices, accents, pitches, tones, vocabulary, dialects. . . . Questions of race are never just about narrative or images or stereotypes, they pervade our grammars, our styles, our forms, and above all our unstated system of preferences, of aesthetic value."[1]

WHOSE VOICE IS "NORMAL"?

One element of privilege is the luxury of having your accent, pitch, tone, vocabulary, and dialect seen as "standard" rather than interpreted and judged as "outside" or different. Having a voice that stands out often affects how that voice grows in reaction to scrutiny. There's a version of spoken English called "all-American," with its Anglo-European amalgam mixed with U.S. Midlands accents often echoed by television newscasters, and that voice overlaps to a large degree with my own. Being able to express oneself under an umbrella seen as standard can give an enormous boost to one's sense of voice.

Writers of color in the United States have regularly been required to "mimic whiteness," as Felicia Rose Chavez describes, before writing in the voices that come from their own experience.[2] Matthew Salesses points out the damaging effects that a framework of "learning the rules before you break them" can have, particularly on writers of color. Because the "rules" imply mastery of a "basic" voice of whiteness, one's culture gets reduced to being a mere addition or decoration. This view privileges white voices. Asking writers of color to "become a part of that tradition" of white voices before finding their own voices thus carries an expectation in which, as Salesses describes it, "the spread of craft starts to feel and work like colonization."[3]

In the era in which I began teaching, the ability to "code switch" seamlessly was seen by many as an essential skill that writers of color learned and employed. But making this ability a baseline expectation requires a writer of color to do twice as much work and to internalize white expression, which puts all the work on writers of color and is another kind of erasure. As David Mura writes in an essay of advice about offering comments on Black writers' expression in particular, "I would try to be cognizant of the fact that SBE [Standard Black English, often also referred to as African American Vernacular English (AAVE)] has been the language of this student and her community; any hint of disrespect of that language from me would be taken as disrespect towards that student and her community."[4]

The rules of craft, as Salesses stresses, are really "about who has the power to write stories ... who gets to write literature and who folklore, whose writing is important and to whom, in what context."[5] In other words, there's no such thing as a selection of writing, a craft tool or term, that does not have a connection to structures of power. The good news, for our voices, is that knowledge of these effects, and of that continuing conversation, gives us options and choices. Writers of color like Chavez, Mura, and Salesses, among many others, offer advice about how to navigate the spaces where voices come together and how to ensure that more writers get the choral support they need and deserve.

GROWING AND PROTECTING VOICES

Racism—overtly intentional or unconscious—often aims to control and curb the free expression of voices and selves, to limit discussion about what is possible. A healthy array of voices reflecting our range of realities gives us all more access to possible forms of expression. As Matthew Salesses writes in *Craft in the Real World*, "How can a writer know the possibilities of what they *can* do without knowing many different ways that things have been done before and where their possibilities have come from?"[6] For people of color and others from marginalized communities, the encounter with voices that reflect or embody one's experience can be lifesaving.

In the book *Just Us: An American Conversation* Claudia Rankine shares the work of poet and philosopher Édouard Glissant, who writes that a person who is a member of the African diaspora "consents not to be a single being" and experiences a "passage from unity to multiplicity."[7] This conscious membership in a multiplicity offers a deep and rich way to see the world, along with the multiplicity of voices that can describe that world. This is a vision that white writers situated in an illusion of universality or an imaginary "normal" often cannot reach.

Writers of color develop voices that reflect multiplicities and also have built institutions to provide the necessary choral support to survive and thrive. Felicia Rose Chavez, in her book *The Anti-Racist Writing Workshop*, offers not only writing advice but also pedagogy and classroom structures and activities to reframe the nature and functioning of the workshop. She writes about how vital it is for writers of color to tune into their inner voices, past voices, and community's voice in order to access power, "to make sense of ourselves, by ourselves, independent of the system of white supremacy that tells people of color that we have no dignity, no history, no art, no voice. . . . We dare to tune in and listen to our own words, in our own tongues, and translate them onto the page with our own fists."[8]

Voices grow stronger when affirmed, reflected, and bounced against rhythms that amplify them and encourage the writer to risk, that tell the writer they're onto something good. Writers of color gather for institutional and personal support through organizations like Kundiman, Cave Canem: A Home for Black Poetry, Radius of Arab American Writers, and Voices of Our Nations Arts Foundation, which offer classes, mentoring, and gatherings for choral support. These organizations and many others allow writers of color to clarify and find voices that feel most resonant, interesting, and challenging, to listen to the threads of emerging voices, and as Chavez writes in *The Anti-Racist Writing Workshop*, to "own up to, and break down, the politics of white narratives."[9]

As we near the third decade of the twenty-first century, people within and beyond publishing and media institutions continue to wrestle with the structures of power that mark certain voices for wide distribution and praise while denigrating other voices and perspectives. This happens not only with who writes the books that receive wide distribution but also how those books are described, how newspaper articles are reported, and what topics and sources and words are chosen to present perspectives on reality. Our educational system, our class structure, our housing policy, our economy, and other cultural and social institutions all play a role in whose voices are included and whose are excluded.

Writing communities and movements have demanded changes that carve out space for writers of color, including online activism such as the #WeNeedDiverseBooks and #PublishingPaidMe hashtags and direct challenges to staff publishing houses and editorial mastheads in a way that reflects the racial and ethnic composition of this country.

After developing and finding her voice, the writer and philosopher bell hooks describes the long journey to publication of her first book. She writes: "Imagine my distress when I answered the call of those voices" of her ancestors and community "and committed myself to writing work only to find that writing mocked, that no one wanted to publish it. . . . I confronted the reality that we may discover the rightness of our vision and vocation before others do."[10]

TRY THIS

1. If you are a writer of color, freewrite using one of the voices you protect or use only for your home communities. Write into one of these voices, channeling joy or insight or a question. What are the voices you use when you feel unfairly judged or policed because of your race, heritage, or other group identity?

2. If you're interracial or your racial background is framed as "complicated" or you find yourself and your voice framed as inauthentic or wrong in more than one setting, write about the voices you've been asked to inhabit and the settings in which your voices are respected. How would you name those voices? Write in the voice that contains that multiplicity.

3. If you are white, freewrite for five minutes about how whiteness affects your speech, your voices, and your vision, including the topics you don't feel comfortable talking about. Who embodied and passed on these models to you? What voices do you hear? Can you name them?

4. Felicia Rose Chavez writes: "Writers must actively address the physical, mental, emotional, and cultural barriers that prevent their full creative realization. They must name their fears and write anyway."[11] Write about a situation in which your own unresolved issues about race provoked a voice in you that you don't often hear. Don't come to a conclusion. What were your anxieties? Can you name this voice? Do you have a voice that can navigate these complexities?

SUMMONING AND NAMING VOICES

Black writer and philosopher bell hooks wrote in a diary as a way to hear herself, "to develop an autonomous voice." Born Gloria Watkins, she chose the writing name bell hooks to honor her great-grandmother and to channel a voice. She writes about needing these structures to support her voice because she'd learned, both from her home community and from other readers, that "having a voice was dangerous." Calling out a reality that others had an interest in hiding provokes reaction and critique from the white world.[12]

People of color have been typecast by the white world of past and present. Nonwhite histories have been reframed in narrow stereotyped voices, with expression both caricatured and monitored for any deviation from white expectations, even as white communities appropriate the brilliance of expression developed and honed by people of color. Tajja Isen, who identifies as mixed-race, writes about the long struggle to remove the "tiny white people" from her head and her writing after a long period in which she had sought to emulate white writers: "In seeking to circumvent the question of race, I wound up replicating the same ideologies that had cornered me into feeling like I didn't deserve to write about it in the first place."[13]

Claudia Rankine writes about how writers of color must constantly choose to write into an unwelcoming silence, to listen instead to a voice that "silently tells you to take your foot off your throat because just getting along shouldn't be an ambition."[14] Writers of color who call out the practices and acts of white writers do the difficult work of making space for themselves to express their perspectives and visions. bell hooks writes, "Black women in the diaspora do not come to writing naturally, for there is always someone standing ready to silence the natural impulse to create as it arises in us, and so to write we must ever resist."[15]

TRY THIS

1. How conscious are you of your own racial and ethnic background as you write? Do you feel pressure when you write to represent the racial or ethnic groups you come from in your writing? Why or why not?

2. Channel a voice that emerges from your racial or ethnic background, something that captures the song or rhythm of some of the

people who formed you. What are the sounds of that voice music? The words and phrases? What name would you give that voice?

WHITE FEEDBACK

White people offering feedback and edits will usually betray their lack of understanding about these dynamics and pressures. Not so many years ago, as the editor of a literary journal, I accepted a wonderful essay that moved back and forth between English and Spanish. Working with my staff, I approved edits to the piece that came from a style guide I'd used over the previous decade, which included the directive to italicize non-English words. I italicized the Spanish in my edits, and I also asked the author to provide more context clues for English speakers.

This writer then generously taught me something with her edits. Her copy came back with *more* Spanish words, not fewer, and with less context. I did the proverbial head-smack to the forehead. I needed to join the current century, as did my style guide.

I went in search of a little education. I was teaching creative writing at a university; I'd read the work of many other writers of color, yet I hadn't brought my behavior or my style guide up-to-date to reflect the work of those writers. I hadn't understood the way in which my so-called neutral edits subtly framed the world as English only. I found articles, read them, and began to understand. I edited my style guide and incorporated this episode into my teaching. If you're interested, the website entitled the Conscious Style Guide, at consciousstyleguide .com, is a helpful resource for tracking and learning about the continual evolution of language and design as they intersect with justice and with self-definition and community making.

I am lucky that I can call this woman a friend in the writing world and that she didn't at all reject me as the result of my mistake. I know that she and countless others face this white pushback from the literary world—not occasionally but every single time they engage and seek feedback or publication.

Writers of color who go into any space where they might receive feedback on their writing usually have to wonder whether they're going to get helpful advice or, instead, coded or blatant racism—either intentional or unintentional—from white readers who may feel entitled to shape narratives of people of color. White people, on the other hand, "do not have to struggle to separate their self-perception from pervasive negative stereotypes of them that are widely and historically held, and also institutionally enforced," writes Paisley Rekdal. This institutional enforcement can be large, or it can be something seemingly small like a single entry in a style guide.[16]

Writers of color may have received many messages—physical, spatial, experiential, verbal—that their realities don't matter or that there is *no* acceptable voice with which to relate their experience. Jenny Zhang writes, "My white teachers and my white classmates told me over and over again they simply didn't believe a Chinese person would ever talk the way my characters did . . . but heaped lavish praise anytime my white peers wrote stories set in countries they've never lived in, narrated by people whose experiences of racism they never personally experienced."[17]

When commenting on the work of writers of color, white people may offer feedback that is at the very least unhelpful and at worst scarring or deeply damaging to writers of color, especially if it dovetails with and reinforces larger racial arguments, with traumatic and generational implications for writers of color.

Feedback on writing from the white world is often going to be two-dimensional and yet spoken with authority. So for white writers, one voice to examine is the voice of the critic, the feedback voice. Where does that voice come from, and how much authority does it have and convey? Where does that authority come from? White people will regularly ask whether the experiences that people of color present in their writing are "realistic." Many writers of color have reported the destabilizing nature of these comments and the grinding pressure of having to represent an entire culture in their writing, while the assumption that dominant white culture represents a "universal" context continues.

Rekdal describes how white readers often expect that the narratives of people of color will address "a continuing trauma that must only be endured, never celebrated."[18] Salesses writes that white writers who pursue this suffering sometimes implicitly expect people of color to "submit themselves for public consumption (consumption that is economic, intellectual, and emotional)."[19] This linkage in white minds between lives of people of color and tragedy can also be a serious danger for white writers who write about people of color. By focusing only on such trauma and tragedy, the net effect is to dehumanize and flatten people of color onto the page, projecting the effects of racism and racist violence onto the people who have had to live through it.

Sometimes, too, white readers will put all the pressure for writing about "political" or "angry" topics onto writers of color or writers from other marginalized groups, avoiding the fact that we are all embedded and connected and, therefore, that we are all unavoidably expressing political viewpoints and various degrees of privilege in our work—even when our life experience informs a perspective that we might see as "not political." That, too, is political. When white writers feel free to write on topics or in voices that are considered not political, they are freed up to do so by an extensive network of power that is doing the political work for them. White writers can change the dynamic partially by running their feedback through an internal filter, pausing to ask themselves whether their feedback would be relevant or helpful if it were reversed, if someone asked "Would white people do x, y, or z?"

If you're working on your writing in a workshop, your instructor might reframe a traditional workshop discussion with new patterns, which Chavez, Salesses, and other writers recommend. If you're part of a writing group or reading someone else's work as an editor or writer, consider asking the author first what feedback would be helpful for them and what feedback they are not interested in. This can benefit writers of all backgrounds.

TRY THIS

1. What kinds of questions or comments from editors and readers have been most helpful to you personally? What kind of feedback makes you want to get back to work on an essay, poem, or story?

2. What activities or narratives might others describe as the most "realistic" portrayals of a stereotypical person who shares your background? Try to write in the stereotypical "realistic" voice that others may expect from your background. What does it feel like? What issues emerge as you write? What limitations are embedded in this voice?

3. Try to write in the deeply internal voice you have for mulling over one of your own biases. What emotional charge do you hear, and what are the habits of that voice? Is there more than one voice struggling to emerge in this internal conversation?

WHITE WRITING AND APPROPRIATION

In *The Racial Imaginary* Beth Loffreda writes, "One way, if you are white, to take note of your whiteness is to pay attention if you feel a little p.o.ed, a little restricted, when asked to think if your whiteness matters to what you write or read or think; or when asked to consider that your writing about race has a content that you have not sufficiently considered."[20] If a person is accustomed to enjoying privilege and having plenty of options, it can be uncomfortable to grapple with the existence of persistent, subconscious racial bias. This bias can't be wished away, and it affects one's unconscious judgments and aesthetic values. When white people think about racism, they sometimes get a brief glimpse of how deep it all goes, and they panic, insisting that they be free of such topics, which feel restrictive in a world in which few restrictions have been imposed on them. To sort through this cognitive dissonance, most white people adopt rigid and simple beliefs they cling to about race, like "Well, I'm not a racist, so none of this applies to me." Or they harbor a dream about a fairy-tale safety zone in which they don't have to talk about race, don't have to think about a system in which they reap enormous benefits at the expense of others, and don't have to act when observing racism in action.

In a moment when I'm criticized for something—and it doesn't have to be about race—I need to listen to my own internal voices. I need to tune into the quiet anxiety in my heart, which picks at me to think about how I might be wrong, over the wave of adrenaline and shouting of my ego, which prefers that I never be challenged.

Racism and the idea of race originated in the rules and structures that white people constructed after they declared themselves "white" to protect their property rights and power. In short: white people started this whole thing, and white people benefit from it, regardless of when your ancestors arrived. Race envelops white people, including writers, in a way that makes it harder for white writers to see it working because we have also benefited from the roadblocks it has built into our thinking. That's a painful thing, so the white psyche tries to hide its tracks. Philosopher George Yancy calls this the "opacity" of whiteness.[21] A white writer's vision is often constrained by forces that remain largely invisible to white people. As writer and thinker bell hooks writes, "The politics of experience and location shape our vision."[22]

White writers who feel defensive will often reject feedback about race or whiteness in their work by saying that any conflicting ideas impinge on their "authentic" voice. This is where the idea of multiple voices is helpful for diffusing a white writer's inability to hear criticism.

The most heavy-handed way a white writer can respond to questions about race and writing is to continue to claim complete freedom, resisting any feedback by labeling it as "censorship." Feedback isn't censorship, but dominant voices often react with outrage when they get any criticism. If it's not backed by state or institutional power, it's not censorship—it's just normal disagreement and resistance.

At this point many white writers will throw up their hands in exasperation that is maybe a little infused with drama, asking "Do I need to be perfect?" (White writers know how to flounce and do a little fake fainting. Bring me the smelling salts! And the logical fallacy here is false dualism.) David Mura states that the requirement for white teachers and writers is not perfection but, instead, a "spiritual humility." The goal here is to be teachable rather than arrogant, and that can include getting upset and overwhelmed, calming down, and then coming back to apologize or continue the conversation.

A white writer may put all the responsibility onto writers of color to tell them what the rules are. And as these conversations develop, a white writer might engage first by wanting simple guides: *Which terms can I use? Can I write about characters of people of color, and if so, how?*

The conversation about writing characters across lines of social identity is long and complex, often resting under the concern about *cultural appropriation* in cases in which a writer in any genre takes on a voice from another culture or community. This doesn't mean there's a simple yes-no traffic light to tell white writers and others when to proceed. Instead, we can take guidance that this is fraught territory and understand the long history of the conversation. Writers are drawn to wonder about and want to inhabit the lives and minds of others. Reading gives us the chance to live other lives. Those are wonderful impulses and opportunities.

Writers writing outside of their own experiences have the responsibility to investigate this conversation and to understand that the less research and listening they do, the more they are likely to stumble into stereotype and caricature. That's the nature of reality; we flatten something until we understand its complexities.

As Rekdal explains in her book *Appropriations: A Provocation*: "Writing requires that we pay attention to others at a level that can only be classified as rude. . . . To observe closely leads the writer to the radical recognition of what both binds her to and separates her from others. It will push her to hear voices she's been taught should remain silent. Oftentimes, these voices, and these truths, reveal something equally powerful, and profoundly unsettling, about ourselves."[23]

For white writers this means becoming aware of what Rekdal describes as the "combined problem of cultural privilege, profit, and self-aggrandizement that must be considered when we appropriate items from other cultures."[24] In other words, there are multiple reasons we might try to write outside of our experience, and one of them might be to seem like a hero speaking for the "voiceless." The choice to speak for others is likely ignoring the fact that those folks are already writing or telling their own complex stories but without the social and institutional supports to gain access to the dominant society's radar.

Rekdal engages with the controversy that emerged around the novel *American Dirt* by Jeanine Cummins, which tells a story about immigration from Mexico. Cummins is a writer who identified as white but revealed that she had a grandmother from Puerto Rico as an added layer of complication. Part of the pushback against her novel emerged from writers of color who lived near the U.S.-Mexico border, who had life experience with the story that Cummins spent only a brief period researching, and who had written with much more realistic and in-depth life experience about the same issue but had not been given the same massive platform or chance to share their stories as Cummins.

Rekdal's book is in the form of a series of letters to a student writer who has wondered about taking on other voices and lives. While Rekdal offers caution against stereotypes, she also pushes against the impulse to say, "No, it's never okay." Instead, she urges writers to actively engage with the impulses behind the desire to take on other voice, to mull over "what appetites I feed when I write from a position outside my own."[25] She asks writers to understand the dangers while refusing to shut down the impulse to transgress, to push, to experiment.

TRY THIS

1. If you have tried to write from a voice outside your own experience, what was that like? What difficulties and roadblocks did you feel as you wrote into that voice? What questions did it raise?

2. If you wrote with the impulse to explore a social issue, what did you learn through the writing experience that complicated your initial impulses? What do you think was at the root of the desire to cross this line in your writing? How did it turn out?

3. Regardless of your background, are there "white" voices in your head? If you are white, do those voices express a little outrage or entitlement at any treatment or inconvenience that limits your movement, the voices that feel entitled to complete freedom? If you are a person of color, what do those voices whisper to you about your

own right to expression, movement, or being? Give those voices space on the page so that you can see them. Delve into them. Where did your body and mind pick up these signals and forms of voice?

MULTIPLE VOICES, MULTIPLE VIEWS

The reality for any of us, writes Felicia Rose Chavez in *The Anti-Racist Writing Workshop*, is that the idea of "authentic voice" is very limiting, and it's important to challenge it because our search for authenticity can be riven with racism. Voice, Chavez writes, changes depending "on the company we keep—it's one way with family, another with friends, and a whole other approach with white folks, who appraise our color, appropriate aspects of our culture, and then critique our performance of race according to their expectations."[26] This is also true for white people, who can loosen their grip on authentic voice to see which of their voices might be revised, challenged, or grown.

White people can decide to take up the challenge of writing into the complexity and the tension, peeling back the areas where the edges of whiteness have come unglued. White people can commit to being teachable and open, to absorbing an array of voices beyond their own experience. Yancy urges white people to "tarry," to stay in this unresolvable discomfort, not to latch onto a rigid idea or quickly imagined solution that only serves to comfort white reality.[27]

Yancy asks us to examine race not as a series of abstract ideas but "as an embodied and messy phenomenon" with "a complexity that often transcends and outstrips abstract conceptual analysis."[28] This messiness is good news because it provides fruitful ground to push, play, and experiment, and it means that the complexity of our observed world in all its detail will support that observation of messiness. And we all need writing that captures our complex life experience in ways that reflect our evolving social views. By pushing against the idea that our own voices, and the voices of others, have to sound a certain essential way, we can look at each other's work for what Chavez describes as "hints of energy, oddity, beauty, proof that writing is inherently imperfect . . . an ongoing attempt, rife with revision."[29]

Experience and challenge grow voices. Throughout my life I've often taken on a new role—a new job, a new position in community leadership, or the role of parent—and felt baffled and lost, lacking a confident voice in that role. I had to do what felt like faking it in those roles, struggling at first to find words and to patch things together with previous voices and borrowed voices. Many of my voices have emerged in points of need and then have been repurposed for other roles. White writers can push into this challenge, risking not knowing in order to gain experience in tangling with ideas that challenge whiteness.

Each writer has a storehouse of messy, complex material to look at every day to use to understand race. I could point to the most blatant racist statements I heard growing up from one relative and the times I fought with him versus the times I stayed silent, complicit.

In addition to constantly patrolling the world of people of color, white people police each other constantly with regard to whiteness. I have an olive complexion, so I've been asked by other white people at various times in my life, "Where are you from?" We scrutinize, as a habit, asking anyone who piques our curiosity, "No, where are you *really* from?" in the search for an essence of otherness. Though the question may come from curiosity, its effect is to flatten an interaction around the subject of race and origin, sending signals of danger in a world where this question is freighted with violence.

This awareness and my own complex experiences around race, ethnicity, and belonging don't make me less racist. They give me a layer of internal resistance and commitment to notice the racism that helped form my reality. My reactions, my speech, my very body, my fears, my options, my bank account, and my history are all shaped in ways that are beyond my control, so there's a racist narrative, a voice, running in my head constantly.

Our writing grows as we acknowledge that this is a systemic issue rather than only one of separate and individual morality. I was raised in the suburban south side of Chicago, which was composed of a patchwork of diverse and white communities, a Rust Belt area where whites attempted to use racism to cordon off areas for themselves. I internalized the constant running narrative around me—from the landscape itself and the people on it—about land and race and the connections among wealth, race, and education. This was a place where white people used segregation and exclusion both to amass wealth and stability and to define marginalized communities as a source of economic and social threat. This was an issue that affected who we lived with, where I went to school, and my daily experiences. Every single day was shaped by the racist decisions of white people. How could I not absorb that into every cell of my body?

We can call these voices and influences out into the light of day. Yancy writes:

> Being a white antiracist and yet being racist are not mutually exclusive. Rather, being a white antiracist racist signifies tremendous tension and paradox but not logical or existential futility. In fact, it is from this site of paradox, tension, frustration, and descriptive complexity, and the weight thereof, that white antiracist racists must begin to give an account of themselves, critique themselves, and continue to reimagine themselves even as these processes will inevitably encounter limitations and failures; indeed, even as these processes will be burdened by the possibility of no *clear* exit.[30]

The work of that description is the work of voices, and it requires voice complexity to engage in that internal and external dialogue. One only has to look at the world to see that racism isn't an individual issue. Understanding how systemic it is—how old, how long, how entrenched—actually takes some of the pressure off of the ego. Sadly, we can't just think our way out of racism by telling ourselves we "don't see color." Not seeing it isn't going to help in dismantling a complex and very concrete system of segregation and discrimination. Seeing the systemic racism around us gives us great material to write about from our own points of view and experience.

This, too, is why having multiple voices is a freeing idea. We can have voices that vehemently disagree with one another. White writers who want to truly hear the voices in their heads and hearts will have to surrender some element of ego and truly listen. That means that when they tune in to the voices that surround and emanate from them, they will see and hear things they don't want to hear. They will have to confront the way race shapes the words, dialogue, and viewpoints of white people, no matter how enlightened those white people might be. Limitation has nothing to do with intelligence. In fact, it's intelligent to admit we are not omniscient.

TRY THIS

1. What messages and voices about race did you absorb unconsciously as you grew up? You might try to name these voices in order to hear them more clearly. What sources of anxiety and tension are they connected to in your body and history? Are there any images attached to these voices? Could you write a conversation that captures that tension?

2. What are the various voices you have developed in order to engage with or reflect on racist conduct? Feel free to write a list, as there may be several. How large are these voices, and what are their sources? What kind of energy does it take to summon and inhabit these voices? Where do they live in your body?

3. What's "messy" about your own background in a good way? What overlaps and confusions and contradictions create a fertile ground for voices? What unique voices do you have access to as a result of that messiness?

9   *Voices of Joy*

Think about the last time you were overjoyed, filled with gratitude or relief, with pride at an accomplishment or surprise at an unexpected bit of luck. What and how did you communicate? For me joy is often accompanied by laughter, by tears, by gestures like hands raised, expressions like closed eyes and wide smiles, postures like sinking to my knees. Joy is a whole-body experience.

We're often almost struck expressionless at joy. We might swear or holler, "I can't believe it!" or "Yes!" We are unguarded and a bit goofy. Joy is an experience rather than a persuasive argument; with joy itself there's no goal to achieve besides celebration, pleasure, or pride. Its rarity on the page makes it a wonderful element for a reader to encounter in text and a nice challenge for the writer as well. Joy, I think, is pure voice, and even a tiny wisp of that magical elixir can make our writing come alive.

Joy focuses our perspective on that which gives us life, helping us to see in sharp relief the qualities and textures of whatever and whoever we love: our favorite foods or pets, a rain shower or a new love or a lottery ticket. When we regard someone or something that brings us joy, we see that person, scene, or object in a loving light that shows us details and characteristics that others might not see. In a sense we are experts about that which brings us joy because we've thought about those sources or have focused on the qualities that we enjoy.

A glowing ode, a long-held interest, or a source of odd delight can help you listen for both joyful subjects and engaging writing. Joy can be subversive: the insistence that Black joy thrives, that a disabled person can take full joy in his or her existence, push against the expectations of tragedy often imposed by dominant culture and voices. And a dash of joy, even in a sorrowful or dense document, can increase the emotional range of the entire work, acting as an oasis for the reader.

Poet and essayist Ross Gay wrote *The Book of Delights* as a kind of self-assignment. He sought to notice and catalog whatever delighted him throughout the course of a year in his life. The book is continually surprising and, true to its title, delightful. But that assignment of "delight" did not constrain Gay to a single voice. Instead, the investigation of small and large joys—taking a tomato plant on a plane ride, reflecting on childhood experiences and consciousness of racial inequality, mourning a friend's illness—is multivocal by design.

Gay frees himself to veer into layered emotions and thoughts, flitting from meditative and angry to comic from one sentence to the next. His voices range from intimate and confiding to silly to awe-inspiring to serious to firm and full of presence, such as the ending of an essay about how we help out strangers and care for each other: "This caretaking is our default mode and its always a lie that convinces us to act or believe otherwise. Always." And then in the very next mini-essay he writes, full of childlike wonder, "How often do you get to see someone slow dancing with a pigeon!"[1] This is an excellent book to read to channel a beautiful palette of voices. And it's a good reminder that a focus on a topic or project is not the same thing as a tight grip on a single voice.

One of the first models of joy in a nonfiction text that I encountered was Steve Almond's memoir *Candyfreak: A Journey through the Chocolate Underbelly of America.* The marshmallow center of this book is Almond's lifelong love of candy. He sets up a road trip to search for the old-fashioned mom-and-pop candies once made in small factories across the United States, which have been threatened by competition from large candy corporations owned now by even bigger multinational conglomerates. Though Almond's research brings him deep into the conflict between small business and corporate America, his connection to his subject matter is the devotion to candy. He demonstrates that joy can also connect you with questions that lead to a fascinating research-driven piece of writing or maybe a piece of fiction about how a love of something can change one's life. And within that joy there can be all kinds of serious questioning and all kinds of emotional range.

Philip Gerard writes about voice: "You can't overlay it on your work. It is intrinsic in everything you do from the moment an idea occurs to you till you turn in the finished draft. . . . Your passion is your voice."[2] Your passions—including the things you really love and care about—are what will awaken your real voices. Start with those passions in order to access voices that are awake and alive, and the voices themselves—fueled by those passions—will light the way in the writing. And you can also take joy in the excavation of something serious or complex in the very act of thinking and reflecting and reseeing and bringing it to light.

The thing is . . . I have seen how many writers have had the connection between joy and the page severed through years of writing only research papers and serious arguments. Some may have learned that writing with passion is *wrong*. When they try it, it feels unintellectual, silly, nonprofessional, and vulnerable. So we need to rebuild that connection in tentative steps until a writer can feel a sense of control and really understand what wealth they have to tap into at any time.

TRY THIS

1. Make a list of what brings you joy during an average day. Coffee? The mail? Bubble wrap? Your dog? Start small.
2. Make a list of your favorite things and people in the world.
3. Make a list of favorite activities or hobbies, music, favorite colors, places, foods, textures, objects, animals, websites, whatever. Keep going with any other category that you can think of. If your joy involves an activity, describe every step in that process. If your joy started at a certain point in time, describe what it was like to first encounter it.
4. Make a list of things that would be part of your perfect imagined life but that you don't currently have, own, or do. (I'm imagining

sitting in a hot tub in my backyard.) Or write about past joys from different eras in your life.

5. Make a list of tiny happinesses that might seem irrational but that make you smile. You might aim for a total of one hundred obsessions and loves from steps 1 through 5.

JOY, WONDER, AND CHILDHOOD

Strong emotions can feel like they are blotting out language. When I see a picture of a hedgehog, for example, my first reaction is "Eeeeeeeeeeeee!!" as in a squeal of joy. Opening up the joy into writing can start with listing the things you love *about* something as a way to begin to inquire into it and discover the questions about it. This writing can feel so personal that one's inner critic might be awakened at once: "Why in the world would *anyone* care about your feelings about hedgehogs?" So, in a way it takes some focus and discipline to write into joy with honesty. I wrote a paragraph as I tried to get to the voice of joy itself, to think about how much I love hedgehogs. I had held a hedgehog for the first time when I was a student in Germany, where hedgehogs just live and walk around in the world like squirrels do in the United States. Here's my first attempt to excavate this memory:

> I remember holding a hedgehog in my hands shortly after I arrived in Berlin for study abroad. I remember the even prickles, and the sense that they were not as sharp as they looked. The quill ends of this balled-up creature were blunt, like the pointed tines of a plastic comb. And suspended upon those tines, inside this ball, was a soft little creature with a snout, tiny eyes, and yet—portable protection. My host mother snapped a picture of me holding it, and I look in that picture so young. I hadn't yet grown out my bangs, and my glasses were still in the round style of the 1980s. My smile is so shy. For that young woman I want quills and armor. The magic of a hedgehog lies in the fact that its little face looks almost like it's smiling. What would it be like to have a suit of quills that one could never take off?

Okay, as is my habit, you can see that I veer into a dash of melancholy sadness. That's a well-worn rut for me. Then I tried again, using that paragraph as a stepping-stone to get *into* my joy, kind of using Pain Woman's vividness to inflate Joy-Hedgehog Woman (I know, she's . . . odd). I managed a sentence:

> Little squishy friend inside a nest of comb-tines with your face a grin and pig-snout, old-man eyes and little hands. I would protect you and we would go through the world bristling our quills and smiling devilishly.

As you can see, the first paragraph is thinking about joy, trying to explain it to a reader. I then used that paragraph as a stepping-stone to get to the second couple of sentences, which is in a voice that more closely inhabits the core of my love for hedgehogs. The first paragraph has voice. And the second experiment results in vocabulary that's child-like and playful, very "voicey." One thing I notice from that experiment is that the first paragraph approaches the subject from an intellectual distance, while the second short paragraph was generated by imagining myself *as* a hedgehog or very near it, talking to it.

I recognize that "Imagine yourself as a hedgehog" isn't what you may have expected in terms of writing advice. But we do have this brilliant ability, as children, to imagine how our bodies would feel if we were animals or objects. Children's books almost train us to do that, with their talking bulldozers and trains and teapots, or else they easily step into that mode because that's the way children think and talk. Parents do this effortlessly, too, as a way to connect with children. The spoon of mashed peas becomes an airplane and the voice a swooping pilot, *Here come the peas!* And children's writing so often captures the joy that adults have been trained to hold at a distance.

Brenda Ueland sees vivid writing as a mode that is "happy, truthful, and free, with that wonderful contented absorption of a child stringing beads in kindergarten. With complete self-trust."[3] The self-trust must be relearned, as we have been trained to abandon that confidence in favor of the sometimes necessary mindfulness of rules and restrictions.

In a few of my essays on chronic pain, I experimented by personifying pain with a touch of joy. This might seem just plain wrong or offensive to those who have had serious pain or watched a loved one suffer. But for me the joy was very connected to the lively pulse of imagination, the persistent idea that even within the pain, my play with language—a joy and a means of survival—continued to exist. So, I used some of that kid thinking to personify pain as a kind of space alien egret. (I know, it doesn't sound like it would make sense. It barely does, but that was the pain talking. And now I love that space egret, and the space egret also helps me weirdly to bear further pain.) Sometimes this play can take the edge off a serious adult topic like pain and make it approachable. And this is not merely a game but a way to resee and reclaim our experience.

Ueland developed this pedagogy of stretching out into joy in the 1930s, and it ended up influencing writers and scholars like Ken Macrorie and Peter Elbow, who then introduced freewriting into writing instruction. Ueland was very clear about taking restrictions, genres, and goals off of the backs of her writers in order to bring life into their writing. She helped her students through encouragement and looseness: "I helped them by trying to make them feel freer and bolder. Let her go! Be careless, reckless! Be a lion, be a pirate! Write any old way."

This approach sounds sloppy, but it's the science of letting voice lead, in the same way that any art aims with great effort and support to capture the spark of life so that others can see themselves in its mirror.

Ueland observed that "after a few weeks of a kind of rollicking encouragement," writers in her community writing workshop "would all . . . break through . . . as from a cocoon, and write suddenly in a living, true, touching, remarkable way. It would happen suddenly, overnight. They would break through from composition-writing, theme-writing, to some freedom and honesty and to writing with what I call 'microscopic truthfulness.'"[4]

I understand what she is saying. The microscopic level of attention to one's experience and imagination, discussed in chapter 7 on detail, requires a de-centering from audience and genre back to one's intuitive understanding of the world. It is a giving over to the liveliness of that experience.

In an interview about her process, Terese Mailhot, Indigenous author of the memoir *Heartberries*, explains: "I'm not trying to create the perfect thing on the page as much as I want to relate perfectly what I want to express to the reader. Everyone has their own narrative voice— and more than any hard-and-fast rules, they should follow that."[5] That voice comes from what we care deeply about. It feels *natural* when we read it on the page because it is, but that doesn't mean it's automatic. It takes some doing to listen to it, to coax it back from where it has been hidden. But it is still there within you. Mailhot discarded an entire novel in a voice that didn't feel real, sweeping aside all that work to turn to another voice that compelled her.

Artist Kay Redfield Jamison describes exuberance as "an abounding, ebullient, effervescent motion." The word *exuberance* shares its root, *entheos* (god within), with *enthusiasm*. Exuberance is an active energy that "leaps, bubbles, and overflows, propels its energy through group and tribe. It spreads upward and outward, like pollen toted by dancing bees, and in this carrying, ideas are moved and actions taken. Yet exuberance and joy are fragile matter. Bubbles burst; a wince of disapproval can cut dead a whistle or abort a cartwheel. The exuberant move about the horizon, exposed and vulnerable."[6]

Writing about art has often described this experience as the "sublime." For me wonder captures the sense of bigness and possibility. Artist Dario Robleto describes wonder as encompassing "passive astonishment and awe, but also active curiosity and doubt."[7] I think this points to wonder as a process one can throw oneself into or pursue, rather than a feeling that requires an external trigger, that overtakes us and fades once that trigger is gone. We can use wonder like a tool when we practice its voice.

Joy and wonder can be sapped from us, or we can get very quick and sly about snatching joy from small and large sources in our lives. We can kindle it, build it, hunt its sources, watch our voices for its clues, and stubbornly refuse to surrender it. This is not child's play. It is something adults need, too, especially when the going gets tough.

The fierce ability to defend joy and enthusiasm is a life-giving skill that will benefit you and those around you and could even change your life.

TRY THIS

1. Take one of your beloved joys from the earlier list of one hundred joys and inhabit it, giving it a voice itself. If it helps, start to write as if you were experiencing that joy. Keep going, and you don't have to stay in that strict point of view. Just write about the images that come to you.

2. Take the same beloved favorite and write about it purely from the senses. If it helps, you can find the object and hold it. For example, when I pick up a binder clip (I love them), I remember that as a kid, I loved the fact that the arms snapped together like clapping. Write about the sensory feelings and the associations. Turn off the inner critic and remember that the goal is a kind of freed-up ecstatic child voice.

3. Make a list of your quirks and obsessions as a child in one column on half a piece of paper. Then in the second column, write whether the quirk has survived or mutated.

4. Now take any entry on this list, and write it at the top of a new page. Don't worry about convincing a resistant reader. Imagine you are writing so that someone understands what it is that you like best about this thing. What are your favorite details? What springs to mind when you think about it? What about this thing or place or person is the best ever? Try to capture how you might talk about this subject if you were talking on the phone to a friend who loves the same thing that you love.

5. Describing what you loved most when you were four or five. What happens to the language and the pauses you use in inhabiting this voice?

WHAT YOU LOVE DOING

When someone describes a source of joy or wonder in their lives, they summon a lilting and vibrant voice, one that draws in a reader. Everyone has their specific joys and attachments, which are part of what makes us human and unique.

Sometimes we sound a little goofy describing what we love, whether it's a sports team or the perfect spicy soup our grandmother makes. Confessing what we love can be as difficult as being honest about a major challenge in our lives. But when we key into that joyful, loopy voice of adoration, a reader can relate because everyone has their *thing*, whether it's thunderstorms or hockey teams. Delving into the details of why you love a particular view of your city or the smell of licorice increases your vulnerability on the page, and the reader gets to see a different side of you. And you might even see a different side of yourself than the one you imagine as the "real you."

It can take vulnerability and courage to set our joys on the page as well as our sorrows, to praise something we delight in rather than to take a voice that seems more appropriate or common, the voice of cynicism and doubt, the voice that is awaiting attack and ready with ammunition. Or the voice of joy can be antiauthoritarian, fierce, a reclamation.

Your confession of joy isn't a persuasive act but, rather, an exploratory act of writing. In the process you might inspire a reader to give your subject another look or teach them something. In reading about the details of someone's obsession, whether it's golf or driving race cars or piloting river barges, I've often come away with a new appreciation for that world.

The most effective way to write about a source of joy is to get into the details, celebrate or access the voice of wonder and awe, the senses and memories and specifics. You can feel free to sound a little goofy. For the purpose of these exercises, you can imagine either that you're talking to a perfect reader or a good friend—or maybe just a beautiful, open, expansive silence.

TRY THIS

1. What are your favorite activities? Take one and describe it in detail, either as a how-to or a free association of all the senses that strike you as you think about doing that activity.

2. Make a list of things that awe you, that you hold in reverence. This can be composed in a very quiet voice or one that is exuberant, or maybe it shifts slightly as you write.
3. Write in a quiet careful voice about something you feel should be approached with care or that you feel deeply attached to.

THE STORY OF JOY

I grew up surrounded with all kinds of glorious pulp paperback books, from Harlequin romances to Reader's Digest Select Editions. In the late 1970s my mom was enrolled in a science fiction mail-order book club. I can't remember whether she recommended one of those books to me or whether I began swiping them, but soon we had a common love: aliens and interspace travel. I remember Arthur C. Clarke's *Rendezvous with Rama* as an early foray: a book about a rotating alien space station that grew strange crops and housed biological-robot hybrids. The plot didn't stay with me, so when I looked it up, I was thrilled to discover that the book was a quiet exploration of the oddness of this constructed world, rather than having a standard narrative. I still remember the distinct feeling of encountering this space cylinder in my teenage mind: an eerie place of complete mystery that was not closed down into the standard storytelling tropes of good versus evil. Just encounter and slightly ominous wonder.

As a child of the 1970s and 1980s, I was surrounded with the science fiction of the television and movie screen: *Buck Rogers*, the original *Star Wars* trilogy, *1999: A Space Odyssey*, and *Star Trek*, among so many others. Many of the shows and movies, however, seemed to map templates of shoot-'em-up conflict sent into outer space. *Star Trek* posed serious questions that came closest to my science fiction reading experience. Almost anything with aliens and robots drew me in, and I sympathized, as only a teenager can, with encounters in which nobody is speaking your language or even breathing the air you need to survive.

I quickly glommed onto the sci-fi shelves at the library and encountered the prodigious output of Isaac Asimov. My mom and I dove into the Foundation series, asking ourselves at regular intervals what the heck was going on. My mom's love of science fiction fits her personality well. She read widely and joyously, taking on the challenging ideas presented in sci-fi as thought exercises. I devoured a book about a clone named Trinity who somehow had a secret compartment in her belly button where she could store contraband. Another book, *The Integral Trees* by Larry Niven, was about a world of a vapor cloud orbiting a sun in which trees floated, unmoored from any dirt or planet, independent worlds in and of themselves. I checked out the "Best of Sci Fi" anthologies in huge stacks and encountered a short story whose premise still creeps up at me during my unsuspecting moments: a world in which personal immortality has been achieved but where artists commit to death for the sake of art. Inside me even still, there is a planet with robots and space people in a star system that helps me keep the airlock open a tiny crack so that wonder can get in.

I happened recently upon Ray Bradbury's *Zen in the Art of Writing*. When I opened the book and reconnected with Bradbury's storytelling voice from *The Illustrated Man*, about tattoos that come to life, or the fires of *Fahrenheit 451* or the stormy carnival day of *Something Wicked This Way Comes*, I also saw the underpinnings of imagination that had sparked my own interest in writing.

In the book Bradbury describes his own journey as a writer. He started with the impulse to "beat, pummel, and thrash an idea" into a story, but then realizing that sheer joy of word association led his stories to spark and ignite. Bradbury writes, "If you are writing without zest, without gusto, without love, without fun, you are only half a writer." And the payoff, for him, is survival: "You must stay drunk on writing so reality cannot destroy you."

What sci-fi opens up in me is the possibility of wonder. And wonder is something that artists and writers pursue, notice, and steer by. The artist Chris Taylor asserts that wonder is "not immature, it's not a gimmick; it is sincere, out of control, and generous."[8] This description evokes the serious sense of play as a continual experiment that stretches into adulthood if we let it, an openness to what is seen and felt and observed.

Activating the voice of self-appreciation or agency is another way to see the wonder of the world expressed in our lives. Audre Lorde, in her important essay "Uses of the Erotic," frames the word *erotic* not as something that's only sexual, in the narrow sense—it's more of a life force. She describes it as "a measure between the beginning of our sense of self and the chaos of our strongest feelings. It is an internal sense of satisfaction to which, once we have experienced it, we know we can aspire."[9] She connects the sense of being in tune and yet vulnerable and open to a joyful feeling of power and agency.

TRY THIS

1. What are you really good at? This can include parts of a job, present or past, or anything else, from washing the dishes to defusing a crisis. What gives you a sense of "flow" or connection to the world? Describe that activity along with this feeling of connection.
2. What is the proudest, most confident voice you've ever occupied? When did you think you were simply amazing? Write in that voice.
3. What elements of your background or identity call up a sense of safety, pride, and openness? What voice do you think or speak in when you feel most relaxed?
4. What superhero would you be and why?

JOY SPARKS QUESTIONS

When you get far enough into something that brings you joy, you may be led naturally to questions about that thing's origins and its economic, spiritual, aesthetic, and political meanings. You might ask about its uses, its costs and benefits. When you stare very deeply at an object or an activity, you will discover gaps in your knowledge, and this is where a writer can take the reader along on a quest to uncover information, creating a narrative of discovery that a reader will want to follow. This was the source of Steve Almond's road trip in *Candyfreak*: where have all the good candies gone?

To take another example, I once saw an image of goats in a tree, each goat standing on a branch. Feel free to look up that phrase online; you won't be disappointed! These goats happen to live in Essaouira, a small town in Morocco, where they climb argan trees to eat the nuts. I love goats, and I love trees, so this combination is delicious but also raises questions. You might want to inquire about the kinds of goats, about whether this hurts the trees, about the larger climate impact, about how long this has been going on, about the impact of people who come to see these goats, about the history of Morocco, and on and on.

As an inquiry into this joy, I gave myself an assignment to freewrite on what goats evoke for me and wrote this: "Goats are unlovely yet resilient. They are a cross between a bug and a mammal. They have bony skulls and bugged eyes with slit pupils. They have been seen as demonic but are so amazingly awesome. Two ex-boyfriends have also loved goats. Goat characteristics I don't love about myself: my knobby toughness, which I maybe need to learn to love."

I then asked myself why I loved the image of goats in a tree and came up with the fact that there's something Dr. Seuss–ish about it, a contrast between the balance needed to stand on a tree branch and the still calm of the goats. And they are so evenly balanced that it's almost as though they were placed there as Christmas decorations.

Then I took a tangent, asking why people like to post animal pictures on social media, how those images function to give us a kind of mental break from reality, how they're cute but also how they let us imagine that they will always be there, that their ecosystems and survival are never under threat, that everything is cute and fine.

Then I imagined I had an unlimited budget and could do a Steve Almond–style investigation of my joy. Could I go see goats who stand in the treetops?

TRY THIS

1. What questions do you have about one of your joys?
2. What's the history, manufacturing process, or origin story of this thing or person, activity or place? What conflicts might lie under the surface of this joy? How is this joy complicated?

3. What do you think your joy means—about you, about your life? Is this a common or uncommon obsession? What comfort are you drawing from this obsession? What insecurity does it address?
4. When did this joy begin in your life? How has it changed over time? Does it have complications and attachment to other emotions?

10   *Voices with Fire*

When I was in my late twenties, I started to vent in little notebooks about a topic that still makes my blood boil: health insurance and health care in the United States. I didn't know I was writing a whole memoir on the topic. Instead, I was trying to process some of my raw rage. This was before the passage of the Affordable Care Act, and my preexisting conditions and the fact that I possessed a uterus made health insurance too expensive for me to afford. This was just the beginning of a long saga for me—and for many—and one that our country has not adequately addressed, one that is a matter of life and death.

Even as I wrote the last paragraph, I was grabbing a hammer and nails and some boards. I wasn't building a soapbox; I was building a *stage*. I have good health insurance now, but I still have ire about the precarious state in which so many people live. The stage I was building wasn't for the purposes of persuasion; all you have to do is say "health insurance," and most people either roll their eyes or stagger as if they've been hit.

As the journal entries piled up, I tried to shape them into essays. But they didn't feel like traditional essays because an essay often takes a journey and uncovers something new. An essay has emotional range, and it turns a subject around in order to create an experience of exploration for the reader. My essays started out as flamethrowers and ended with flames. A personal revelation about this issue was not going to erase or exorcise the source of my anger. I shared the writing in a few workshops and received comments that something was missing. Writing on a topic that provokes anger is a challenge, but that's not because anger is bad.

I wish someone had told me that because I began to tell myself that I was too angry to make something of literary worth on the topic. It turned out that part of my underlying question was what living in this situation had done to me, how it had shaped my sense of self, of past, present, and future. I was both angry and wondering about that anger.

Many of us have received the message that voicing any anger makes us sound "too aggressive." We might feel an internal censor that asks us to be agreeable. If we've been raised around people who expressed their anger in scary or violent ways or if judgments about our anger made us into targets of violence, we might have shut down that part of ourselves, forbidding any utterance that betrays emotion. While characters in canonical literature might get angry, it's fascinating to think about how often a character in a play or novel gets angry and then comes to a tragic end. How often is anger redemptive or positively transformative in what we read?

Voices formed by anger are often seen as taboo because anger provokes anxiety, even as it can be truly transformational and life-giving. We've all sent off angry emails or text messages we later wished we could retract, and releasing anger into the world can, at the very least, lead to hurt feelings and misunderstandings. The negative consequences of anger can make many of us shy away from the voice of anger. But writing about things that make us angry—from memoirs about family dysfunction to exposés about oppression and corporate abuses—can help change the world. The world needs writing born of righteous anger. As an activist, I've channeled anger into complicated action plans and campaigns, and the anger was used like gasoline in an engine, delivered in measured doses, to keep an effort going and maintain contact with the reason for our work.

Anger can do so much damage if it isn't focused. Aristotle wrote, "Anybody can become angry—that is easy, but to be angry with the right person and to the right degree and at the right time and for the right purpose, and in the right way—that is not within everybody's power and is not easy."[1] This idea also connects to Aristotle's interest in rhetoric. Expressing anger is easy, but using it in combination with reason and precision and for a good goal is harder. We have probably all seen examples of political campaigns in which raw, unfocused rage, often directed at groups of people, was used as a stand-in for focused political messages. That group rage lures people in, promising some vague transformation but really only accomplishing pain and division. In her important essay "The Master's Tools Will Never Dismantle the Master's House," Audre Lorde draws a distinction between anger and hatred: "Hatred is the fury of those who do not share our goals, and its object is death and destruction. Anger is a grief of distortions between peers, and its object is change."[2]

Lorde is talking about expressions and audiences and goals. Her insight about the connection between anger and grief feels very accurate. And she highlights something important: through the expression of anger, change can happen.

Robert Cohen writes, in his essay "The Piano Has Been Drinking," about the rant as a particular feature of American fiction, in particular what he calls "hyphenated ethnic rage," in which a writer straddling two identities rails against "being squeezed into categories and wanting to break free—but not too free, not so free that you can't recognize yourself or be recognized by your people, who drive you crazy, or rather, reflect back at you how you drive yourself crazy—is perhaps the great American complaint."[3] The word *complaint* here shouldn't be read as a negative but, rather, as a form. Cohen shares how this complaint—with its animating back-and-forth tension—has brought forth fantastic writing from many writers, including Ralph Ellison, in *Invisible Man*.

I wish someone had told me as a young writer that there was a massive body of social change writing in which anger has been channeled into beautiful literature. I also wish I'd learned that the way to turn that anger into literature is not by shaming yourself into being less angry but, instead, by being free on the page, letting anger bloom in a first draft so that you as a writer can see what you're dealing with and so you can see anger mature, branch, and transform. The branching complexity and insight fueled by anger can light the way to change and to writing that works.

During one introductory composition class in a windowless basement classroom, I introduced a research essay assignment and gave my students the option to write about any topic that interested them. They looked up at me and shrugged, not knowing what to write about.

"What?" I asked. "Don't you *care* about anything?"

The thing was, they had rarely been allowed to care about things in their school-related writing. They had shut off that invested part of their brains when they walked into school, and they had left their interested, curious, angry, and irritated voices in their dorm rooms. Instead, they'd been told to care in measured doses about whatever topic was set in front of them.

Okay, I said. I want you to throw away all the rules of good writing and even logic. Instead, I want you to vent spleen on the page. What pisses you off? (I find that invoking this exercise with colorful "non-classroom" language is essential to get the ranting engine started.)

They laughed, raising their eyebrows in skepticism. When I said "Go," they wrote furiously, intently, right up until the time I said "Stop." And they had smiles on their faces—the smiles of discovery—or the furrowed brows of intense concentration.

We talked about what they uncovered: little life annoyances, old grudges, huge issues in current events and social injustices, family feuds—every single one of them a research topic. And every one of the students had uncovered complexity in their topic. And they had also experienced a measure of self-respect that I think happens too seldom in formal education: they saw that what was happening in their souls, minds, and hearts was perfectly legitimate as a source of serious academic attention.

What I found most interesting was that many of them observed a "turn" in their anger, even in the space of five minutes. They had to scrape off a bit of rage to learn something new about themselves and to uncover something else beneath the anger.

After that experiment I committed to becoming more honest about the fact that my irritability and anger are both a major asset for my own writing. I began to collect and share "angry" essays. I began to talk about how I dive into what annoys and enrages me. My books don't often end up as rants, but they often sure do start that way. And as I began to let myself be angry on the page, I learned that within that angry voice were many different options. I could write in a voice that was pointedly specific, with numbered lists, or broadly heated and full-throttle mad. I could explore the anger, drawing upon a past experience that made me angry because it was wounding, or I could stand firm, drawing a line and using my sentences to sharpen my point. I could discover that my real topic was to the left, to the right, or beneath that anger.

TRY THIS

1. Give yourself ten minutes and write about everything that makes your blood boil or gets your goat.
2. If you loved that, do it again. Do it every day. You can give each of the voices you uncover in your anger writing a separate name. Watch whenever you're judging yourself for that anger.
3. Look back at what you wrote. Did you notice any internal resistance or urge toward censoring or editing your anger? Or did the anger turn into insight, into a discovery? How did the voice change?
4. As you go about your day, listen for a moment in which someone expresses anger. It could be "live," overheard in a restaurant, or on TV. If at all possible, write down the sounds that were uttered. Were sentences completed and responded to? What was the pitch of the voices?

ANGER TRANSFORMS

Writers who work on these exercises often find that they don't stay angry. They vent, and then once they clear out the pipes, they see what's under the anger or ask a question or realize that they're onto another topic entirely. Anger is a strong emotion, and suppressing it means that we're losing an opportunity to understand how it operates, including important elements of ourselves and our world. Our anger may be connected to an experience or a memory. It may show us a solution or reveal our limitations or our courage.

When we feel angry about something, we need to witness it. Exploring anger is research. Audre Lorde writes: "I have come to believe over and over again that what is most important to me must be spoken, made verbal and shared, even at the risk of having it bruised or misunderstood. That the speaking profits me, beyond any other effect." Carina del Valle Schorske, in writing about Lorde's quotation in the context of silences in literature, wrote that it's important to become "fluent in both rhetorical modes" of anger and silence "in order to hear ourselves think, hear each other talk, and tune the dial toward the survival of our many voices."[4] In other words, if we don't listen to the voice of anger, if we try to suppress it, we may not be able to hear the voice conversation inside us.

At the same time, if anger *is* a habitual voice for you as a writer or if your anger has often found eager ears based on your social privilege, it might be helpful for you to lean into silence or to listen to the anger of others. If you find your mind pounding with rants directed at a certain group or identity or social issue, you might try to write from underneath that habitual anger. What other emotions are driving it—anxiety, maybe, or fear of the unknown? Sometimes I find that a blast of strong emotions like this can be focused and settled with the prompt "What I wish I could say is . . ."

bell hooks writes, "Coming to voice is an act of resistance." She also quotes Carol Gilligan, who says that getting in touch with these voices provides "possibility for resistance, for creativity [and] for a change whose wellsprings are psychological."[5] Lorde connects the articulation of anger to the ability to "make common cause with others" and to "seek a world in which we can all flourish."[6]

Writers often say "writing isn't therapy" to draw a line between journal writing and a finished piece with literary merit. People working for social change around the world know that there isn't a simple wall between personal well-being and community change. Often we have to share and explore our stories in order to change the world. The Latin American form called "testimonio" "has been inscribed and sanctioned as a literary mode since the 1970s, in large part as a result of the liberation efforts and the geopolitical resistance movements to imperialism in Third World nations." Chicana and Latina activists and scholars identified and used *testimonio* as critical to the "struggle of people of color for educational rights and for the recovery of our knowledge production."[7] These texts change both the writer and the listener or reader. This model of social change was also popularized and shared by liberatory educator Paulo Freire.

The important thing about such testimony is that it is created with a community in mind, and the sharing of personal pain and anger is a means to liberation. It is research: gathering of life experience in order to examine and understand it. While the trigger may be discomfort or pain or grief, the goal is insight. A blog post, a memoir, and an essay can all have these goals in mind. To me the mode of testimonio does not automatically disqualify one from also producing literature. That would be logically suspect; why would certain emotions or certain speakers be excluded from making expressions with beauty or significance? This also begs the deeper question of who gets to decide the merits of a piece of writing and what those standards are.

In *Wounds of Passion: A Writing Life* bell hooks describes that while the use of a pen name from her great-grandmother was partly undertaken with the goal of separating from her own ego, the name was also meant to summon a particular voice and persona: "Talking like her meant I spoke my mind—clearly and decisively."[8]

Sometimes it's helpful to say things on the page that we can't hold as thoughts within the isolation of our own heads. Sometimes the page is the first audience, and seeing our words and our anger on the page is a kind of much-needed confirmation and admission to ourselves. Sometimes the page and the right voice make us brave.

TRY THIS

1. Write a manifesto. Start with "I believe . . ." if that's helpful.
2. Start writing in a voice in which you "speak your mind," as bell hooks summoned her great-grandmother. Who is that? Can you

give that voice a name? Is it someone you know, have read about, or imagine?

3. Try to start with an overly bombastic statement like an aphorism: "There are two kinds of people in this world." Or maybe work your way into anger by jumping off from a point of view with which you disagree: "The most terrible piece of advice I ever received was . . ."

4. Write about what you do when you're angry in the present day, including behaviors and concrete details, to make a portrait of "myself when angry" and also maybe sketch out how various family members behave when they're angry, kind of a family tree of anger behaviors. We often have an idea of anger in our heads that is more akin to Audre Lorde's definition of *hatred*. Anger can be quite clear and rational. What does it look like?

5. As mentioned, if anger is the easiest thing in the world for you to tune into, or if you find yourself ranting and getting affirmed by nods and encouragement, try to pause and dig beneath that rant. Can you access other emotions that might be its source? Try writing about a topic that makes you angry with the prompt "What I think I want to say is . . ." or "What I can't quite explain is . . ." or "I think this makes me so angry because . . ."

ANGER AND RANGE

After a night out with my friends, I am restored through hearing about the trials and humor in their lives and through sharing my own. What I love about talking together with friends is how much the talk slips and twists, launches and pools. We change and layer topics and reactions at lightning speed, with emotional and intellectual agility. We rest for a moment in sadness, and then someone makes a comment, and we are laughing and gasping for air. There is movement and surprise, and this—because it is so innate to who we are—is also what's beautiful about writing. If I aim to be a friend to the reader on the page, I want to create that emotional and intellectual agility. That is range, and it's especially important when writing with anger.

As I wrote my book about health insurance, I learned that a single note of anger doesn't give the reader enough complexity. Odds are good that if they've picked up the book, they might be angry, too, and looking for a way to carry their own anger more easily or to figure out what to do with it. Or else they're not sure how they feel about the topic. Either way, they don't want to be shouted at. They want complexity as well as the story of where to put or use that anger. This isn't because anger is bad. It's because we don't live in one key or theme. During the average day, our emotions are all over the place, and those layers should also be in our writing.

One day during my era of venting about health care, I saw a flyer in the local food co-op for a workshop entitled something like "Living Serenely without Insurance." First, I got angry at the flyer (of course). Then I began to have an argument in my head with the flyer, and I realized I had a question to explore: is it possible to be okay with this situation?

For me the answer was no. But it led me to a second question: what has living in such an unsettled state done to me and have there been lasting effects? I began to wonder how far back this went and at what point my rage had sparked. What experiences had I already accumulated, and how had those shaped my life? I needed to offer testimony and witness, but I also needed to inquire and to complicate and to really *see* and reckon with the larger issue and its effects.

If you've been in a creative nonfiction writing workshop, you may have heard the comment that your readers want "more you" on the page. You may have related scenes from your life, but what the reader might want is more mulling over, more reaction, more of a sense of what you make of the experiences. Similarly, internal dialogue in fiction gives readers a sense of connection to the inner world of the narrator or main character. This, by the way, goes to show you how limiting the "show, don't tell" framework is. Showing is fine. But the telling—the inquiry, the detailed research in scene, the wondering what it all means—is often the beating heart of a piece of writing.

After a few years of telling the stories of my life when I had no or not enough insurance, each of the difficult episodes had developed a slightly separate voice and separate topics. Each was about a different phase of my life, and each arrived at a different insight. Putting them back together as a book was the next challenge.

I had a conversation with a fellow writer, who read the whole manuscript. He asked the dreaded question: "What is this really about?"

I was frustrated. "It's about how much this has affected me and, as a case study, how it's affected all of us—how awful it is to live like this."

"But how is it to live like this?"

I was angry. And the whole book had been born of anger. But then, it turned out, I was so intent on showing that I hadn't let myself speak to the reader. I hadn't really gone inside. I realized I hadn't been following my own premise. I wanted to see how the health insurance crisis had shaped me, but I was only looking at my health insurance experiences, not at myself. I wasn't subjecting myself to full scrutiny.

When I began to take my own question seriously, I began to move more deeply into material that scared me. At this point I was seven years into the project. I didn't like what I saw. I was scared by my own conclusions: namely, that living in a state of health care precarity had affected me very deeply, more deeply than I wanted to admit. The claw marks are still all over me, to be honest.

Strangely, as I began to look at those claw marks, I also began to see cracks of light. Once I began to see myself as a normal human being affected in all kinds of messed up ways by health insurance anxiety, I began to view myself with the kind of sympathy and empathy that took me seven years to find. It became a game: pick a random moment from the time I was writing about and see if I could see health insurance in it.

At this point I was ripping through each chapter with dread, trying to pull out and add material to answer this question, to locate points where I had come in contact with health insurance and health insurance had won.

In shifting to look at the small material of my life and in discovering empathy for myself, I began to move toward the big questions:

how is this possible and acceptable? How do we live like this? This is not a righteous rhetorical question; this is a serious question I cannot answer. What soup of denial and self-hatred and fear and money and disconnection from our bodies creates and fuels this inability to talk about our physical lives and deaths as ruled by this system? The book couldn't answer any of those questions, but it could ask them. I had taken seven years to articulate a cascade of life questions, some of which forced me to admit how much I'd been harmed, how much it hurt, and what got me through that hurt.

If you're interested in a masterful, perfect, slim, and breathtaking example of the complexity of anger, please read Jamaica Kincaid's *A Small Place*. Her exploration of colonialism in Antigua and its long-reaching impact starts with sheer fire, first drawing the reader in and then turning outward to explore centuries of history with a keen eye, shifting between humor and mournful sadness and questioning. And the anger is not reserved for one target; it turns and deepens.

Thomas Merton, the contemplative monk who was also an engaged activist, mulled over how he might write about social issues, "not to preach, not to dogmatize, not to be a pseudo-prophet," but nonetheless to "take a moral stand." He asked, "Am I so far gone that I can't do this without putting a brazier on my head and running about like Solomon Eagle in the London fire?" His question, too, came back to listening for the voice allowed him to speak, a voice he heard as "quiet, definite and pure."[9] Merton in his diaries wrestled with the same question I grapple with when the news makes me almost froth at the mouth, when my text messages to friends are all capital letters and I am sitting at the rim of despair.

That, then, has been one of the questions that I have run across again and again in my writing. When one is at the rim of despair, sitting at the edge of that gray canyon, what happens? What is *that* scene like?

The last draft of the health insurance book went through a read by my boyfriend (now my husband). He had a very wise thing to say, which was that the book needed "more of me." Specifically, he said, what the book needed was evidence of what exactly got me through all those years. And—as obvious as the fingers on my hand—what I hadn't said was that my survival had been stitched together by my friends. They marched with me at demonstrations, shared information about home cures and doctors who would accept payment on a sliding scale, heard my anger, and laughed when it turned to bleak humor. The bodies and minds of my beautiful friends had helped me stay alive and in my body.

So, the book about health insurance was also a book about how I had survived, and the answer to that was with a lot of help and love. And that was something I wasn't able to see in the beginning, but it was an answer that I would never have been able to see deeply without my anger.

TRY THIS

1. What is inside your anger? What is the world you're longing for? Try with a freewrite that starts out, "It's not about the anger. It's about..."

2. What is the voice that emerges in a setting where you are supported and heard about something that makes you angry or breaks your heart? What is the voice that supports another person in their constructive anger?

ANGER AND STYLE

In her wonderful essay on politics and anger, "An Axe for the Frozen Sea," Megan Stielstra writes about taking up axe throwing after the 2016 presidential election in the United States.[10] The essay is structured in numbered segments, and within those segments Stielstra makes frequent use of line breaks and very short sentences. At one point she gives the reader two short sentences: "I want to split open, my guts on the table. I want to see this rage." Then there's a break for a new numbered section, comprised only of the sentence, "I have recently started therapy." Then there's another numbered section that starts, "And axe-throwing."

The essay isn't all short sentences; as a whole, it feels generous and spacious, giving the reader a welcome into the writer's experience even as she contemplates and explores the feelings of helplessness and deep anger in the face of political acts and decisions that affect the lives of millions. There's a saying among writers that the "hotter" the subject matter is, the "cooler" the telling should be. Basically, if you're heated up about something emotionally, you can turn down your language so that the experience of reading doesn't overwhelm the reader. I think that's part of what Stielstra is doing here. At the same time, it's interesting to contemplate: is the voice cooler? The short sentences, in their pared-down directness, hit the page like blades of an axe, directed and sharp.

Sentence length and word choice are two tools that writers have to create and capture a voice on the page to express and reveal their point of view and to pare down a voice to its essence. These short sentences, rather than being cool or distant, allow Stielstra's anger to be clearly visible to the reader, allowing the reader space to contemplate the image "I want to split open, my guts on the table" and what it means to get to a visceral level of rage that chooses violent images while clearly also refusing to either engage in real violence or to direct that violence even conceptually at others.

Heidi Czerwiec, in her essay "Anatomy of an Outrage," explores her own anger after she sees an ROTC exercise on the campus where she works; she had not been warned about the exercise and assumed she was living through an active shooter situation. She writes a letter to the editor and is then subjected to hate mail. Like Stielstra, Czerwiec employs a mix of short, punchy sentences and longer sentences, given the reader time to focus as a drumbeat creates a strong rhythm. This rhythm is a bodily experience, and both of these essays focus on the body's experience of anger. Czerwiec writes, "My adrenaline has a hair trigger now, spikes at the slightest threat."[11] Stielstra also reflects on where her rage has become located in her body, what it feels like and what physical impressions it produces.

These are choices of craft, but they are also a good example of how a voice is accessed and constructed to claim authority in a setting in which the speaker's authority might be undermined by the very anger she is expressing. The grounding in the body, the controlled sentences, and the structure and reflection all create the feeling of an embodied human marshaling resources, taking a strong stance, and claiming the right to make clear declarative sentences from a specific and personal point of view. Some writing advice starts with an awareness of audience to construct an argument, but Stielstra, Kincaid, and Czerwiec don't begin with their opponents' views in mind. Their aim is to explore and also to clarify their own experience, beginning in their own bodies and realities. If that ends up convincing someone, that's fine, but in reading their work, I come away with the experience I know well in my own body: wavering, enraged, scared, and yet emerging focused and stronger. In going through that experience vicariously with the writers as I read, I am reminded of and draw upon my own experience. Voice, as expressed in the complex physical and emotional experience, is what drives these essays and gives them power.

Especially if these strong emotions cause discomfort, naming these voices is quite liberating. In my book about chronic pain, I let Pain Woman say and do things that I myself felt ashamed of, and she showed me the way forward.

TRY THIS

1. Think about a global or local issue that evokes a wide range of emotions, even if those feelings seem negative or overwhelming. Then name a voice that is strong enough to contain all the fire of your reactions. What does that voice say? Since this is a large voice, what are the varied moods and viewpoints that it contains? Try to write for five minutes in that voice. What questions are raised for you about the issue? Does it shift to another voice as you write?
2. Who in your life do you admire as a source of well-spoken and well-lived anger? Try borrowing that voice and writing into it.

11 *A Whisper of a Voice*

I look at the white rectangle of a document on my screen, with a few fragments of black squiggly lines. I'm tired. I don't know what I feel, but I can't make anything happen today. It feels like a heavy frozen blanket of snow, like an uneasy silence. While some people call this "writer's block," I think there's more going on here than feeling blocked.

Sometimes when I listen inside and hear silence, I can unwind it to understand that it's made up of voices in tension with each other, of fears and self-judgment and inner conflict. An inner conversation, or a conflict of voices, can be a fruitful source of intelligent and complex perspectives. Conflicting voices give us the ability to express nuance and contradiction and to juxtapose two chords, creating an interesting dissonance. Sometimes silence can be externally imposed. A writer might face harsh judgment or restrictions from family or community or might have no time or space to string sentences together and hear a voice.

Still other silences come after a big project is finished or between writing projects. Many writers describe this as a "fallow" period, a word that refers to a farming practice of letting a field rest between years of cultivation to allow nutrients to return to the soil. A fallow period is uncomfortable, even for an experienced writer, because most of us like the momentum and structure of a project. Taking a pause to gather feelings and impressions, to face the raw confrontation with oneself and one's doubts, is confusing.

Still other days of silence contain a "full" feeling. That day of blankness I described had an edge; I felt like I might cry, but I didn't know what I was sad about. It felt like a wordless silence. I sat and tried to piece it together, and I couldn't analyze it intellectually. I often think in images and pictures, instead of words, when I am trying to figure out complicated topics, so I asked myself to imagine any kind of container. What kind of container was I, and what was I filled with and to what level? Was I empty like a worn glass bottle found on the beach, with wind whistling at its neck?

I got the answer almost immediately in an image: I felt like I was filled to the brim, that I was angry and sad. I didn't want to feel that way, and one of the things I was angry about was very complicated, so a second voice had come in subconsciously to wrestle with those feelings, saying in effect: "You don't feel this way. That's too big. Try to think about something else." In my heart the effect was a kind of noisy static that might have sounded like "nothing" if I hadn't taken the time to unwind it.

I stayed with the visualization a bit longer and realized I had two other voices in my head. One was a sort of hangover of reading some of my old journals, which I'd needed to do for research, and I'd fallen into a scared voice to echo a scary time in my life. But then, beneath these layers, the image I had was that the container in my visualization was full to bursting, about to explode.

The voice I heard beneath these top layers of silt was a resounding NO (it really did feel like capital letters). That no was about certain things I didn't want, and it was also a yes about strong feelings and wants and needs. It gained its force from the conflicting voices—some of them happy and proud and anxious and strong—that needed to be expressed.

Trappist monk and writer Thomas Merton wrote in his journals about wrestling with layers of identity as a writer, which he felt was "still a false identity, although it has a temporary meaning and validity. It is the cocoon that masks the transition stage between what crawls and what flies."[1]

TRY THIS

1. When you are feeling unsure about what you want to say, imagine yourself as a container. What does it look like, and what is the voice inside it? How full is it?
2. Are you in any kind of cocoon, in transition to a new voice? Can you give it a name?

FEAR

Jacqueline Woodson, an award-winning author of over thirty books in multiple genres, writes: "What people identify as writers' block, I see as fear. . . . The first step to getting over it is recognizing what you're afraid of: Are you afraid to reveal something about yourself, are you afraid your story will fail, are you afraid someone will judge you? Whatever is keeping you silent is the thing you need to look at deeply and move beyond."[2]

The good thing about acknowledging this fear is that once it comes to the surface, it can be evaluated. Is it a fear of not being good enough? That's a risk that one can write into. Maybe the fear is a worry that the telling and publishing of a story in any genre might have real-world consequences, including the loss of family connections, friendships, and community ties. Or maybe it's a resistance to seeing or hearing something complicated about oneself.

I have a story from my life about a childhood experience that has felt like the foundation of every book I've written. I've then cut the story from multiple books because I couldn't bear the reactions from people I loved about this admission. The story I keep cutting was an anchor and yet one that was too "heavy" for the individual books I'd written.

Finally, I managed—after twenty years of writing and rewriting—to construct a book (not yet published) that utters this story. Because I didn't want to give many details, I realized I could "tell it slant," in Emily Dickinson's lovely advice, and give enough information without feeling too revealed. I realized that I'd been seeing this chunk of text as a courtroom transcript, a piece of writing in which I had to tell the whole truth and nothing but the truth.

I didn't have to do that at all. The paragraph, as it ended up, was safely told from my adult point of view, with the goal of expressing what it's like to regard this conflict now and what it has been like to carry it. I found, with the feedback of trusted fellow writers, that I was giving enough to be clear and yet withholding enough to create a safe margin for myself.

Several sets of expectations in the writing and publishing world can pressure a writer to feel as though a complete transcript of a difficult experience is necessary. Especially during the peak of the memoir boom throughout the 1990s, writers were told to focus on a narrative arc, to show and not tell, so that their reflective voices were suppressed and "what happened" was foregrounded.

The traumatic stories and experiences of marginalized people are often seen to be mere transcripts, "material" or raw content of trauma that writes and sells itself. These accounts are then unfairly judged to be nonliterary because of their content and because of who is writing them. Traumatic material is often assumed to be "easy" to write because the material itself is dramatic. With all of these experiences and judgments circling, it is essential to take back the power to decide for oneself what to show and what to tell.

Other fears about writing can include the vulnerability of taking strong stances or the anxiety of being judged or even of revealing one's unique sensibility or maybe of offending the sensibilities of one's communities. All of these fears are important, and they are easier to address once we are conscious of them. If we are afraid of being judged for our odd stories, for example, an awareness of this can help us realize that many writers share this fear, and many writers have advice and experiences to offer from their own experiences of having navigated through this.

Peter Elbow writes, "The foundation of verbal meaning often lies in the silence of what is felt nonverbally and bodily."[3] We can pause in these difficult heady and blocked moments to check in with ourselves. Pat Schneider writes, "Fear is a friend of the writer. Where there is fear, there is buried treasure."[4] We can see fear as a marker for a place that offers riches for writing and excavation.

Years ago a young woman turned in an essay to my workshop class about her struggle with family violence. She chose words—sharp edges of black on a white surface—with a cool precision, shining a narrow spotlight on moments and scenes but revealing little else. The margins and page breaks marked out a numbing silence.

In workshop I encourage participants to reflect carefully on the writer's words rather than to spin judgments and conjectures about the author's actions or motives. I have always believed this approach offers a buffer or safe zone to allow the writer to present ideas and stories without risking personal judgment. But this young woman's text left us all wanting to read between and beyond the lines. I gave her the option to add a reader's note or talk to the class about what feedback would be most helpful before we started, but she shook her head, clearly not yet able to ask anything of the reader. We read through the pages, searching for clues about the person clearly still in the midst of this crisis, experiencing the pain that offers no easy epiphany and no way out.

We all wanted the easy escape hatch of closure.

Readers raised their hands to comment, and they requested "more." They wanted to learn about causes of and help for this devastating and harrowing personal challenge. Scrawling in the margins seemed an inadequate response; the readers as human beings needed to know if the author needed help. What they wanted from the text were words that indicated emotion so they could understand whether the narrator / writer / main character was in danger.

Back in my office, I emailed her with a carefully chosen mix of words: casual, general, concerned, asking how "it" went for her, eliciting what I knew was there—that rage and all the emotions beneath it. I asked if she wanted to meet, to talk. She responded with a paragraph simmering with resentment. There was too much discussion of emotion in our workshop, she said, too much judgment. She wanted feedback on the writing, she said, on the text.

Now, upon reflection, years afterward, I begin to hear this writer again. She may have heard my advice to "add more emotion" as a nauseating request to sprinkle some tears into her text, to pander to an imagined audience that wanted an after-school special of pain and easy redemption, a talk show tearjerker narrative.

Clearly, the sobbing, the drama, or the anguish were not what she wanted to talk about. She was maybe aiming for a kind of documentary account to mirror the functional numbness of getting through a crisis, or she was exploring the events for herself by starting with the facts, or maybe something else altogether. I believe she was not writing with the desire to wound or manipulate her audience but, instead, to get at the lived truth of her experience. Our workshop didn't feel supportive enough for her to say more.

I read her words with despair. As a student, I'd shared my life and pains in essays early in my own writing career, then felt anger rise like a tornado when I heard my life and my text being chewed over like a meal, misinterpreted because I hadn't learned how to direct the reader's attention. It was hard enough to admit the facts to myself and others on the page.

I later came to see that my own anger flowed not from a simple misunderstanding over word choice, theme, or image. Instead, the act of sharing the text had somehow reminded me that the words were more than words. My own experience had been *real*. The reality check of a workshop shocked me into anger and sadness, as my readers and fellow writers reflected the pain I'd walled off with text. They struggled to express their human concern and reactions. They felt my subject matter, and so I felt it again. I felt less in control of my text and more plainly reminded of its real-world source. It was grief, and the grief was huge.

As writers, we are free to tell and to not tell. If we decide to leave out our reactions and interpretations about an event, it is natural for a reader to want more direction about how they should interpret a text. But if you as the author are not ready to give such direction, that's okay. However, that might mean the writing—and the living—are still in progress.

Sometimes we have a lot to say but we can't find the right voice. And some voices are by nature sedate, and they withhold information that they're not comfortable sharing. They want to say less, maybe because what they have to say is very focused and doesn't want to get muddied or lost. Cutting a text down to the most essential points, honoring what doesn't need to be shared, can also be an important choice.

Carina del Valle Schorske meditates on Audre Lorde's political advice that "your silence will not protect you," which is directed at people with privilege who use that privilege to remain apart from controversy rather than to speak up on the side of the disenfranchised. Schorske writes that silence can also be a way to protect others, especially "when you face down demands to confess or condemn, when you refuse to sing for the master, when you speak not at all rather than speak the words they've scripted for you. Go ahead, claim your *right to remain silent*. Of course, the protection of silence is not absolute—it's just a tool in the toolkit. But it is also, potentially, a source of spiritual solace."[5]

Refusal to play into expected narratives is an important way to conceptualize silence and one that can allow other voices to come forth.

TRY THIS

1. Start a freewrite with the phrase "What I am afraid of is . . ." Try to tackle one of your greatest fears and the roots of why you fear it. You might come to a silence, a sign that there's a lot underneath that you can't unearth. And that's okay.
2. If this voice was a character in a movie, what would it look like? What does this voice sound like? What does this voice want? What advice does it have for you?
3. What do you choose not to write about and why?

SELF-CENSORSHIP

Fiction and nonfiction writer Tillie Olsen's 1978 book, *Silences*, expresses the struggle of a working-class white woman trying to write amid the demands of work, family, and community involvement. A writer must have the desire, time, support, and space, Olsen writes, but also "much conviction as to the importance of what one has to say, one's right to say it."[6]

Internal and external censorship can drive a person to edit out or suppress voices before they even speak. Olsen writes, "These pressures toward censorship, self-censorship, toward accepting, abiding by entrenched attitudes, thus falsifying one's own reality, range, vision, truth, voice, are extreme."[7]

For writers who are battling self-censorship, freewriting is a great foundational practice for discovery, expression, and playing with language. And the compressed nature of freewriting can also nudge a writer to dive into something that feels forbidden or risky, something that would be daunting to explore without a time limit. Through the practice of freewriting, we begin to know what's in our minds, below the surface. Diaries and other forms of personal and private writing, often disparaged as confessional, can help us write into difficult material that might be preoccupying us. We might feel torn between wanting to voice something and not wanting to voice it for an audience. To put something on the page in the form of a journal entry or a freewrite allows a writer to bear witness to something that is in process, something that may find its public expression years later or never. As Virginia Woolf writes, "If you do not tell the truth about yourself you cannot tell it about other people."[8] This seems, too, to draw a linkage between nonfiction writing and other forms and genres.

These forms of private writing help us hear the full range of voices, including the voices we might discount. This practice helps us know ourselves better, which can even lead to revelations that affect our real, lived lives. How separate is this from "real" literary writing? Some might say it's completely separate, but in my experience I have needed to know myself in order to decide to make long-term changes that allowed me to stay alive and happy in order to produce literary work. I also needed to see my own thoughts on the page during many times in my life when

I heard that my perceptions of the world weren't accurate, which is a difficult experience for a writer and for any human.

Carol Gilligan, in studying the voices of adolescent girls, tracked how they lose the authority to speak and begin to doubt themselves. The truly alarming thing is that as these girls stop speaking about what they feel and know, they actually *stop knowing* things they once knew. They come to experience their feelings as not real and struggle to articulate their inner realities.[9] The loss of voice either causes or is an effect of a lack of agency in the world. When your inner reality is not reflected or affirmed in the outer world, when your voice isn't responded to and your words aren't given support, your very sense of self is affected, and this can impact whole communities. In other research it was found that what helped these girls retain their "sense of self and voice" was the presence of an adult to confide in, someone "who could stand outside the culture and affirm the girl's vision through these developmental years, affirming the binds and inequities."[10]

When I look over the journals I still have from high school and earlier, I see that I was trying on voices to figure out who I was supposed to be and who I was allowed to be. One voice that inhabits a series of green-tinted steno notebooks I filled in high school is plucky, like a teen mystery series narrator who is always supposed to look on the bright side, pick herself up, and dust herself off for the next challenge. Yet the voice is frayed, conscious of its audience, conscious of being watched and evaluated, though I'm not sure who would be peering over my shoulder. The voice performs a kind of housekeeping of the soul, sweeping depression under various rugs and doilies, promising to make the best of things, chirpily vowing to look forward to a time after finals or after something else. It is a voice in the act of fighting with and silencing another voice, the voice of the girl who walked along the roadside in the rain crying. It is a voice afraid of its source, afraid of the future, afraid of what might be expected of it and what it might be asked to turn into.

TRY THIS

1. Choose a topic that you'd like to write about but can't seem to find a way in. Try to start with one of these sentence starters and do a freewrite:

   What I know fovr sure is . . .
   What I couldn't say then is . . .
   I know the difficulty of . . .
   What saved me was . . .
   What brings me joy is . . .
   What I want to tell you is . . .
   What I'm not sure about is . . .

2. Ask a voice to talk about something it has been carrying that is heavy.
3. The secret I have learned to surviving is . . . .

NO TIME

One of the most concrete and daunting limitations a writer can face is a lack of time or space to write. Virginia Woolf's essay "A Room of One's Own" brings up the painful realization that so few people have a place where they can shut the door, have time to be alone, and have space to think. These days I have a job that gives me one of the most precious things in my life: an office door. I still have to push against people's requests for favors, for my time, against expectations of "friendliness" and female caring and availability, even against my students and coworkers and supervisors, to protect the time to write and think, even if it's only an hour a day. And yet that hour a day is a massive privilege. People around the world who yearn to express themselves live in situations in which they have no private corner, no access to education, and no space to explore ideas.

Prevented from writing by family obligations and child-rearing and the need to work to support her family, Tillie Olsen wrestled with the unmet urge to write: "My work died. What demanded to be written, did not. It seethed, bubbled, clamored, peopled me." Years of this unmet need for writing changed her. Expression is not a faucet that can simply be shut on and off. When she finally had space to write, Olsen "had to learn response, to trust this possibility for fruition that had not been there before. Any interruption dazed and silenced me. . . . When again I had to leave the writing, I lost consciousness. A time of anesthesia."[11]

Especially in trying conditions like these, a writer might be doubly daunted with the thought that tiny snippets of time are not enough to produce anything finished or any work of literary significance. The "dream deferred" that Langston Hughes describes in his poem "Harlem" can be an incredibly painful one to carry, and the numbing, the anesthesia, that Olsen writes about might be preferable to being in contact with the daily pain of thoughts unexpressed.

Writing in a journal, or writing just a few phrases when one has time at work, can be incredibly significant under these conditions. This contact with one's writing sensibility can be both painful and renewing, like the prickle of blood flowing through the veins after a limb has fallen asleep. The writing I did in spiral notebooks while working various busy jobs and while riding public transportation—jotting phrases in my head when I didn't have anything else coherent to say—gradually formed into poems and snapshots and short lyrical essays that I now treasure because they allow me to "remember what it was to be me," as Joan Didion describes in her classic essay "On Keeping a Notebook."

There are times in some people's lives when writing anything down can be dangerous. These stories are so necessary. And even a stray detail—a favorite lunch, a snippet of a glimpsed pedestrian's hat—can bring that whole era back with stunning clarity. Save the snippets of what it was to be you so that all the deep feelings beneath the silence can be accessible later.

TRY THIS

1. When you think about a silent period in your own life, what memories emerge? What were the feelings, as you remember them, beneath that silence? What were you wrestling with?

2. Sometimes a silence is held together with a very functional and adult voice, one that is taking care of us. What's the name of the silent-keeping voice, and what is it like to write in this voice? What's the vision that this voice urges?

EMERGENCE

A writer might be daunted by the empty white space of the page and assume that it reflects a similar emptiness inside. Often, however, complicated ideas take time to emerge, like a plant unfurling in stages from the soil. The leaves of a plant have to capture the sun's power before a flower can bloom. Good ideas need space to grow. When I feel that odd "full of nothing" feeling, I know that I'm carrying something that's developing in me, and I have to carefully analyze it, invite it, or wait for it to emerge.

Sometimes in writing I've felt stuck as I cast around for the right voice. But as soon as I hit on the right one, the words start rushing out. When writers report a feeling of being transported by their work, of the sentences spilling forth, it can be an after-effect of this agonizing "carrying," a time when complex and braiding ideas have had time to build under the surface so the right voice can emerge.

This "full of something emerging" feeling can be uncomfortable. It often feels like a bubble trapped in my throat, a bodily expression of something I will eventually be able to voice but that makes me edgy and restless. A writer might easily interpret the physical and mental unease as a signal that something has gone awry. Worse yet, a writer might assume that writing and thinking deeply always feels blissful and clear, so these weird intense feelings might indicate that one is "not a good writer" or is "doing it wrong."

Writers have our weird rituals—favorite pens, snacks, times of day, sounds, need for quiet—as sources of comfort because we're often edgy and half-freaked-out. We often don't know what we're doing. We're trying to comfort ourselves as we tiptoe out onto the plank and as we listen to voices that are new or maybe uncomfortable.

As I mentioned in the example with the container, I discovered strong feelings when I looked into a silence, but those feelings were trapped under a layer of judgment, a sort of internal censor that rejected those images or that didn't want to excavate them. These inner conflicts don't signal a lack of clarity. They are a richness. If you are embarrassed or afraid to feel a certain way, that feeling or voice might be a risky, new, or bold voice you haven't had much practice with. It might be right on the edge of where you need to write and live.

In chapter 3 I shared the work of Sondra Perl on felt sense. Peter Elbow recommends checking in with one's body and gut to steer the writing: "The foundation of verbal meaning often lies in the silence of what is felt nonverbally and bodily. . . . When writing goes badly, it is often because we don't make these pauses for quiet consultations with felt sense."[12]

Elbow describes silence, and the pause for reflection, as "one part of the self ministering to another part of the self."[13] Maybe it's an odd image—that one part of us can care for another part of us—but it's very present in the culture with the prevalence of the phrase *self-care*. In this case, however, it's not about comfort but about a deeper conversation and about pushing expression forward.

Elbow quotes author Eva Hoffman, who describes writing in her journal in a resonant way that I first shared in chapter 1 and that we can return to now, seeing a different side: "I make my way through layers of acquired voices, silly voices, sententious voices, voices that are too cool and too overheated. Then they all quiet down, and I reach what I'm searching for: silence. I hold still to steady myself in it." This is an important point in a long quotation, so I'll stop in the middle to say that many writers don't talk about this feeling, which to me is like a "dropping in" or focusing. I had this exact sense, too, when I begin to write, the feeling of trying on outfits, hearing a chatter of language, looking for the right tool in the drawer, and then a quieting.

Hoffman continues: "A voice begins to emerge: it's an even voice, and it's capable of saying things straight, without exaggeration or triviality. As the story progresses, the voice grows and diverges into different tonalities and timbres. . . . But the voice always returns to its point of departure, to ground zero."[14]

It's fascinating to me that a beat of stillness can be a kind of landmark to help us navigate toward what we want to say. It's a sign from our body and our gut, which Elbow calls a "click," that lets us know a certain approach feels right, "an experience that is *foundational* for learning how to write well."[15] And nobody can hear that silent click; it's inside you.

FEAR OF WEIRDNESS

Terese Mailhot, author of *Heartberries*, once struggled to write a novel that wasn't working. She went away on a writer's retreat and then began writing from her life experience out of chronological order, abandoning the conventions she'd learned. "I can hear workshop leaders in white graduate programs telling me to slow down—that the setting needs to be described before you jump into dialogue," she says about the writing. "Or to evenly dispense setting, dialogue, exposition, and description."

It's a common refrain that writers should learn the rules first in order to break them, but from my own experience, it's not that easy. Mailhot's boldness as an Indigenous writer should not be underestimated. As an eager student who wanted to write well, I took to such rules wholeheartedly, but it then took another ten years to really feel comfortable in breaking them. That's a lot of time in a short life when many things went unsaid on the page. I wasn't completely separated from my writing voices, but I had to relearn my range of options later, then build confidence in trying them.

Mailhot reflects on her own experience in the classroom: "It's so difficult and important for teachers to try to bring that weirdness out. Student writers are usually so guarded that the way they write is sometimes only a glimpse of what their potential is."[16]

After I left school, my touchstones were the weirdest books I'd read, the ones that balanced reliable technique with wild experimentation, each devising a method to reach the reader that was all their own. Walking out into one's own weirdness can feel like the loneliest experiment, an effort bound for failure. It can make us feel so vulnerable. And realizing that you're about to get weird can feel like a move of complete desperation—after you've tried all the traditional approaches and nothing is working.

That silence of desperation can often lead to wonderful discoveries.

STOKING THE FIRE

Sometimes the need for a bold voice comes from an inner examination of a subject and the slow building of resolve. Sometimes we know we are writing something that will spark fights, that will make certain readers angry, and yet we have to write. We are ready to write because the words are an expression of what we believe, where we come from, and where we need to go.

In these situations the question of audience is a delicate one. Becoming aware of a critical audience too early can blunt our voices, our wonderful weirdness, and our fire. Elbow recommends that at the beginning we "don't write to enemies who disagree with you and who think you are crazy or stupid." Instead, we can "write to friends and allies who are eager to know what you have to say; then after you have gotten your ideas clear the way you like them, you can turn to the job of making adjustments for the enemy."[17]

I think Elbow would be equally fine with the opposite tack of spitting fire onto the page and to an imagined specific audience. The point is to stay with whatever impulse or generous audience sparks a voice. Elsewhere he writes: "Even though we often develop our voice by finally 'speaking up' to an audience or 'speaking out' to others . . . the opposite effect is also common: we often do not develop a strong, resonant voice in our writing till we find important occasions for *ignoring* audience— saying, in effect, 'To hell with whether they like it or not. I've got to say this the way *I* want to say it.'"[18]

Traditional composition classes focus on audience awareness as a key to a writing task, but writers have many other options. Writing can be for oneself, and Toni Morrison offers a wise piece of writing advice: "If there's a book that you want to read, but it hasn't been written yet, then you must write it." Our first audience is oneself. If there's a book you need and have never found, writing with yourself as an audience can confirm your own reality and speak a suppressed truth into the world. Put your weird and necessary brilliance onto the page so that you can find the audience who knows how to see and hear you and so you can teach the audience to understand in new ways.

TRY THIS

1. What issues have you had the privilege to be silent about? What is the voice of that privilege? What is that privilege afraid of?
2. Do you have a voice that is best for delivering bad news or speaking the uncomfortable truth? You might call this voice "the one who knows." You can try controlling the pace and letting the quiet, knowing voice speak if you like. Or not.
3. Is there a voice inside you that only speaks in a whisper? Write a list of the voices that don't often get to speak.

12 *The Voice of Spirit*

I often write as a way to ask difficult questions of myself and the world. Though these questions might start out as a whisper or silence, the voices of asking and listening can turn to something louder, firmer, weirder—or even to a voice that offers sustenance.

Writing with spirit is often about listening to the quiet voices within ourselves, but it also involves gathering the courage to act in line with our ethics in the world. "Spirit" is an idea that's not helpful to everyone's voice. For some the legacy of encountering a repressive spiritual context has meant that a deity or higher power has always been there watching for sin. In this context one's voice and one's thoughts become a constant source of danger. But sometimes naming a voice that guides us can help reclaim that private territory.

Some writers have drawn a connection between making art and connecting to spirit. Brenda Ueland writes, "It is when you are really living in the present—working, thinking, lost, absorbed in something you care about very much, that you are living spiritually."[1]

Thomas Merton contends that "to write is to love: it is to inquire and to praise, to confess and to appeal. This testimony of love remains necessary. Not to reassure myself that I am ('I write, therefore I am'), but simply to pay my debt to life, to the world. . . . The bad writing I have done has all been authoritarian, the declaration of musts, and the announcement of punishments. Bad because it implies a lack of love, good insofar as there may yet have been some love in it. The best stuff has been more straight confession and witness."[2]

We often think of witnessing in terms of trauma or atrocity, but I find it such a helpful reminder that witness includes inquiry, watching the roiling sea inside us, and loving the world. At the opposite end of the spectrum, writing that tries too hard to be "inspiring" can end up focusing on the feel-good moments without understanding the struggle.

Spiritual writing can include both moments of strong inspiration and clear feeling as well as times of doubt and internal wrestling. One thing that impacted me deeply about my time in the Catholic Church were the regular reminders from priests and nuns that doubt, too, was part of faith, that the wrestling—the churning, the moments lost, the days wandering in the desert—matters as a part of our stories.

The writer Marge Piercy has written, "I belong to nothing but my work carried like a prayer rug on my back." She evokes the image of writing as a ritual, one that she goes to regularly for connection to something larger than herself. This reminds me of another quotation about inspiration from poet Carolyn Forché: "If I just work when the spirit moves me, the spirit will ignore me." Forché is referencing spirit as muse, as that vague flow that guides the pen, and implying, as many other have, that it is regular contact with the muse that leads to inspiration. Even that word, *inspire*, has spirit as "breath" at the root.

Brenda Ueland writes, "Inspiration comes very slowly and quietly."[3] So, whether or not you feel comfortable with outright "spiritual" writing, you can channel the voice inside that has wisdom, that offers reassurance; maybe this is the voice of someone from your past or present who loves you unconditionally. You can think about the voice inside that connects with awe and wonder, whatever it is about this whirling universe and its wheeling galaxies that blows your mind.

TRY THIS

1. Who or what provides you with guidance? Who or what do you belong to? Try to write in a voice that is addressing a letter to that presence or person or one that is imagining what that presence or person would say to you.

2. What is the voice that speaks about awe or wonder? If channeling this voice is not comfortable, you can also write about the voice of intuition or your inner source of wisdom or reassurance. Maybe this is the voice of someone in your life that you can adopt as your own. How does that voice speak to you?

REFLECTION, SEEING, AND HONESTY

Getting in touch with voice and spirit also pushes me to look honestly at the details of my life until they become luminous. The everyday is its own form of holy, the "thinginess" that reveals itself when you look closely, as described in chapter 7.

I am continually altered by observation of detail, a process that the writer Annie Dillard explores exquisitely in her work. She notes two kinds of seeing, one honed by the details and a second "kind of seeing that involves a letting go."[4] We can, as Dillard did, go to the woods to look for muskrats and sycamore trees, and we can absorb the details we see. And the details—what we notice as our capacity for seeing them grows—allow our voices to emerge. The more specific we can be, the more we get the chance to both hear ourselves and see the world.

The root of the word *analysis* comes from the Greek root of *ana*, which means "up," and *lyein*, which is "to loosen." Today the word carries with it a sense of cold dissection or the act of tightening an argument around a thesis, battering the details into place. Instead, imagine analysis as a letting go of preconceived notions, loosening one's rigid assumptions and beliefs in order to see otherwise, diving into complexity.

TRY THIS

1. One of the most fruitful assignments I gave writers during a recent class was to read Dillard's book *Pilgrim at Tinker Creek* and then choose a place to visit for a total of about two hours, broken up into shorter segments. And then just *see*. You might try this, and in recording details, a new voice might emerge, one that wonders and records.

2. The voice of not-knowing can be equated with ignorance and weakness. What a loss for our spirits! Listen to the voice of not-knowing and imagine its strength. Write what it tells you about what to "loosen" in order to resee.

THE HARD STUFF

A writing guide on voice is probably a weird place to describe one of the most spiritual places I've ever been: sitting in a circle of strangers around a large double stove in a kitchen, which sat near an access road and a Mexican-Chinese buffet in a cinder block building in southern Georgia.

It was there, in a support group for family and friends of those who struggled with addiction, that I came with all of my raw pain as my family fell apart. I came and cried in that kitchen; the alcoholics and addicts were meeting beyond the door in the main function room. I don't remember a single name of anyone around that table, and the faces changed often. There was a rehab nearby, and sometimes families came whose loved ones were in treatment, with stunned and shell-shocked looks on their faces.

I have been trying to write about that long journey that has criss-crossed my entire life, beginning with confusion, traveling through rage, and ending with love in continued struggle. I'll never be completely done with all the fault lines scored in my soul as the result of those experiences.

Spiritual writing, for me, is not about an Instagram picture of a sunset and some weird quotation attributed to the Buddha that the Buddha never said. Many people pursue redemption, salvation, and rebirth as kinds of spiritual touchdowns, but personally, I will always just be on the road toward functioning a little bit better, carrying all those lines in my soul with me, screwing up and trying to make amends. This is the salvation of someone handing me a toolbox and telling me to go build a house. It doesn't save me the scrounging for nails and sweating in the sun and swearing and splinters and thinking that I'll never get it right.

Sometimes, in writing about our fiercest difficulties, the lessons do not emerge until much later. In many cases there are no clear lessons, but the balm of the passage of time allows us to layer one of our lives over the other, and only in marking that passage and the distance traveled do we get some kind of peace.

TRY THIS

1. What, for you, is the voice of trying? Listen to the voice inside you that urges you to just keep making another effort. What does that voice sound like, and what does it tell you?

2. Think about the most broken-down, shattered place you've ever been in your life. For someone very dear to me, that place was the parking lot of an Arby's fast-food restaurant, so I will call it your "Arby's moment." Write that moment, including what got you through it and what happened afterward, what it was like to be that close to the electric edge of giving up.

3. For a difficult time in your life, it might be helpful to write a scene that has the main character in the second person of "you" or even the third person of your preferred pronoun or maybe your name. That can help to introduce enough distance that you can see yourself moving through a past scene, to describe the action that muddies when you put yourself into the memory of a time still livid with emotions. Write about a difficult time with that observing voice.

4. Now try writing to that "you" or "they" character, describing what you see. As an example, this sentence came out when I described myself in the second person when writing about myself at work in my early twenties,: "You had to have a swagger, a ready laugh, an ability to make fun of someone else before they made fun of you." What I wrote surprised me because when I feel back into that time using the first person, I only remember a sense of feeling lost.

5. Now write about what has happened to the other people in the scene, if there were any, and what has transpired in the time gap

in your life between then and now. Mine included, "Now I am a professor, and at least one of those others in that house died soon afterward."

HONORING WHAT YOU KNOW AND WHO YOU ARE

Many of us are very hard on ourselves. Depending on our backgrounds, some of us may have inherited from cultural and faith traditions a kind of fiery self-hatred or critical eye that catalogs our weaknesses and failings. Living in an economy and culture like the United States, in which weaknesses and fears are turned into marketing campaigns for products promising to fix those "flaws," we may have become adept at identifying what we don't like about our bodies and our minds, and we might compare ourselves mercilessly to famous people on social media and to our friends and family.

One of the painful exercises I was forced to do in meetings like the one at the Mexican-Chinese buffet was to see myself more accurately. I hated that because I was really, really good at savaging myself before anyone else could do it. That was my main defense mechanism: simmering in self-hatred so that no one could beat me to the punch.

So, even if you have no formal faith or religion, the remaking of your relationship with yourself, outside of this weird cultural obsession with self-hatred, is a spiritual act. Developing a voice that praises yourself feels *weird*. And yet it just might be the voice that delivers stability beyond your imagining. This voice doesn't have to be sunshine all the time. It just has to see accurately or see otherwise, to list the good that is there.

The act of witnessing one's own life without the veil of vicious self-criticism can feel so odd. To start, you might describe the things you do physically during an average day, being conscious of not veering into the negative but, instead, just seeing. I don't remember why I started working on this prompt, but here's an example from my own attempt to see myself better:

In my car I rehearse necessary speeches while driving down the road, and my steering wheel is very impressed at my eloquence and insight.

I buy things on clearance that I don't love in weird colors and wrong sizes, thus getting a temporary burst of pride at saving money and a more lasting sense of annoyance at these strangely colored pieces of clothing that don't match with other things. I vow to change my life by changing my posture. I sit up straight, yoga style, and feel my vertebrae stacking up like a righteous Jenga game. When I am stressed or thinking, my spine curls and cups. In meetings with women, my friends especially, we curl over almost double as if bowing to each other. I refuse to judge this. It is an expression of how tired we are and how sometimes it is good to slump.

Some of this makes me smile. It is what it is. And I feel a burst of compassion for this woman who is just a person trying her best.

The Chicana philosopher, writer, and activist Cherríe Moraga writes: "All writing is confession. Confession masked and revealed in the voices of our characters. All is hunger. The longing to be known fully and still loved. The admission of our own inherent vulnerability, our weakness, our tenderness of skin, fragility of heart, our overwhelming desire to be relieved of the burden of ourselves in the body of another, to be forgiven of our ultimate aloneness in the mystical body of a god or the common work of a revolution."[5]

We can confess not only our sins but also our longings, our human frailties, our "tenderness of skin, fragility of heart," as Moraga brilliantly describes it. This confession of humanity, pursued through the details of our vulnerable lives, lets us be known to ourselves and others and, in the writing, lets others also recognize themselves.

TRY THIS

1. Start a writing prompt with "I am often right about . . ," and then for balance you can follow it up with "I am often wrong about . . ." Where does that voice of perspective seem to come from? Does it connect to any voice from another person in any part of your life? That might be a voice worth exercising.

2. Make a list of your repeated actions and attitudes in the present tense during an average day: your physical motions, your habitual

thoughts, where you place your shoulder bag or how you carry your keys, your gestures and how you use your hands.

3. Write for five minutes on either the prompt "What I didn't want to see is . . ." or "What I didn't know at the time was . . ." Now look over that piece of writing and name that voice. Who is speaking, the one with insight?

SPEAKING FOR US AND WITH US

One of James Baldwin's many gifts as a writer is his ability to raise spiritual issues in an approachable and urgent way. He addresses spirituality not in terms of dogma but in terms of living as humans in an aching world and making choices. Baldwin's writing has a wide range of voices, all related and completely his, infused with the power and cadence of the sermons he gave, preaching as a boy in the Pentecostal Church. In his essay "Take Me to the Water," he writes: "Incontestably, alas, most people are not, in act, worth very much; and yet, every human being is an unprecedented miracle. One tries to treat them as the miracles they are, while trying to protect oneself against the disasters they've become."[6]

What I feel in these sentences is the vocal intonation, the units and rhythm. The rhythm is a conceptual container that holds aloft layers of insights. Baldwin frequently works with pairs of sentences, stacking complications to steer toward complexity. And those two sentences do such spiritual work, joining together in a kind of prayer that contains the messy array of humanity and urging the reader to hold together two ideas that seem to cancel each other out. It is that containing of an uncontainable mystery that makes his writing so deeply spiritual for me.

In the essay "Nothing Personal," he writes: "I am aware that we do not save each other very often. But I am also aware that we save each other some of the time."[7] Whether or not you have a specific spiritual belief system, writing with spirit in mind can provide an opening to allow us to explore our own sense of the world. This is another area that is often explicitly prohibited with the advice of "show, don't tell."

Baldwin is a master of detail and storytelling, and his power comes from building that action and then using it to say the complex things that need to be said in a voice of telling that plucks such complexity from the abyss of suffering.

Because we focus so much on argumentative rhetoric in the United States, many of us, even if we are trained as writers, have missed the exposure to other elements of ancient theory about communication. Aristotle writes about ethos in a way that is often captured as the authority of the speaker. But even the word *authority* sounds different to us than what *ethos* meant to Aristotle, and we can't hear it the way his audience heard it. Our often authoritarian and consumerist society adds a sharp edge that implies that ethos is mostly about manipulation, about *seeming* good while being bad or about getting what you want at the expense of others.

What often gets left out of writing textbooks is the sense of "eunoia": the care and attention toward the audience. Rather than trying to shame, harm, provoke, manipulate, or badger through language, we can write to give something to the reader. Commercials, political speeches, emails, letters from employers . . . text is so often used to wound and cut down and divide. Often, if we focus on a "hostile" reader, there's no way that we can channel care toward those who read our work. *Eunoia* is nonetheless latent as potential and something we use every day in the encouraging texts we send to friends, the comments on a picture posted to social media, or the love expressed in a letter.

TRY THIS

1. Write a letter of admiration to someone whose presence in your life has sustained you, either as a friend or relative or as a stranger. Be honest and generous. What does it feel like writing in that voice? This voice, too, the voice of praise, can grow and grow if you exercise it.
2. Try a similar prompt with "What has saved me is . . ."
3. Write for five minutes to describe "a day in which I love my life."

The voice of spirit can also be collective rather than individual, and one of these tools for accessing it is the choice to speak for a "we" rather than a "me." This can feel odd at first, but the voice can inflate our souls and let us glimpse a sense of spiritual authority that we might not ever have been given before.

I turn again to Baldwin, who channels this "we" effortlessly, having earned the observations through experience. He had lived through enough racism and homophobia and other forms of pain to be embittered, and yet in writing for the "we," he refuses the impulse to cut himself off from a community and from his right to speak with authority. He continues, in a bold way, to speak for humanity, thus including himself obstinately in the very community that some would deny him: "The evil is, in some sense, ours, and we help to feed it by failing so often in our private lives to deal with our private truth—our own experience."[8] This, to me, rings clearly with the command that we look at our own lives so that we avoid the evil of not seeing what Baldwin calls our "private truth."

Ultimately, Baldwin uses the keen observation of his own life, including its pain, to heave up from deep places such startling sentences and insights that they become precious, these pairings of self-contradiction that fold like two halves of a locket, both true. Look for the hinge of this locket at the *yet* in this quotation: "Every good-bye ain't gone: human history reverberates with violent upheaval, uprooting, arrival, and departure, hello and good-bye. Yet, I am not certain that anyone ever leaves home. When 'home' drops below the horizon, it rises in one's breast and acquires the overwhelming power of menaced love."

Baldwin's brilliance can be intimidating, but an extended immersion in his work can change your voice, as if you are practicing scales in a completely different key. By observing your own struggles and details or by seeing, as Dillard asks us to, you can let in the varied voices and watch as these insights shimmer on the surface, brought up through a writer that has found his or her authority. These forms of writing are not solutions to any practical problem. They are statements that hold complexity and mystery.

TRY THIS

1. Start a freewrite with "we" and see where it takes you. If nothing starts, you can add any strong verb, like *love* or *judge* or *forget*. The "we" might end up referring to humanity or to a group of people, and that group might be speaking for a real or fictional world.
2. Try a pairing like Baldwin's with the "we": "We so often . . . ," for example, or "And yet we . . ."

SPIRIT AS NOT KNOWING

One of my Buddhist teachers, Elizabeth Mattis Nyamgel, wrote a book called *The Heart of an Open Question*, which seems to me to be a manifesto for living inside the attempt to see and explore the world. The idea of questions without answers and the goal of being open to look at life with an open, questioning heart have become what I find most compelling about the essay form, which is often driven by a difficult question that doesn't have to be answered or can't be answered. Writing such an essay allows me to practice reflection. Mattis Nyamgel taught me about the root of the word *analysis*, and she teaches about how often humans want to cling to a single explanation or clench their version of "rightness." I love these ideas because I struggle with them so much. I am hostile and irate about political events. I have yelled at family members so hard that I've hurt my throat and their souls. I am fiery, angry, and sad about so many things.

Buddhism has nudged me to wrestle with the fact that I am not unitary or singular, that my "self" is constantly shifting. That's helped me in the practice of watching what is going on in my mind and seeing how it's like a lava lamp, how my feelings constantly shift and how even a "stuck" feeling passes and changes into something else. I hope that in getting to know myself better, I might become better able to watch for the surges of strong emotion that could propel words to hurt another person.

Buddhist practices have asked me to examine my experience and watch my mind. Another Buddhist idea is to test out received truths for oneself rather than to passively accept what is handed down, which has strengthened my voice as an essayist and writer. Strengthening those muscles has given me permission not necessarily to come to conclusions but to record the process of looking and then to speak with authority from that experience. The notion of interdependence, too, has a deep resonance with my experience in the world as a nonfiction writer: it's all connected. I love burrowing into a tangent and finding that it opens into discoveries and themes I need to explore, helping me to get to know my own life.

And again, from Baldwin, on his time in the church:

> It was very important for me not to pretend to have surmounted the pain and terror of that time of my life, very important not to pretend that it left no mark on me. It marked me forever. In some measure I encountered the abyss of my own soul, the labyrinth of my destiny: these could never be escaped, to challenge these imponderables being, precisely, the heavy, tattered glory of the gift of God. To encounter oneself is to encounter the other: and this is love. If I know that my soul trembles, I know that yours does, too: and, if I can respect this, both of us can live. . . . For, I have seen the devil, by day and by night, and have seen him in you and in me: in the eyes of the cop, and the sheriff and the deputy, the landlord, the housewife, the football player: in the eyes of some junkies, the eyes of some preachers, the eyes of some governors, presidents, wardens, in the eyes of some orphans, and in the eyes of my father, and in my mirror. It is that moment when no other human being is real for you, nor are you real for yourself. The devil has no need of any dogma—though he can use them all—nor does he need any historical justification, history being so largely his invention.[9]

I know that's a huge quotation . . . but where could I stop? It's all there. And Baldwin summons spiritual wisdom *not* from the false confidence of an aphorism, a commandment, or a judgment of others. And he doesn't aim for the simple inspiration of "I learned from it and now I'm stronger." Instead, he finds the devil "in my mirror," and through that experience, and the experience of seeing it in the eyes of others, he understands both evil and love.

TRY THIS

1. Think about the voice that would offer advice to a younger version of yourself.
2. Aim for the voice that reflects on hard-won experience by starting, "It was hard, but I learned . . ."
3. If you were writing a letter to a friend, encouraging your friend to keep going in the face of a challenge or to stick with a difficult task, what would you say?

13 *Editing and Revising with Voices*

Writing with vibrant voices has two hallmarks that work in tension with each other to make the sentence feel alive: consistency and fluidity. When I'm revising, I'll often get out a pen and circle places where the voice has shifted in a jarring way, has gone dead or dull, to see what is hiding or why I had unplugged. Because a voice is so often a portal to content, inextricably linked with what's been seen, sensed, or said, a voice shift isn't merely a place where the icing on a cake needs to be smoothed over. It's a sign that something might need to be cracked open or more deeply delved into.

As your skill at watching for voice grows, you can edit with an eye to capturing and enhancing liveliness. And learning about your own voices—including your quirks and turns of phrase—can also help you edit your work to strengthen and layer those voices.

PICKING UP VOICE IN A DRAFT

Because voices reveal and create patterns of thought, each voice comes with its own weaknesses and zones where its signal isn't very strong. Often there's a "safe" voice that we fall into habitually with a certain kind of writing task, but that might not be the best tool for the job. So first, when you're puzzling over a draft, ask yourself what the voice sounds like. What is that voice trying to be, and what is that voice afraid of? Is the voice stuck in a certain mood or view of its material that is limiting you? If you're excited about the subject but somehow your writing isn't conveying that excitement, you might try a freewrite, separate from the document, where you go off about how cool you think the topic is, and then see whether you've generated pieces or words that can be infused into your document.

So many times in my own writing struggles, I have been stuck on voice. I've confused my feelings about the material or my audience with the voices that might reveal more about my own thinking. For example, in writing a memoir about loving those with substance abuse issues, I would sink down into a voice that felt as trapped and constrained, as I did during some of those years. I allowed my feelings about the topic and experience to close off my writing voice, to make my depiction of those days as numb as I felt at the time. This, then, further limited the reconstruction work I was trying to do with words and limited my ability to see those events in a new light. I wasn't allowing myself to figure out what I felt *now* about what I was writing. I couldn't even see my material—or really get curious about it—until I opened up some space for other voices that asked new questions and focused on different angles of my topic.

Sometimes, too, the sense of audience is what's constraining my voice or my sense of how I think I *should* feel about a topic or an echo of another story that has influenced my thinking. As a result, I'm missing opportunities for adding greater depth to both my thinking and my writing. Usually, I'm hiding. If the topic feels risky, I might pull away and write more abstractly or more numbly, tiptoeing into the topic.

Another challenge I often see in my own drafts is that I'll fade off into abstract language at transition points. Sometimes I veer into vagueness because I am trying to connect to a point that I know needs to come next but I can't figure out how to get there. Often I find that when I'm cutting out the vagueness in a draft, I have to break it into pieces and reglue them somewhere else. I also know, from looking at my own writing, that I have trigger words—usually ending with *-tion*, like *abstraction*, or sentences starting with *in*, like "in the event of"—that tell me I've detached from a guiding voice.

TRY THIS

1. Look at a piece of writing you'd like to revise and scan it for voices. You can even mark the names of the voices you've encountered while reading this book or add to your voice list if you discover a new one. Or maybe what you hear in the draft is an amalgam of two voices. Now scan your list of voices. Do any of them jump out as being able to provide a fresh view of the topic? Write on your topic for a few minutes in an unexpected voice to see what comes up. Or try a voice that seems to have nothing to say on the topic.

2. Do you see any trigger words that tell you to notice a voice that's vague or veering away?

3. If you're working on a specific revision of a story or poem or essay, describe the voice you see and hear on the page. Or if you're reading someone else's work, describe for them how the voice feels to you. What image could capture that voice—a slow and persistent snail? A fierce and powerful bulldozer?

4. When you're offering feedback on someone else's draft, try to put into words the voice that is speaking to you. Maybe even name its qualities: point of view, tone, emotional cadences, psychological distance from the reader, level of shyness or confidence, undertone of shame, and anything else that comes to mind. Hearing those details articulated might help a writer to understand what needs to be adjusted in a text.

REVISION, ANXIETY, AND VOICE

Most writers have some level of revision anxiety, and often that is what's behind the term *writer's block*. Sometimes we might be afraid to look at a page with our words on it because we can't get the voice right. The work feels fake because the voice feels constraining. The words ring false because we haven't been able to channel the voices that we can *almost* hear or to find the one that can tell the story right.

Toward the end of one class, I asked my students to write about their revision anxiety, and I wrote along with them. I described my revision anxiety—still ever present—partly as "the feeling that maybe this time there will be no magic. It is confronting the gap. It is the sickness of looking down off a bridge to the ravine below. It is the worry about my identity being in question, my core coming undone."

That sounds quite drastic, but I think revision can feel like a threat to the self particularly if we're not able to hear or identify the voice that's underlying and fueling the work. A first draft often feels so fluent because we are channeling a voice, whether or not it's the right one for the final draft. Returning with a critical eye, that "flow" can feel absent. We may examine our work with a withering gaze, forcing the voice into hiding. For that reason, it's very important to identify that even if a draft isn't working, you may be onto a voice that you need to pursue, or you may need to channel other voices.

In my freewrite on revision, I also wrote that a first draft feels like "a ladder, crashing waves, stepping outside, studying molecules, fun, unpacking." Revision feels like "shattering a sculpture, repetition, all the options and questions, two ways of seeing the work, losing language, a chance to redo, folding laundry, surgery." Now that I'm looking at these sentences, I am not exactly sure what they mean, but I know that my metaphor voice is strong and has a lot to say because I've let that voice grow free. That voice offers a wealth of images and mystery.

And then one more slightly terrifying image, courtesy of horror movies on television in the 1970s: "Exactly where I am most sure of an essay's spine or skeleton is exactly where it needs to split its skin and molt into a werewolf."

My view of revision has been influenced by one of my most important writing teachers and mentors, Lee Martin, who writes beautiful fiction and nonfiction (though none of it is about molting werewolves). He also has a great blog on craft in which he published a piece called "Felt Sense: Focusing on Revision." Martin takes Sondra Perl's insights on felt sense, described in chapter 3, and uses them in the service of reseeing a draft. He advises, "Identify a place in your draft that makes you feel uncomfortable, or a place that seems too vague but also important"—there's that vagueness again—then write about what might be the *consequences* of being more specific. This can help us home in on our fears about revision. He also asks writers to think about what they know about the topic, what excites or interests them about it, and "where does this essay want to go?"[1]

TRY THIS

1. Try Lee Martin's prompts about "felt sense." What is missing from a draft, and where does the draft of your poem, story, or essay want to go?
2. What does revision feel like for you? What are you worried about when you revise?
3. What do you *love* about your topic? What first sparked your interest in it? This might mean going back to chapter 9, "Joy Is the Seed of Voice," and channeling some of those voices.

HOMING IN ON THE PLACES TO SPLIT OPEN WITH VOICE

Many writers need to start each day with a voice encounter to "prime the pump" of language. They might either read their own work aloud or start a writing session by reading a bit of poetry. What they are doing is reconnecting with voice in the form of speech or expression and the music in its cadences. Taking in another voice—often more meditative, musical, even lively or challenging—can clear the fog and subconsciously start a writer on a new path into the material.

As my focus on voice developed, I began to have conversations with myself in a journal about the voice I wanted to reach. During the drafting process of my memoir about a loved one's addiction, I *knew* voice was the problem, but I couldn't crack the code. On the page my voice sounded strangled and mournful. I didn't even want to slog through the pages to reread them, which was a sign of trouble.

The heart of the problem was that I was ashamed of so many details in the narrative, including some of the behavior that I had tolerated from others. So I was defensive, and I approached the reader as a kind of judging confessor who would assign me penance. I began to see that my voice was the problem, but I couldn't figure out what my other options were. Behind that voice, in my heart and head, I didn't have a mournful view of my past. I had intense and fiery feelings about it that were both positive and negative. My voice wasn't right for this project because it was constraining all that I could say. And my sense of the audience as a judge wasn't helping either!

So I rewrote the book several times in different voices to shake myself out of the doom and the shame. First, I chose to write from the point of view of a present-day me who is just a bit wiser, explaining the narrative to a younger me—and in the second person, no less. My voice was the tone you'd take in talking to an eight-year-old: explaining, encouraging, pointing out what went right.

Then I realized that I'd left out the inherent joy of my approach to life, so I rewrote it again from one of my joyful voices, a hayseed–punk rock young woman from a good day in my twenties.

I'm not sure if any of these voices worked, but this was great conscious practice to learn about my wild voices.

I decided, through this process, that I needed a thread of spiritual insight through the book because the story was also about coming to believe in help and hope and because a trusted reader pointed out that this was a theme but not one that I'd allowed much room for. I was writing from the experience but not from the wisdom that the experience had generated.

So I turned to a favorite book, Annie Dillard's *Pilgrim at Tinker Creek*, which is often described as nature writing but is as much about fieldwork of the soul. I have always admired Dillard's confident irreverence on the page. I decided that I wanted to write sentences like the sentences in Dillard's work—evocative, careful, joyful, alive with the surprise of unexpected words and devoted to noticing details in the concrete outer world. And sometimes, in the midst of a carefully meditative paragraph, Dillard will lay down a plainspoken, gum-cracking voice like a royal flush at a poker table. That resonance of the unexpected—the minute voice shifts from sentence to sentence—is part of what makes the book such a pleasure to read.

A shot of Dillard's voice, filtered through my sensibility, helped me write sentences that had more loft and music. This is using voice as a foundation for writing, as a generative tool, rather than as decoration.

Then—finally, finally—I came to the understanding that I didn't have to write a book in one voice. By watching myself rewrite and rewrite this book, I realized that in each draft, shadows of the previous voices remained like layers of rock in a mountainside. That is how we are; as living, breathing beings, our minds contain all the layers of our past. One minute we're thinking of a person who makes us worry, and the next minute the sight of a coffee cup given to us by a friend makes us smile and lighten. We veer and tack. We layer ourselves.

Some of the voices in our heads are "sticky," like that voice of shame from my memoir's first draft. This voice came from stigma and social pressure, gender and class and other real-world problems. Such voices adhere to us, get in our heads, and tell us how to see ourselves and the world. Sometimes you have to write a whole book to realize that you don't need a certain voice to tell your story. Getting rid of such voices is a matter of deep editing and soul wrestling. It's not a matter of tapping the delete key a few times. The draft that was full of shame and apology helped me to see exactly how deep that voice was embedded in my life. It's still there, but I catch it more quickly these days.

Practicing other voices mattered. Rewriting and reseeing my past through a joyful lens was a weird assignment to give myself, but it also shifted something slightly in my life. To be honest, I still haven't figured out the right voice for that book. But when I began to play with the possible voices to tell the story, something frozen in me broke open, and I saw that at least I had a choice about the way to see my story. This is part of why I recommend that writers rant, lament, and rage on the page about the things they barely allow themselves to think. This is why the solution to a frozen relationship to writing is to practice with more voices.

Writing isn't therapy, just like basketball isn't chess. There are different rules, different scoring systems, and different goals. But that doesn't mean that I didn't learn a whole lot about myself in the process.

Now, as I think about whether I want to take the reader's time with my current draft, I know I haven't yet found the right voice to convey the urgent unsaid things the story wants to say. So, back I go for a bit more reading and living in order to find it.

What can you do if you don't know which voice fits to tell a complex story? Say you have a sentence in a voice that feels wrong. Try to write into the disagreement. "I sound so frozen here, but why? Another way of looking at it is . . ." This conversation with yourself on the page embodies Phillip Lopate's advise to capture the "mind at work." Maybe this is a few notes to yourself, but maybe it will also generate sentences that stay in your draft. As you write about the challenge of telling a story, you build a bond with the reader. This conversation with honesty, depth, and struggle is often what thinking and living feels like. The dilemma about how to tell a story well mirrors the dilemma about how to live a life.

Each piece of writing and each book has a different narrative voice or range of voices with different volumes, different stances, different moods and energy. Sometimes the narrative of a book traces the change of a voice through its pages. When you're conscious of voice, you can do a little quick juke from one voice to another, livening up a bland document. It's like a magic trick—readers will say: "Oh, you're such a good writer! I love this, and I'm not even sure why—it just sounds like a real person!" And you can smile and nod, knowing the truth is voice.

TRY THIS

1. If you receive feedback from another reader about the voice of a work or if you catch an image that expresses a voice, try to imagine a voice that's as near to opposite of the draft voice as possible. Say you're hesitant and quiet about a topic you're feeling your way into. Now envision an ogre, a bulldozer, a fire-breathing dragon. Catch the wisp of that voice, that version of yourself, and write into it.

2. Sit down with a draft of something you're writing, and in the margins, make notes about the voice of each paragraph. What

do you see? Is it the same voice for pages and pages? Think now about another comfortable voice that you've discovered through the work in this book and try writing in that voice drawn from another time period in your life.

3. Try arguing with a voice on the page or turning consciously from one voice to another while describing what it feels like to shift voices, to resist the habitual voice.

4. Voice can be a tool for analysis, and certain voices tend to reach certain conclusions. You might have been asked in an introductory writing class to play the "believing and doubting" game, in which you channeled a voice of bombastic confidence and a voice of academic skepticism. These are only two among endless channels. What about a voice of slow consideration or a voice that cuts in and always disbelieves a binary either-or view of the world? What about a voice that always tends to look for the comedy in a serious topic or an irreverent voice that rejects the topic in favor of a more important question?

REWRITING AGAINST VOICE

In my first full-time writing gig for an alternative weekly newspaper, I was asked to take on the specific voice of that newspaper: writing with a kind of snarky, wry humor that looked for the ridiculous in the world but was never outright funny. There was a touch of cynicism to it, which didn't really fit with my worldview, but it was a paycheck, and I learned a lot from the experience. Until I learned "house style"—or really, "house voice"—my drafts came back as a sea of corrections in red. Then, over time, I learned how to push a bit against house voice and finally to use it as a tool. We often have a house voice assigned as a kind of thinking template for a task, whether it's a quarterly report or an annotated bibliography. And now I still have that voice as an option I can use, an ingredient that I can add into my other writing when it seems helpful.

Even when we write documents for work or school, shreds of our voices inescapably come through, and if we want to be successful at this work-for-hire or house style writing, we can learn to inhabit it like a costume. Behind the mask, a person still breathes. And once we fully inhabit that voice, we can also borrow it as a template for other writing.

In *Tell It Slant* Brenda Miller and Suzanne Paola, share the technique of the "hermit crab" essay, which is an essay that takes an unexpected form—a grocery list, a how-to manual, a horror movie script—and uses it to tell a personal story. Each of those "container" forms carries an expected voice. The delight for the reader comes in the tension between two layers of voices: the expected surface voice devoted to the form and the deeper material that animates it. Similarly, many poetic forms come with an expected voice, like an ode that captures a voice of praise and devotion or a lament that catalogs a state of misery and its causes. These containers are really voice experiments that over time became voice costumes for writers to try on.

TRY THIS

1. What would your current piece of writing look like and feel like if it were revisited as a "how-to"? An invoice for services rendered or a bill for damages to an insurance company? Such experiments often work because they airlift us right out of a habitual voice into a new one that has the potential to explode our point of view.

2. If you're writing in a form that feels like it has rigid constraints, the way to write a *great* version of that form is to break those voice expectations, in subtle or overt ways. You can often see this in the "turn" at the end of a poem, which might be a new layer unearthed in a poet's thinking, or it might be a breath of air let in by a shift of voice. Is there a piece of writing that might be turned by tinkering with a second voice at the conclusion?

THE VOICE OF ABSTRACTION

Often one of the underlying constraints of house style is vagueness and abstraction. If you're writing a technical or business document, the voice is completely prescribed, with very narrow openings for voice. This rigidity constrains a reader's view of the topic by design. Instead of "We fired a bunch of people," the quarterly corporate earnings statement might have to read, "Market conditions necessitated a right-sizing of the workforce."

We can understand what's going on here. And as writers, we can fully see what George Orwell meant in "Politics and the English Language" when he wrote that such word choices begin in vagueness but end up somewhere much more significant: "A speaker who uses that kind of phraseology has gone some distance toward turning himself into a machine. . . . And this reduced state of consciousness, if not indispensable, is at any rate favourable to political conformity."[2]

Many, many writers have had to write sentences like the "market conditions" sentence in order to eat, to not get fired, and to earn a paycheck. We might also be polishing our résumés and cover letters as we do so in order to stave off desperation, but sometimes market conditions necessitate that our bosses make us do horrible stuff. It's important that writers who aim to connect their voices with their bodies, minds, and hearts *understand* what is happening with these sentences. Only in that way can we take Orwell's advice to heart and grasp how our gifts will be used. Just call it what it is: spin. It's better to admit what's happening than to give away one's voice and not realize what has been sold.

In these and many other situations, genre dictates voice. Today many writers learn to write by practicing various genres: the cover letter, the review, the summary, the letter to the editor. But genre is not voice. Ultimately, the idea of genre is a package of stylistic choices made over and over again until they become ossified. Practicing a genre is fine as a first step in learning to write, but writers should also learn about what genre is: a series of writing gestures that often obscure power relationships and that demand a drastic limitation of voice.

I think about Orwell's advice almost every single day. As I revise, I see—to an uncomfortable extent—how my writing brain tends toward abstraction. The voice of abstraction is very sticky and very comfortable. The sentences with passive verbs, in which the action is hidden and the words all end in -tion, grow up in my paragraphs like creeping poison ivy. This voice is a fantastic way to avoid conflict or action, and I've been trained by that "official" voice of abstraction, very related to the worst of academic and work-for-hire writing. It constrains my thinking.

This issue is delightfully and seriously captured in Danielle Evans's novella "The Office of Historical Corrections," from her short story collection of the same name.[3] The narrator works at an imaginary government agency where employees travel around the country putting sticky notes on public inaccuracies. Her colleague, Genevieve, visits historical markers because her "most persistent and controversial grievance was the passive voice atrocity: wherever there was a memorial, she wanted to name not just the dead but the killers."[4] In uncovering the victim of a racial hate crime, Genevieve raised the hackles of those who wanted to remain nameless and their descendants. History is so much more comfortable when we don't name names, but that, too, is a worldview that resists accountability and change.

Orwell's essay snaps and buzzes with a voice that cuts through tired turns of phrase, and I highly recommend reading the whole thing. At the end of "Politics and the English Language," he boils down his advice to a set of guidelines:

i. Never use a metaphor, simile or other figure of speech which you are used to seeing in print.
ii. Never use a long word where a short one will do.
iii. If it is possible to cut a word out, always cut it out.
iv. Never use the passive where you can use the active.
v. Never use a foreign phrase, a scientific word or a jargon word if you can think of an everyday English equivalent.
vi. Break any of these rules sooner than say anything outright barbarous.[5]

Orwell's rules diagnose, for me, the points in my own writing that need to be sharpened. But as a complication, it's important to note his last point: "Break any of these rules." Orwell doesn't always follow his own advice in his novels and nonfiction. But that's okay—what Orwell wants is to give the writer options and to hone the writer's editing sensibilities so they can be wielded like a knife, freeing voice from the tether of spin.

TRY THIS

1. Go through a draft and circle the passive verbs. You don't have to change all of them, but if they occur in a cluster, you might ask whether the cloud of passivity is shielding you or others from an angle, voice, or topic that has rich possibilities and important things to say.

2. If there's a point in your draft where you're shifting into abstraction, try to write about what you or a character *did*, even if the doing didn't seem very dramatic. We often miss quiet actions and small decisions. Instead of "It was a day in which nothing happened," what about "She mulled over what to do, sifting through her doubts, and washed a coffee cup."

OUR VOICES, EDITED AND SHARPENED

To edit for voice, we first become aware of our choices and our range. Then we begin to see when we are veering into the shadowlands of spin or abstraction that Orwell describes. As much as our family has shaped us by years of interaction, our consciousness has been constructed by the voices we have been asked to inhabit as well as the voices we've read. The more we see this in our writing, the more choices we have as writers and as humans.

Here we enter a paradox: sometimes a first draft is like an open window, inviting in lively phrases so delightful that they'd never emerge in a longer goal-oriented piece of writing. An inexperienced writer might close down around the feeling of fluency in drafting and claim that every first draft expresses pure voice and that editing is a kind of violation. In truth, it all depends on our ability to see what we've got in the raw material. Sometimes our first expressions really do have what Pat Schneider calls the "freshness of voice" that reminds us why we like to write.[6] Sometimes . . . but sometimes not. We can develop editorial discernment and clarity to find the treasures, to lift them up from plodding prose and slushy sentences.

As bell hooks writes, "To be serious we must dare to be critical of our urge to tell our stories, of the ways we tell them."[7] She's talking here about not just our sentences but our very selves. How we write, hooks says, is a function of who we are and where we come from: our class, race and ethnicity, gender identity and sexual orientation, region, disabilities, and more as well as our habits and prejudices.

She recounts her struggle against the expected voices as she strove to move beyond "a mere imitation of the fake academic neutral sound I had learned to cultivate in academic settings."[8] She wrote her book *Ain't I a Woman* multiple times, drafting and redrafting until she found the right voice, which pulsed with her lived experience as a Black woman from a particular time and place. This is not at all a "dumbing down" or translation out of complexity into simplicity. Like Orwell, hooks uses "a thinking and writing process where I am pushing myself to work with ideas in a way that strips them down, that cuts to the chase and does not seek to hide or use language to obscure meaning . . . to transfer to the act of writing vernacular modes of verbal exchange that surface in the expressive culture of the southern black working class."[9]

You might notice that hooks melds direct short words and phrases like *strips them down* and *cuts to the chase* with academic turns of phrase like *writing vernacular* and *modes of verbal exchange*. She's weaving voices. I would argue she's doing this to elevate plainspoken language and to consciously build a bridge between academia and the way folks talk, to show that both are equally able to carry complex ideas. She's articulating something that the world would have us forget: the brilliance of the people we come from.

She's not saying that our first drafts express the innate purity of that brilliance. What she's saying is that we're all a mixed bag, and we sometimes write muddy and sometimes write clear, and that we have to observe the eddies and swirls of our mixing voices, then exercise and navigate them consciously.

Her point is also illuminated by poet Ira Sadoff in an essay, "Open Letter," in *The Racial Imaginary: Writers on Race in the Life of the Mind*. Sadoff writes: "Late in the revision process, I wonder if the poem asks difficult enough questions? I think about the cultural forces on my language—where did that feeling or phrase or idea come from: am I appropriating someone else's pain? . . . Am I globalizing, stereotyping, over-generalizing about a group of people, white or black? Am I writing about people I know and understand? If not, do I honor their strangeness?"[10]

Voice is not what happens to fly onto the page or the screen in the first draft. Instead, writing with voices is about getting to know your options, then thinking consciously about *which* voice you are attempting to channel so that you can see the strengths, limitations, and implications of where you're writing from.

When I am editing for voice, I realize that I am a white midwestern woman but not one who can speak for that whole demographic. I've got a nasal twang in my speech that strangers pick out as Chicago, but I've got a green bean casserole lowbrow thrum that comes from my place on the planet in a working- to middle-class South Side suburb riven with class angst. I've got a chip on my shoulder from growing up creative and sensitive in a knockabout place. And I've got a scrappy tomboy edge from growing up there, too, a pushing back against what pushed me.

Not everything that Green Bean Casserole Woman comes up with is brilliance, but she's got a song that, in certain situations, works. And in certain other situations, there's entirely too much cream of mushroom soup for her current role. And in certain other situations, that girl—the one who was teased on the school bus in the 1980s—hides. She doubts herself with *I think* and *just* and *maybe* when her voice should be listened to, so I, as the adult editor, have to lure her out of the shadows, strip away those corn husks she's using to cover up her strangeness.

And that casserole girl thinks she doesn't know anything, but her bombastic academic cousin, the professor I am today, sounds like she knows everything. So somewhere in the middle, roping in both those tendencies, is the nearest I can get to true, especially if I carefully add in touches of several other voices. The community organizer voice cuts in, wanting to ask about social forces and power. And then I realize how little I know. As a white girl growing up along Interstate 80, I never stood in those mono crop fields and really *got* that the soil was land of the Kickapoo, the Myaamia, and the Potawatomi, that people had been passing through that land for eons before the Europeans arrived. Listening—taking in, too, what you don't know, recognizing when you need to step back and lower your own voice to acknowledge the voices of others—is also part of voice.

bell hooks writes in *Remembered Rapture* that awareness of our voices is ultimately what allows us to build bridges and connect: "Unless we are able to speak and write in many different voices, using a variety of styles and forms, allowing the work to change and be changed in specific settings, there is no way to converse across borders, to speak to and with diverse communities."[11]

ALL THE WOVEN VOICES

Peter Elbow writes that "polyvocal or multivalent kinds of discourse"— those sorts of communication woven from multiple voices—introduce options for playing games in writing, allowing a writer to express "what is ambivalent and complex." The sound of one voice breaking through another, like a wink of yellow in a gray painting, often comes in the form of asides or digressions. These places in the text, he writes, are "where suddenly we feel an added infusion of weight, richness, presence."[12] He adds, however, that these voice breaks can signal places where something more needs to be uncovered and that pulling at that stray thread will reveal a key point still submerged.

The rhythm and melding of voices in my work provides a kind of substructure that is even below the level of content or meaning. I think of that woven substrate as the tectonic plates of the writing. Sometimes I hear elements of the voice urging on the sentences, and sometimes I have content and can't hear the voice.

The poet Sandra Beasley wrote that wonderful and concise description of voice, mentioned earlier, as a series of craft decisions involving six areas: "Point of View, Tense-Aspect-Mood, Image, Sound, Structure, and Diction." Voice is, in her words, is "the aggregate, the delivery system for your craft decisions." She mentions that when a piece is identified as having a "strong voice," it's because a writer is making these choices with consistency throughout the piece.

In my view this consistency doesn't have to mean using one voice. Rather, it can be a consistent weaving of more than one voice, a shifting or braiding that itself has a kind of deep rhythm and music. Imagine you can see or feel the rhythm of voice in a piece: maybe it starts out plainspoken, then veers into your Dillard voice, then your plain voice, your abstract voice, your Dillard voice, then back to plain, creating a kind of voice melody throughout a piece.

Elbow quotes Arthur Palacas, who describes voice as "the factive and the reflective." Palacas sees "fluency" as the ability to shift back and forth between the seeing/describing/action and the internal/reflection/thinking.[13] As Annie Dillard shows me, you might have one voice for observing the outer world, a biologist in the field, and one reflective voice for thinking about memory and spirit, and a third—a crashing kid who wants to jump in puddles—that romps through both of those adult voices. Or as Baldwin demonstrates, you might have one voice that fixes the scenes of the past with inexorable truth and another that draws deep into an echoing well to bring sustenance from the gap between desire and reality.

Don Fry, in an essay in the book *Writing Voice*, describes several characteristics of voice that are a helpful start.[14] I've taken his list as starting point and moved the elements around, adding a few entries as well as some description and elaboration after some of them. You can use this list to analyze the voices of the speaker, narrator, or character in any genre.

The first group feels like the thumbprint of life on language:

level of diction (formal, medium, informal);
slang and dialect (marking place and time);
wit and humor;

ethnicity, race, region, disability, and class background as well as
    work history;
gender and sexual orientation as they affect expression and voice;
insertions and interruptions: place marker syllables (for example,
    "ummmmm," "know-whadda-mean?" or "put it this way");
confidence;
sophistication;
references: music, literature;
name-dropping.

The next group has to do with voice and how official and abstract
or concrete it is:

formality of grammar and usage;
punctuation;
sentence clarity and economy;
sentence length and variety of length;
dependent clauses at the beginning of sentences;
active, passive, and linking verbs (remember Orwell);
contractions;
abstract or specific and, if so, what kind of language and focus
    (academic or corporate abstraction, the specific diction of a
    plumber or naturalist)?

These choices are also part of these three elements, which express
deep rhythm:

repetitions: words, phrases, imagery;
parallel structures (also are a way of creating a deep structural
    rhythm);
rhythm and flow: speed of speech and pausing; where pauses
    happen and what is emphasized.

Voice features are affected by the audience, by what needs to be said
and to whom, and by the context:

audience: who the speaker is speaking to and how that listener is responding or imagined to be responding (sometimes this isn't clear, and sometimes it is very clear) and what the speakers goal seems to be;

view of others and self (respectful, irreverent, with regard to society, a group);

point of view and tense (for example, first-person voice fits a character/persona with a limited viewpoint but one that goes deep into a person's inner thoughts; this can include the real or false beliefs the speakers have about themselves in a situation and or inner conflicts).

These seem to have to do with deeper personality traits and orientations toward the world:

enthusiasm, zest versus sarcasm, cynicism;

degree of reflection and self-insight;

mental state and physical state;

descriptive versus cryptic;

level of directness or indirectness;

level of associative or linear thinking;

imagery;

values and ideals; positioning for or against certain values in a chosen school of thought;

grammatical patterns that reveal thinking and conceptual patterns (for example, "we" versus "I" did something, all passive voice, spatial metaphors, focus on problem solving or feeling);

self-interrupting, other-interrupting, focus, tangents.

TRY THIS

1. Look at a piece of your own writing, using the lists to describe yourself as a speaker through that text. Try it with someone else's writing. What does the list leave out?

2. Think about yourself in high school or in fifth grade. Channel that voice and that feeling. What would the voice from that person sound like? Can you write a paragraph in that voice?

3. Sketch out a five-minute autobiography using only a list of nouns. Now do one using only a list of verbs. Now look back: what voice is implied in your choices?

4. How would your friends and family describe you? Now look back at that list of words. What kinds of voices do they seem to capture? How does your voice vary depending on who you're talking to? You can use this list to add to the full range of voices you might embody and use in your writing.

WEAVING VOICE COMPLEXITY

So much of what happens with voice is beneath the surface of writing. Often that felt sense of revision that Sondra Perl and Lee Martin write about is a nonverbal bodily impression or awareness. The list of voice elements in the previous section might be equally helpful in analyzing the voices in texts by other authors first, so that you can then go back and see these factors working in your own writing. Sometimes looking at our own voices with such precision can cause a sense of self-consciousness that freezes the very fluidity we are trying to achieve.

Ultimately, as Orwell says, a writer can "break any of these rules." The most important thing is to observe your own process and see what works for you. Getting to know what makes the voices flow—whether it's reading poetry or watching for trigger words, whether it's channeling your inner teenager or your inner silence—is the most valuable part of this experience. In the course of your living, you may encounter a voice within you that you've never brought to the page. That might be the exact voice that needs to speak. Or you may open a book and hear a voice that calls out a new response from within. As you grow and change, your voices will develop, fade, and shift, with each one offering a new window to the world.

A Few Final Words

I hope that experimenting with voices in these chapters has opened up some space for the unsaid things in your drafts and your work, and I appreciate you taking the time to try these voices out with me. As always, at the end of something big, my voice turns to doubt: what made me think I had the right to say any of that? Did I miss something major? (I undoubtedly did.)

In the aftermath of unfurling your strongest statements, inhabiting your wildest visions, carefully crunching those shells of protective voices, and sewing voices to each other in a multicolored quilt of boldness, you may find yourself a little tired and a little daunted from the challenges you've given yourself on the page. Inhabiting our full selves can feel like molting, and it takes time to get used to. As I've come to learn, that sense of fatigue is a recoil voice, one that indicates the tiredness of hard work. I know, at that point, to put the pages aside. I know that I've risked what I needed to risk and that tomorrow, when I look at my work, I'll see—with a fresh cup of coffee and a night's sleep—my own life in a new way, as filtered by the words I managed to put down.

And the excavation of voices will continue. Every time I encounter a new voice on the page, maybe one written by you, it will call up a response in me, and maybe it will be one I want to try on for size. Or I will go for a walk to mull over the felt sense in revision and realize—triggered by the sight of a wave or a tree or nothing I can even name—that another voice layer is asking me to articulate what remains unsaid.

May your list of voices grow long and wild. May you say the bold thing. May you cut the dull rind of the fruit with your editing knife to show its colorful, soft, sweet insides. May you mix your voices and season them with control and abandon and joy. May you take the woody seed of an old voice and, instead of discarding it, plant it to grow more voices.

GRATITUDE

Thank you to everyone who protected and challenged and grew my voices, including my mother, Gerhild Heidi Huber, who bought me a typewriter and thought I might like to write a newspaper column. To my teachers: from Ms. Haynes in second grade and her laminating machine to Mr. Pain in fifth grade to Mr. and Mrs. Bounds in junior high and high school. And deep thanks to Mr. Joe Miller, high school English teacher and friend, and Mrs. Grabowski. Thank you to my aunt Sister Rosarita Huber, who lives in my heart and told me I could be a writer. Thank you to teachers who heard and saw me: the kind and generous Lee Martin, the inimitable Lee K. Abbott, Bill Roorbach, fellow writers and editors Dinty W. Moore and Joe Mackall.

Thank you to the activists who taught me boldness and power: AWOL, the Avengers, Maria Lugones, JwJ, Labor Notes. Reframing the world is voice work.

Thank you to my friends who treated me like a "real writer" and to friends Jason S-W and Mike and everyone else who edited zines and articles with me. Thank you to Jenny Grabmeier and Kathy Bohley, Nicole Stellon O'Donnell, Sharad Puri, Brooke Davis, Laura Shelton, and Monica Kieser, always and forever. Thank you to the AFG.

Thank you to the women: Anna Lawrence and Kris Sealey, Gwen Alfonso and Emily Orlando, and to my colleagues at Fairfield University. Thank you to every single writer who has offered me encouragement. Thank you in particular to Kris Sealey, whose conversation with me about race pointed me to the work of George Yancy.

Thank you to the writers whose work I found in the used book stacks of the bookstore where I used to work: Anne Lamott, Brenda Ueland, bell hooks, and first and last, Peter Elbow, who sent me an encouraging email in response to my long fan letter. I've tried my best to "give 'em hell."

Thank you to the fellow writers who sustain me: Elizabeth Hilts, Nalini Jones, Heather Kirn Lanier, Amy Monticello, Adriana Páramo, Sarah Einstein, and Barbara Tyler. Thanks to Anna Leahy for vital comments on this book. Special thanks to Sejal Shah for working with me on an (unsuccessful) AWP panel proposal that got some of this thinking going. Thank you to Daisy Hernández for her generosity. Thank you to every single writer who wrote to me about *Pain Woman* and gave me the courage to continue. Thank you to all of the wonderful folks at the University of Nebraska Press, including Courtney Ochsner, Rosemary Sekora, Elizabeth Gratch, and many others, for giving my books a home and helping them into the world, for giving my books a home.

Thanks to Cliff and Ivan for their choral support and challenge. And thank you, dear reader, for taking the time to wander through voices with me.

NOTES

NOTE TO THE READER

1. Chavez, *Anti-Racist Writing Workshop*, 34.
2. Rekdal, *Appropriate*, 62.

1. LISTENING TO VOICES

1. Quoted in Elbow, *Everyone Can Write*, 206.
2. Burroway, *Imaginative Writing*, 49.
3. Chavez, *Anti-Racist Writing Workshop*, 41.
4. Larson, *Memoir and the Memoirist*, 131.
5. Hoffman, *Lost in Translation: A Life in a New Language*, quoted in Elbow, *Everyone Can Write*, 181.
6. Elbow, "What Do We Mean When We Talk about Voice," 13.
7. Salesses, *Craft in the Real World*, 92.
8. Elbow, "Inviting the Mother Tongue," *Everyone Can Write*, 341.
9. Sher, *Intuitive Writer*, 119.
10. Elbow, "Fragments," *Everyone Can Write*, 143.
11. Elbow, *Vernacular* Eloquence, 78, 91.
12. Wexler, "Interview with Patricia Hampl."
13. Elbow, "Voice in Writing Again."
14. Elbow, "On the Concept of Voice," *Everyone Can Write*, 222.
15. Lopate, "Reflection and Retrospection."
16. Schneider, *Writing Alone*, 96.
17. Schneider, *Writing Alone*, 198, quoting Elbow's essay "Inviting the Mother Tongue," *Everyone Can Write*.
18. Schneider, *Writing Alone*, 35.
19. Elbow, *Vernacular Eloquence*, 155, 169.

2. THE VOICE LINEAGE

1. Burroway, *Imaginative Writing*, 360.
2. Elbow, "Pleasures of Voice," 216.
3. Elbow, "Reconsiderations," 168.
4. Elbow, "What Do We Mean When We Talk about Voice," 20.
5. Ko, *Leavers*, 9.
6. Elbow, "What Do We Mean When We Talk about Voice," 5.
7. Elbow, "What Do We Mean When We Talk about Voice," 6.
8. Beasley, "What We Talk about When We Talk about Voice."
9. Mambrol, "Key Theories of Mikhail Bakhtin."
10. Bayles and Orland, *Art & Fear*, 60.
11. Elbow, "What Do We Mean When We Talk about Voice," 19–20.
12. Elbow, "What Do We Mean When We Talk about Voice," 6.
13. Hoagland and Cosgrove, *Art of Voice*, 114.
14. Elbow, in "Reconsiderations of Voice in Text," writes in 2007: "George Bush was probably elected because his voice was more persuasive and believable to voters. We're left with a widespread perplexity about whether that down-home 'nucular' voice is him or a clever ruse" (171).
15. Rankine, *Just Us*, 200.
16. Zeiger, "Personal Essay and Egalitarian Rhetoric." 236.
17. Ueland, *If You Want to Write*, 24.
18. Hoagland and Cosgrove, *Art of Voice*, 20.
19. Chavez, *Anti-Racist Writing Workshop*, 55.
20. Healey, "Rise of Creative Writing," 23. https://www.bookdepository.com/Rise-Creative-Writing-New-Value-Creativity-Stephen-Peter-Healey/9781244039834.
21. Páramo, *Looking for Esperanza*, 71.

3. VOICES LIVE IN THE BODY

1. Elbow, "What Do We Mean When We Talk about Voice," 5.
2. Hackett, *I Gotta Crow*, 33.
3. Tversky, *How Action Shapes Thought*, 71–72, 124.
4. "But no doubt I shall think differently next year," Virginia Woolf writing to Vita Sackville-West, March 16, 1926. *Letters of Virginia Woolf*, vol. 3.
5. Van der Kolk, *Body Keeps the Score*, 331.
6. Livingston, "Thumb-Sucking Girl," 17.
7. Elbow, "What Do We Mean When We Talk about Voice," 14.

8. Perl, *Felt Sense*, 2.

9. Perl, *Felt Sense*, 50.

10. Ueland, *If You Want to Write*, 47.

11. Ueland, *If You Want to Write*, 32.

12. Ueland, *If You Want to Write*, 43.

13. Mirvis, "Lost Voice."

14. Lunsford et al., *Everything's an Argument*.

15. Merton and Montaldo, *Year with Thomas Merton*, journal entry from October 2, 1958, 3:296.

4. MIND IS THE SOURCE OF VOICE

1. Lopate, "The Essay Lives—In Disguise."

2. Elbow, "Pleasures of Voice," 216, 249: from Clifford: the idea of stopping students at points throughout an essay to have them react and respond in order to reveal the essay's structure, from Fish's belief "that the mind needs to investigate its own activities."

3. Matthew Smith, "Constraints Breed Creativity: OuLiPo," MattyMatt.co, July 23, 2015, http://mattymatt.co/constraints-breed-creativity-oulipo.

4. Hackett, *I Gotta Crow*, 31.

5. Sommers, "I Stand Here Writing."

6. Filloy, "Orwell's Political Persuasion," 53, 54.

7. Orwell, "Hanging."

8. Wexler, "Interview with Patricia Hampl."

9. Kim, *Calligrapher's Daughter*.

10. Lopate, "My Drawer."

11. Lopate, "My Drawer."

12. Knight, "Interview."

13. Leilani, "'Luster' by Raven Leilani."

14. Lopate, "Reflection and Retrospection."

15. Macrorie, *I-Search Paper*.

16. Larson, *Memoir and the Memoirist*, 129–31.

17. Rutledge, "Every Word Is an Act of Resistance."

5. TIME AND PLACE GROW VOICES

1. hooks, *Remembered Rapture*, 67.

2. Chamberlain, "From 'Haunts' to 'Character.'"

3. Metcalf and Simon, *Writing the Mind Alive*, 58.

4. Schneider, *Writing Alone*, 94.
5. Schneider, *Writing Alone*, 94.
6. Warrell, "Jacqueline Woodson's Windows."

6. VOICE OF CHALLENGE AND CHANGE

1. Elbow, "Pleasures of Voice," 222; Mambrol, "Key Theories of Mikhail Bakhtin." Elbow wonders if this lack of choral support is the reason why women tend to use many more expressions of emotion, exclamation points, and so on in their professional communications, possibly because they are trying to compensate for being less "heard" in certain settings.
2. Hackett, *I Gotta Crow*, 84.
3. Ueland, *If You Want to Write*, 6.
4. hooks, *Remembered Rapture*, 5.
5. Hackett, *I Gotta Crow*, 73.
6. Giménez Smith, "Parts of an Autobiography," 37.
7. Giménez Smith, "Parts of an Autobiography," 38.
8. Slomski, "Journal Therapy."
9. DeSalvo, *Writing as a Way of Healing*, 210.
10. Gornick. *Situation and the Story*, 24.
11. Watkins, "On Pandering."
12. Montaigne, *Essays of Montaigne*, xvii.
13. McPhee, "Draft No. 4."
14. Burroway, *Imaginative Writing*, 50.
15. Metcalf and Simon, *Writing the Mind Alive*, 32–37.

7. DETAIL IS THE SEED OF VOICE

1. Morrison, "Site of Memory," 92.
2. Morrison, "Site of Memory," 99.
3. Nowak, "Complicated History of Einfühlung."
4. Doty, *Still Life with Oysters and Lemon*, 6.
5. Gewen, "Staying Power," 12.
6. Baldwin, "Notes for a Hypothetical Novel," *Collected Essays*, 229.
7. Baldwin, "Notes of a Native Son," *Collected Essays*.
8. Goldberg, *Writing Down the Bones*, 50.
9. Kaygill, *Kafka*.
10. Gregg, "Art of Finding."
11. Woolf, "Modern Fiction."

8. EMBODIED VOICES, RACIALIZED LIVES

1. Charles Bernstein, "Open Letter," in Rankine, Loffreda, and Cap, *Racial Imaginary*, 64.
2. Chavez, *Anti-Racist Writing Workshop*, 95.
3. Salesses, *Craft in the Real World*, 10.
4. Mura, "White Writing Teachers."
5. Salesses, *Craft in the Real World*, 22.
6. Salesses, *Craft in the Real World*, 102.
7. Rankine, *Just Us*, 31–32.
8. Chavez, *Anti-Racist Writing Workshop*, 98.
9. Chavez, *Anti-Racist Writing Workshop*, 126.
10. hooks, *Remembered Rapture*, 127.
11. Chavez, *Anti-Racist Writing Workshop*, 52.
12. hooks, *Remembered Rapture*, 11.
13. Isen, "Tiny White People Took Over My Brain."
14. Rankine, *Citizen*, 55.
15. hooks, *Remembered Rapture*, xiii.
16. Rekdal, *Appropriate*, 121.
17. Zhang, "They Pretend to Be Us."
18. Rekdal, *Appropriate*, 56.
19. Salesses, *Craft in the Real World*, 84.
20. Loffreda, "Open Letter," in Rankine, Loffreda, and Cap, *Racial Imaginary*, 209–10.
21. Yancy, *Look, a White*, 168–69.
22. hooks, *Remembered Rapture*, 89.
23. Rekdal, *Appropriate*, 121.
24. Rekdal, *Appropriate*, 25.
25. Rekdal, *Appropriate*, 50.
26. Chavez, *Anti-Racist Writing Workshop*, 79.
27. Yancy, *Look, a White*, 158.
28. Yancy, *Look, a White*, 19.
29. Chavez, *Anti-Racist Writing Workshop*, 33.
30. Yancy, *Look, a White*, 175.

9. VOICES OF JOY

1. Gay, *Book of Delights*, 135, 137.
2. Gerard, *Creative Nonfiction*, 134.

3. Ueland, *If You Want to Write*, 52.

4. Ueland, *If You Want to Write*, 64.

5. Fassler, interview with Terese Marie Mailhot.

6. Jamison, "Exuberance," 261–63.

7. Dario Robleto, in Markonish, *Explode Every Day*, 227.

8. Chris Taylor, in Markonish, *Explode Every Day*, 281.

9. Lorde, "Uses of the Erotic: The Erotic as Power," *Zami, Sister Outsider, Undersong*, 54.

10. VOICES WITH FIRE

1. Aristotle, *Nicomachean Ethics*, bk. 2, 1108b, *Oxford Essential Quotations*, ed. Susan Ratcliffe, 4th ed. Online. 2016. Accessed December 4, 2021, https://www.oxfordreference.com/view/10.1093/acref/9780191826719 .001.0001/q-oro-ed4-00000434.

2. Lorde, "The Master's Tools Will Never Dismantle the Master's House," *Zami, Sister Outsider, Undersong*, 129.

3. Robert Cohen, "'Piano Has Been Drinking,'" 247.

4. Audre Lorde's essay "The Transformation of Silence into Language and Action" quoted in Schorske, "On the Perilous Potential of Feminist Silence."

5. hooks, *Wounds of Passion*, 180.

6. Lorde, "Master's Tools."

7. Blackmer Reyes and Curry Rodríguez, *Testimonio*.

8. hooks, *Wounds of Passion*.

9. Merton and Montaldo, *Year with Thomas Merton*, journal entry for June 2, 1961, 4174.

10. Stielstra, "Axe for the Frozen Sea."

11. Czerwiec, "Anatomy of an Outrage."

11. A WHISPER OF A VOICE

1. Merton and Montaldo, *Year with Thomas Merton*, journal entries for June 3 and 4, 1963, 4:188.

2. Warrell, "Jacqueline Woodson's Windows."

3. Elbow, "Silence: A Collage," *Everybody Can Write*, 176.

4. Schneider, *Writing Alone*, 4.

5. Schorske, "On the Perilous Potential of Feminist Silence."

6. Olsen, *Silences*, 27.

7. Olsen, *Silences*, 256.

8. Virginia Woolf, in Olsen, *Silences*, 143.

9. Hackett, *I Gotta Crow*, 50.

10. Hackett, *I Gotta Crow*, 50, quoting Jill McLean Taylor, Carol Gilligan, and Amy M. Sullivan, *Between Voice and Silence: Women and Girls, Race and Relationship*.

11. Olsen, *Silences*, 20.

12. Elbow, "Silence: A Collage," 176.

13. Elbow, "Silence: a Collage," 178.

14. Hoffman, *Lost in Translation*, 181.

15. Elbow, "Discourses," *Everybody Can Write*, 231.

16. Fassler, interview with Terese Marie Mailhot.

17. Elbow, introduction, *Everyone Can Write*, xvi.

18. Elbow, "Closing My Eyes as I Speak," *Everybody Can Write*, 94.

12. THE VOICE OF SPIRIT

1. Ueland, *If You Want to Write*, 59.

2. Merton and Montaldo, *Year with Thomas Merton*, journal entry for April 14, 1966, 6105.

3. Ueland, *If You Want to Write*, 28.

4. Dillard, *Pilgrim at Tinker Creek*, 31.

5. Moraga, *Last Generation*, 162.

6. Baldwin, "Take Me to the Water," *Collected Essays*, 357.

7. Baldwin, "Nothing Personal," *Collected Essays*, 700.

8. Baldwin, "This Nettle, Danger . . . ," *Collected Essays*, 687.

9. Baldwin, "The Devil Finds Work," *Collected Essays*, 571.

13. EDITING AND REVISING WITH VOICES

1. Martin, "Felt Sense."

2. Orwell, "Politics and the English Language."

3. Evans, *Office of Historical Corrections*, 163–265.

4. Evans, *Office of Historical Corrections*, 186.

5. Orwell, "Politics and the English Language."

6. Schneider, *Writing Alone*, 197.

7. hooks, *Remembered Rapture*, 68.

8. hooks, *Remembered Rapture*, 90.

9. hooks, *Remembered Rapture*, 40.

10. Ira Sadoff, "Open Letter," in Rankine, Loffreda, and Cap, *Racial Imaginary*, 240.
11. hooks, *Remembered Rapture*, 40.
12. Elbow "What Do We Mean When We Talk about Voice," 12, 13.
13. Palacas, "Parentheticals and Personal Voice," 121.
14. Fry, "Creating Your Own Voice," 51–80.

WORKS CITED

Alvarez, A. *The Writer's Voice*. New York: Norton, 2005.

Baldwin, James. *Collected Essays*. Edited by Toni Morrison. New York: Library of America, 1998.

Bayles, David, and Ted Orland. *Art & Fear: Observations on the Perils (and Rewards) of Artmaking*. New York: Image Continuum Press, 2001.

Beasley, Sandra. "What We Talk about When We Talk about Voice." *Writer's Chronicle*, February 2017.

Blackmer Reyes, Kathryn, and Julia E. Curry Rodríguez. "*Testimonio*: Origins, Terms, and Resources." *Equity & Excellence in Education* August 3, 2012, 525–38. Chicana/Latina Testimonios: Methodologies, Pedagogies, and Political Urgency, no. 3.

Burroway, Janet. *Imaginative Writing: The Elements of Craft*. 3rd ed. New York: Pearson, 2010.

Chamberlain, Charles. "From 'Haunts' to 'Character': The Meaning of Ethos and Its Relation to Ethics." *Helios* 11, no. 2 (1984), 97–108.

Chavez, Felicia Rose. *The Anti-Racist Writing Workshop: How to Decolonize the Creative Classroom*. Chicago: Haymarket Books, 2021.

Cohen, Robert. "The Piano Has Been Drinking: On the Art of the Rant." *Georgia Review* 59, no. 2 (Summer 2005): 233–53. https://www.jstor.org/stable/41402586.

Czerwiec, Heidi. "Anatomy of an Outrage." *Roar*, April 25, 2017.

DeSalvo, Louise. *Writing as a Way of Healing: How Telling Our Stories Transforms Our Lives*. Boston: Beacon Press, 2000.

Dillard, Annie. *Pilgrim at Tinker Creek*. New York: Harper's, 1974.

Doty, Mark. *Still Life with Oysters and Lemon: On Objects and Intimacy*. Boston: Beacon Press, 2002.

Elbow, Peter. *Everyone Can Write: Essays toward a Hopeful Theory of Writing and Teaching Writing*. New York: Oxford University Press, 2000.

———. "The Pleasures of Voice." In *Literary Nonfiction: Theory, Criticism, Pedagogy*, edited by Chris Anderson. Carbondale: Southern Illinois University Press, 1989.

———. "Reconsiderations: Voice in Writing Again: Embracing Contraries." *College English* 70, no. 2 (2007): 168–88.

———. *Vernacular Eloquence: What Speech Can Bring to Writing*. Oxford: Oxford University Press, 2012.

———. "What Do We Mean When We Talk about Voice in Text?" In *Voices on Voice: Perspectives, Definitions, Inquiry*, edited by Kathleen Blake Yancey. Urbana IL: National Council of Teachers of English, 1994.

Evans, Danielle. *The Office of Historical Corrections: A Novella and Stories*. New York: Riverhead Books, 2020.

Fassler, Joe. Interview with Terese Marie Mailhot. "On the Necessity of 'Willful Blindness' in Writing." *Atlantic*, February 14, 2018.

Filloy, Richard. "Orwell's Political Persuasion: A Rhetoric of Personality." *George Orwell: Contemporary Critical Essays*. New York: St. Martin's Press, 1998.

Fry, Don. "Creating Your Own Voice." In *Writing Voice: The Complete Guide to Creating a Presence on the Page and Engaging Readers*, edited by Cris Freese. Foreword by Reed Farrel Coleman. Cincinnati: Writer's Digest, 2017.

Gay, Ross. *The Book of Delights: Essays*. Chapel Hill NC: Algonquin, 2019.

Gerard, Philip. *Creative Nonfiction: Researching and Crafting Creative Nonfiction*. Long Grove IL: Waveland Press, 2004.

Gewen, Barry. "Staying Power." *New York Times Book Review*, September 2, 2012.

Giménez Smith, Carmen. "Parts of an Autobiography." *Milk and Filth*. Tucson: University of Arizona Press, 2013.

Goldberg, Natalie. *Writing Down the Bones: Freeing the Writer Within*. Boulder CO: Shambhala Publications, 2005.

Gornick, Vivian. *The Situation and the Story: The Art of Personal Narrative*. New York: Farrar, Straus & Giroux, 2001.

Gregg, Linda. "The Art of Finding." Poets.org, October 25, 2006. https://www.poets.org/poetsorg/text/art-finding.

Hackett, Jill. *I Gotta Crow: Women, Voice, and Writing*. New York: Watson-Guptill Publications, 2002.

Healey, Stephen Peter. "The Rise of Creative Writing and the New Value of Creativity." PhD diss., University of Minnesota, 2009.

Hoagland, Tony, and Kay Cosgrove. *The Art of Voice: Poetic Principles and Practice*. New York: Norton, 2020.

Hoffman, Eva. *Lost in Translation: A Life in a New Language*. New York: Dutton, 1989.

hooks, bell. *Ain't I a Woman: Black Women and Feminism*. South End Press, 1981.

———. *Remembered Rapture: The Writer at Work*. New York: Henry Holt, 1999.

———. *Wounds of Passion: A Writing Life*. New York: Henry Holt, 1997.

Isen, Tajja. "Tiny White People Took Over My Brain: Learning to Rethink the Canon and Find My Voice as a Mixed-Race Writer." *Electric Literature*, September 12, 2017. https://electricliterature.com/tiny-white-people-took -over-my-brain.

Jamison, Kay Redfield. "Exuberance: The Passion for Life." In *Explode Every Day: An Inquiry into the Phenomena of Wonder*, edited by Denise Markonish. New York: DelMonico Books, 2016.

Kaygill, Howard. *Kafka: In Light of the Accident*. London: Bloomsbury Publishing, 2017.

Kim, Eugenia. *The Calligrapher's Daughter*. New York: Henry Holt, 2013.

Knight, Lania. "Interview with Creative Nonfiction Writer Phillip Lopate." *Poets & Writers*, May 16, 2008. https://www.pw.org/content/interview _creative_nonfiction_writer_phillip_lopate.

Ko, Lisa. *The Leavers*. Chapel Hill NC: Algonquin Books, 2018.

Larson, Thomas. *The Memoir and the Memoirist: Reading and Writing Personal Narrative*. Athens OH: Swallow Press, 2007.

Leilani, Raven. "'Luster' by Raven Leilani: An Excerpt." *New York Times*, August 6, 2020. https://www.nytimes.com/2020/08/06/books/review/luster-by -raven-leilani-an-excerpt.html.

Livingston, Sonja. "Thumb-Sucking Girl." *Brevity*, May 11, 2005, 17. https:// www.creativenonfiction.org/brevity/past%20issues/brev17/livingston _thumb.htm.

Loffreda, Beth. "Open Letter," in Rankine, Loffreda, and Cap, *Racial Imaginary*, 209–10.

Lopate, Phillip. "The Essay Lives—in Disguise." *New York Times*, November 18, 1984.

———. "My Drawer." *Getting Personal: Selected Writings*. New York: Basic Books, 2003.

———. "Reflection and Retrospection: A Pedagogic Mystery Story." *Fourth Genre* 7, no. 1 (Spring 2005): 143–56.

Lorde, Audre. Quoted in Carina del Valle Schorske. "On the Perilous Potential of Feminist Silence." *LitHub*, November 1, 2016.

———. *Zami, Sister Outsider, Undersong.* New York: Quality Paperback Book Club, 1984.

Lunsford, Andrea, John Ruszkiewicz, and Keith Walters. *Everything's an Argument.* 7th ed. New York: Bedford / St. Martin's, 2015.

Macrorie, Ken. *The I-Search Paper: Revised Edition of Searching for Writing.* Portsmouth NH: Heinemann, 1988.

Mambrol, Nasrullah. "Key Theories of Mikhail Bakhtin." Literary Theory and Criticism (website), January 24, 2018, https://literariness.org/2018/01/24/key-theories-of-mikhail-bakhtin.

Markonish, Denise, ed. *Explode Every Day: An Inquiry into the Phenomena of Wonder.* Munich: DelMonico Books, 2016.

Martin, Lee. "Felt Sense: Focusing on Revision." LeeMartin.com blog, November 11, 2013.

McPhee, John. "Draft No. 4: Replacing the Words in Boxes." *New Yorker*, April 22, 2013.

Merton, Thomas, and Jonathan Montaldo. *A Year with Thomas Merton: Daily Meditations from His Journals.* New York: HarperOne, 2004.

Metcalf, Linda Trichter, and Tobin Simon. *Writing the Mind Alive: The Proprioceptive Method for Finding Your Authentic Voice.* New York: Ballantine Books, 2002.

Miller, Brenda and Suzanne Paola. *Tell It Slant.* 3rd ed. New York: McGraw Hill Professional, 2019.

Mirvis, Tova. "A Lost Voice, Writer's Block, and a New Life." *LitHub*, September 17, 2017. https://lithub.com/a-lost-voice-writers-block-and-a-new-life.

Montaigne, Michel de. *The Essays of Montaigne.* Vol 1. New York: Modern Library, 1946.

Moraga, Cherríe. *The Last Generation.* Boston: South End Press, 1999.

Morrison, Toni. "The Site of Memory." In *Inventing the Truth: The Art and Craft of Memoir*, edited by William Zinsser. 2nd ed. New York: Houghton Mifflin, 1995.

———. "Toni Morrison's Most Notable Quotes about Life, Race, and Storytelling." Associated Press. *USA Today*, August 7, 2019.

Mura, David. *A Stranger's Journey: Race, Identity, and Craft in Narrative Writing*. Athens: University of Georgia Press, 2018.

———. "White Writing Teachers (or David Foster Wallace versus James Baldwin)." *Journal of Creative Writing Studies* 1, no. 1 (2016). 1–15. https://scholarworks.rit.edu/cgi/viewcontent.cgi?referer=&httpsredir=1&article=1010&context=jcws.

Nowak, M. "The Complicated History of Einfühlung." *Argument: Biannual Philosophical Journal* 1 (2011): 301–26.

Olsen, Tillie. *Silences*. New York: Dell, 1979.

Orwell, George. "A Hanging." *The Adelphi*. 1931. Accessed December 5, 2021, via Orwell Foundation, https://www.orwellfoundation.com/the-orwell-foundation/orwell/essays-and-other-works/a-hanging.

———. "Politics and the English Language." *Horizon*, April 1946. Accessed September 12, 2020, via Orwell Foundation, https://www.orwellfoundation.com/the-orwell-foundation/orwell/essays-and-other-works/politics-and-the-english-language.

Palacas, Arthur L. "Parentheticals and Personal Voice." In *Landmark Essays on Voice and Writing*, edited by Peter Elbow. New York: Routledge, 1995.

Páramo, Adriana. *Looking for Esperanza: The Story of a Mother, a Child Lost, and Why They Matter to Us*. Hopkins MN: Benu Press, 2012.

Perl, Sondra. *Felt Sense: Writing with the Body*. Portsmouth NH: Heinemann, 2004.

Rankine, Claudia. *Citizen: An American Lyric*. Minneapolis: Graywolf Press, 2014.

———. *Just Us: An American Conversation*. Minneapolis: Graywolf Press, 2020.

Rankine, Claudia, Beth Loffreda, and Max King Cap, eds. *The Racial Imaginary: Writers on Race in the Life of the Mind*. Albany NY: Fence Books, 2015.

Rekdal, Paisley. *Appropriate: A Provocation*. New York: Norton, 2021.

Rutledge, Renee Macalino. "Every Word Is an Act of Resistance: Finding My Voice as a Filipino Writer." *LitHub*, February 10, 2017.

Salesses, Matthew. *Craft in the Real World: Rethinking Fiction Writing and Workshopping*. New York: Catapult, 2020.

Schneider, Pat. *Writing Alone and with Others*. Foreword by Peter Elbow. Oxford: Oxford University Press, 2003.

Schorske, Carina del Valle. "On the Perilous Potential of Feminist Silence." *LitHub*, November 1, 2016. https://lithub.com/on-the-perilous-potential-of-feminist-silence.

Sher, Gail. *The Intuitive Writer: Listening to Your Own Voice*. New York: Penguin, 2002.

Slomski, Genevieve. "Journal Therapy." *Answers.com*, April 1, 2007. http://www.answers.com/topic/journal-therapy.

Sommers, Nancy. "I Stand Here Writing." *College English* 55, no. 4 (April 1993): 420–28.

Stielstra, Megan. "An Axe for the Frozen Sea." *Believer*, September 28, 2018.

Taylor, Jill McLean, Carol Gilligan, and Amy M. Sullivan. *Between Voice and Silence: Women and Girls, Race and Relationships*. Cambridge: Harvard University Press, 1996.

Tversky, Barbara. *Mind in Motion: How Action Shapes Thought*. New York: Basic Books, 2019.

Ueland, Brenda. *If You Want to Write: A Book about Art, Independence, and Spirit*. Minneapolis: Graywolf Press, 1997.

Van der Kolk, Bessel. *The Body Keeps the Score: Brain, Mind, and Body in the Healing of Trauma*. New York: Penguin, 2015.

Warrell, Laura. "Jacqueline Woodson's Windows." *Writer*, October 21, 2018.

Watkins, Claire Vaye. "On Pandering." *Tin House* (Winter 2015). https://tinhouse.com/on-pandering.

Wexler, Laura. "An Interview with Patricia Hampl." *American Writing Program Chronicle* 30, no. 3 (March–April 1998).

Woolf, Virginia. *The Letters of Virginia Woolf*. Vol. 3, *1923–1928*, edited by Nigel Nicolson and Joanne Trautmann. New York: Harcourt Brace Jovanovich, 1980.

———. "Modern Fiction." In *The Essays of Virginia Woolf*. Vol. 4, *1925–1928*, ed. Andrew McNeille. London: The Hogarth Press, 1984.

Yagoda, Ben. *Memoir: A History*. New York: Riverhead Books, 2009.

Yancy, George. *Look, a White! Philosophical Essays on Whiteness*. Philadelphia: Temple University Press, 2012.

Zeiger, William. "The Personal Essay and Egalitarian Rhetoric." In *Literary Nonfiction*, edited by Chris Anderson. Carbondale: Southern Illinois University Press, 1989.

Zhang, Jenny. "They Pretend to Be Us While Pretending We Don't Exist." *Buzzfeed*, September 11, 2015.

INDEX

Bradbury, Ray, 106, 141
braided voices, ix, 32, 63, 74, 204
Brand, Dorothea, 12
breath, 8, 36–40, 176; panic and, 39, 41;
as pause, 46–48, 111
Buddhism, 44, 185–86; sense of self in,
6, 185. *See also* meditation
Burroway, Janet, 2, 95

Cameron, Julia, 12
Chavez, Felicia Rose, vii, 2, 32, 115–18,
122, 127
childcare and writing, 168
child voice, 42, 51, 61, 75–76, 78, 80,
83; memory and, 109, 132, 140, 161;
as narrator, 19, 42, 135; as original
voice, 12, 17; pedagogy and, 31;
wonder and, 132, 134–35
choral support, 28, 32, 79, 82, 87, 94,
97, 116–17, 216. *See also* Bahktin,
Mikhail
chronic pain. *See* disability; pain
class. *See* social class
cliché, 105, 107
Cohen, Robert, 147
colonialism, 25, 56–57, 115, 155
comedy, 18–19, 21, 196. *See also* humor
community, as voice encourager, 5, 9,
81, 184
compassion, 34, 180
complexity, 34, 58, 107, 127, 153, 155,
177, 182, 185, 201, 203, 207; James
Baldwin and, 105–6, 182–83; racism
and, 127, 129; weaving multiple
voices and, 34, 182–83
composition classes, 16, 91, 136, 173;
audience in, 91; pedagogy in, x, 31,
49; rant assignment in, 148
conclusion. *See* endings
confessional writing, 166. *See also*
healing; therapy; trauma

confidence, 8, 42, 51–52, 58, 74–79, 128,
186, 193, 196, 205; characteristic of
voice, 35, 74, 190; childhood and,
81, 93, 135; naming voices and, 11, 17;
practice and, 51, 76, 172
conflicting voices. *See* dissonance
consistency, 188, 204
Cosgrove, Kay, 28
courage, 175
creative constraint, 54
crisis, 84, 142, 163–64
criticism, 8, 79–80, 89, 146; effect
on voice, 79; internalized, 91–92;
whiteness and, 124
cultural appropriation. *See*
appropriation
Cummins, Jeanine, 126
curiosity, 45, 90, 137, 148, 189;
whiteness and, 128
Czerwiec, Heidi, 157–58

Darwin, Charles, 13
denial, 13, 29, 112, 155
depression, 4, 81, 167
DeSalvo, Louise, 87
detail, 17, 57, 62, 99–113, 127, 136, 139,
177, 183; memory and, 169
diaries, 31, 82, 105, 155, 166. *See also*
journals
Dickinson, Emily, 161
Didion, Joan, 169
digression, 203
Dillard, Annie, 177, 184, 193, 204
disability, 4–5, 37, 44, 54, 132, 205. *See
also* ableism
disembodied, 30, 37. *See also* embodied
writing
dissociation, 36–37, 41, 48. *See also*
body; disembodied
dissonance, ix, 159; whiteness and, 123
Doty, Mark, 105

doubt, 35, 159, 167, 176, 209; as criticism, 139; as quality of voice, 35; as wonder, 137

dualism, 18, 31, 36, 41, 124, 196

editorial. *See* letter to the editor

Elbow, Peter, x–xi, 9–10, 12, 16–17, 20, 26, 53, 79, 171–73, 203–4

embodied writing, 36, 43–44, 97, 114, 118, 158, 207; race and, 127. *See also* body

empathy, 104; and reading, 61, 104; for self, 154

endings, 93, 132

enthusiasm, 21, 80–81, 138, 206; as quality of voice, 206

essay, 30, 51, 56–57, 61–63, 74, 90–92, 132, 142, 147–148, 156–57, 182; goals of, 151, 185; hermit crab, 25, 197; Montaigne and development of, 94; questioning and, 185; workshop of, 100–102, 163. *See also* exploratory writing

ethics, 64, 175. *See also* appropriation; political writing

ethos, 16, 28–29, 34, 48, 67, 183

eunoia, 183. *See also* audience

Evans, Danielle, 199

experience, voice of, 63

experimentation, 12, 27, 45, 97, 126–27, 135, 141, 145, 172–73

exploratory writing, 13, 26–27, 97, 140, 145, 155, 172; versus persuasion, 139

expressive writing, 17, 59, 68

fallow, 159

fear, 4, 73, 112, 118, 150, 159, 161–67, 188; of judgement, 162; and privilege, 174; of revision, 86, 190; of weirdness, 172

feedback, 67, 162–64, 167, 195; and naming voices, 190, 195; and

whiteness, 120–24, 167. *See also* workshop

felt sense, 46–48, 50, 59, 84, 162, 171, 191–92, 207, 209. *See also* embodied writing; Perl, Sondra

fiction, 17–19, 56–57, 59, 62, 92, 102–3, 110; internal dialogue in, 153; science, 73, 140–41

figures of speech. *See* speech

Filloy, Richard, 56

Fish, Stanley, 53

fluency, 188, 191, 200, 204

Fórche, Carolyn, 176

form, 17–18, 23–30, 45, 55–56, 94, 185, 197; and audience, 95, 197; breaking, 12, 45, 197; complaint as, 146; letter as, 126; list as, 86. *See also* diary, essay, hermit crab, journalism, journals, letter to the editor, rant, testimonio

freewriting, 12, 143, 166, 183; and revision, 97, 189, 191

Freire, Paulo, 151

Frost, Robert, 9

Fry, Don, 204–6

Gay, Ross, 132

Gendlin, Eugene, 46

genre, 2, 17–18, 23–25, 33–34, 74, 125, 161, 204; disregarding, 136; and power, 198

Gerard, Philip, 133

gesture, 1, 13, 21, 38–39, 66–67, 131, 182

Gibson, Walker, 34

Gilligan, Carol, 46, 48, 150, 167

Glissant, Édouard, 116

goals: in writing, 27, 30, 85, 147, 206; and audience, 21, 88; and persona, 151; and persuasion, 30–31; reflection as, 10, 162, 185; setting aside, 49–50, 131, 136, 200; and testimony, 151. *See also* purpose

McPhee, John, 94

meaning, 10, 68, 95–96, 101–2, 106, 110–12, 162, 171, 201

meditation, 25, 31, 39–40, 47, 53. *See also* breath

memory, viii, 61, 76, 102–6, 109, 134, 150, 179, 204

mental health, 80, 90. *See also* depression

Merton, Thomas, 51, 155, 160, 175

messiness, 33, 96, 127–28, 130, 182

metaphor, viii, xi, 4–5, 11, 33, 40, 45, 191, 199, 206; and voice, 10

Metcalf, Linda Trichter, 75, 97

Miller, Brenda, 25, 297. *See also* hermit crab essay

mimesis, 104

mind at work, 53, 59, 63, 195. *See also* Lopate, Phillip; stream of consciousness

Mirvis, Tova, 49

Monson, Ander, 90

Montaigne, Michel de, 94

Moraga, Cherríe, 181

Morrison, Toni, 8, 102–3, 172–73

movement, x, 48, 97–98, 107, 126–27, 152; of mind, 62. *See also* walking

Mura, David, 115, 124

Nabokov, Vladimir, 106

naming voices, 5, 22, 34, 51, 59, 135, 152, 158, 175, 190, 202

narrator, 12, 19–20, 32–34, 56–57, 63–64, 111, 153, 167

not-knowing, 178. *See also* doubt

numbness, 164, 169, 189

Olsen, Tillie, 165–66, 168–69

oppression, systemic, 7, 79, 89, 105, 114, 117, 122, 124, 128, 146

Orland, Ted, 25

Orwell, George, 56–57, 105–6, 198–201, 205, 207

pain: emotional, 184, 186; physical, 3, 17, 36–38, 44–45, 54, 59, 87, 135, 177

Palacas, Arthur, 204

panic, 39, 59. *See also* anxiety

Paola, Suzanne, 25, 197

Páramo, Adriana, 32–33

passive voice, 198–200, 205–6

past, voice of, 22, 42, 63, 204

performance, 18, 48, 98, 127; of self, 7. *See also* persona

Perl, Sondra, 46, 171, 191, 207

persona, 16, 18–19, 21, 29, 33–34, 45, 87, 90–91, 151, 206

persuasion, 23, 30–31, 34, 145; narrator and, 56; problems with, 31, 50, 54

Piercy, Marge, 176

platform, 126

play, ix, 4–5, 13, 15–17, 24–25, 73, 135–37, 141, 194, 203

poetry, 19, 25, 29, 45, 59, 82–83, 86, 169, 190, 197, 202

political writing, 29, 56–57, 64, 122, 147, 165, 183; and abstraction, 56, 105; and context, 99, 198; and writing identity, 3, 65, 122. *See also* activism; Lorde, Audre; Orwell, George

practice, 24, 74, 77, 137, 166

prayer, 53, 176, 182

primary voice. *See* home voice

privilege, 73, 114, 122–23, 150; silence and, 165, 168, 174

process, viii, 13, 49–50, 54, 59; wonder as, 137

Proprioceptive Question, 97–98

purpose, in writing, 6, 31, 33, 145. *See also* goals

questions, 23, 31, 49, 97, 118–19, 142–43, 149, 151–55, 175, 185; pace of, 29, 69, 77, 114, 119, 127, 201–2, 205; in workshop, 100

racism, 8–9, 29, 79, 114, 116, 118–19, 121–24, 127–30, 184, 201–2; effects on voice, 8, 77; and landscape, 44, 128–30; in workshop, 120–21, 124. *See also* whiteness

range, 15, 20–22, 28, 99, 200; emotional, 22–23, 76, 77, 132–33, 145, 152; of subject matter, ix, 82, 99, 116, 166, 172; of voices, 1–3, 11, 18, 30–34, 37–39, 549, 59, 86, 166, 182

Rankine, Claudia, 29, 114, 116, 119

rant, 11, 27, 44, 147–50, 152, 194. *See also* anger

reader, 28–34 53–54, 59, 61–63, 86, 90–95, 111, 137–39, 151–57, 163–64, 182–83, ; care for, 94, 183; connection with, 22, 53, 67–68, 195; ideal, 94, 138–39; identification and, 62, 97, 139; trust and, 57, 88. *See also* audience; eunoia

reading aloud, 36, 192

recursion, 31

reflection, 31, 53, 77, 96, 111, 171, 177, 184–85, 204

Rekdal, Paisley, viii, 121–22, 125–26

research, xi, 29–31, 63–64, 125–26, 132–33, 148, 150–51, 153; immersion as, 110; journaling as, 160; memory as, 103; research paper, 11, 30, 91, 133. *See also* I-Search paper

resonance, ix, 7, 19, 29, 88, 193

respect, 79, 109, 148, 186

revision, 16, 86, 101, 127, 190–92, 198, 202, 207, 209

rhetoric, xi, 6, 18, 27, 29, 31, 56, 94, 146, 183

rhythm, 9–10, 21, 29, 38–41, 47–48, 72, 81, 157, 182, 203–5; movement and, 39; walking in, 38, 47

Rich, Adrienne, ix, 1

Robleto, Dario, 137

Roth, Philip, 15

rules, 20, 23, 26, 54, 115, 124–25, 137, 172, 199

Rutledge, Renee, 64

Sadoff, Ira, 202

Salesses, Matthew, 8, 115–16, 122

satire, 17, 25

scene, 51–53, 92, 101–3, 110–13, 131, 153, 155, 179; internal 53, 56

Schneider, Pat, 12, 75, 162–63, 200

Schorske, Carina del Valle, 150, 165

science fiction. *See* fiction

second person, 179, 193

self, notions of, 6, 17–18, 20, 34, 64, 78, 116, 185, 201, 209. *See also* identity

self-care, 171

self-criticism, 91, 180

sentence length, 156, 205

setting, 48, 65, 68, 70, 75, 94, 118, 156–57, 172, 201, 203

sexism, effects on voice, 8, 76–77, 91–92, 194

shame, 80, 90–91, 183, 190, 192–94

"show, don't tell," issues with, 45, 51, 62–63, 92, 99, 153, 162, 182. *See also* detail; tell it slant

silence, 48, 90, 139, 150, 159–60, 162–65, 169–71, 173, 175, 207; and listening, 7, 29, 48, 139, 169–71; as power, 150, 165; and privilege, 119, 128, 165; as self-censorship, 77, 148, 166; as social stigma, 90, 119; and writer's block, 159–60, 169–71. *See also* listening; tell it slant